FACING MY LAI

MODERN WAR STUDIES

Theodore A. Wilson
General Editor

Raymond A. Callahan

J. Garry Clifford

Jacob W. Kipp

Jay Luvaas

Allan R. Millett

Dennis Showalter

Series Editors

• • • • • • • • • • • • • • • • • • • •

FACING MY LAI

MOVING

BEYOND

THE

MASSACRE

EDITED BY

DAVID L. ANDERSON

University Press of Kansas

© 1998 by the University Press of Kansas

All rights reserved

Published by the University Press of Kansas (Lawrence, Kansas 66049), which was organized by the Kansas Board of Regents and is operated and funded by Emporia State University, Fort Hays State University, Kansas State University, Pittsburg State University, the University of Kansas, and Wichita State University

Library of Congress Cataloging-in-Publication Data

British Library Cataloguing in Publication Data is available.

The paper used in this publication meets the minimum requirements of the American National Standard for Permanence of Paper for Printed Library Materials Z39.48-1984.

Facing My Lai : moving beyond the massacre / edited by David L. Anderson.

p.   cm. — (Modern war studies)

Includes bibliographical references and index.

ISBN 0-7006-0864-8 (alk. paper)

1. My Lai Massacre, Vietnam, 1968.
2. Vietnamese Conflict, 1961–1975—Atrocities.   I. Series.

DS557.8.M92F33   1997

959.704'3—dc21   97-24409

Title page photograph of the Son My memorial courtesy of Randy J. Fertel.

Printed in the United States of America

10 9 8 7 6 5 4 3 2 1

*This book is dedicated to Ron Ridenhour and Hugh Thompson
in recognition of their patriotism and commonsense morality,
and it is also dedicated, lest we forget, to the memory of the 504
Vietnamese who died in Son My Village (My Lai 4 and
My Khe 4) on March 16, 1968.*

We used to get intelligence reports
from the Vietnamese district offices.
Every night, I'd make a list
of targets for artillery to hit.

It used to give me quite a kick
to know that I, a corporal,
could command an entire battery
to fire anywhere I said.

One day, while on patrol,
we passed the ruins of a house;
beside it sat a woman
with her left hand torn away;
beside her lay a child, dead.

When I got back to base,
I told the fellows in the COC;
it gave us all a lift to know
all those shells we fired every night
were hitting something.

— W. D. Ehrhart, "Time on Target."

In our village today,
A big battle was fought.
Old ladies and children,
Were sent straight to hell.
Our eyes fill with tears
While we watch and ask God:
Why is the enemy so cruel?

— Vietnamese song

CONTENTS

PREFACE

· · · · · · · · · · · · · ·

The My Lai massacre—the murder of 504 unresisting Vietnamese civilians—was one of the darkest events in recent American history. During the first three days of December 1994, a remarkable gathering convened on the campus of Tulane University to reflect upon the massacre and related issues of war and atrocity. In his opening-night address, Robert Jay Lifton, author of *Home from the War: Vietnam Veterans: Neither Victims nor Executioners,* offered a theme for the conference in the idea of witness, both legal and religious. He invited those in attendance to listen and to learn from each other about My Lai, the Vietnam War, atrocity, modern warfare, and themselves. As Jonathan Shay has written in *Achilles in Vietnam: Combat Trauma and the Undoing of Character,* "Healing from trauma depends upon communalization of the trauma—being able to safely tell the story to someone who is listening and who can be trusted to retell it truthfully to others in the community. So before analyzing, before classifying, before thinking, before trying to *do* anything, we should *listen*" (p. 4).

This book is intended to enable its readers to "listen" to what the conference participants heard. It is not a conventional book of conference proceedings because the gathering was not one in which formal papers were presented. Although a few of the sessions featured one speaker, most of the issues were addressed in roundtable format. The sessions were videotaped or audiotaped, and transcripts were prepared from the tapes. The book consists of selected portions of the transcripts that have been edited to make the oral statements more readable and to keep the focus on My Lai. It is not a verbatim record of the conference. Since there were no formal papers, participants' remarks do not include source citations for quoted material. Footnotes and information in brackets have been added by the editor, but they have been kept to a minimum. Due to various technical limitations of the audio and video recording systems, all or portions of some sessions were not recorded and are not included.

The contents are organized topically, although most of the chapters focus on individual conference sessions in order to maintain their roundtable character. The Introduction and chapter 1 provide some factual and interpretive context for the discussion of the My Lai incident, atrocities in warfare, and combat trauma. Chapters 2 through 4 represent different types of witness. Chapter 2 is a thought-provoking and sometimes emotional recounting of personal experiences and reflections by three men directly connected with the My Lai massacre. The third chapter provides the journalists' perspective, and the fourth is based upon the remarks of authors who have written fiction and poetry about atrocities in Vietnam. Chapters 5 through 10 deal in some way with "facing the darkness." Chapter 11 is from the conference's concluding session, in which several participants from other round tables and some invited observers came together to address "healing the wounds."

The reality of My Lai, of atrocity, and of the violence of warfare is confronted in these pages as different witnesses from varying perspectives hear from and respond to each other. The participants reach no definitive or agreed answers to all the questions, but the final product is distinctively American. In the best democratic tradition, citizens openly confront and analyze harsh facts about their society in a shared effort to heal both personal and national trauma.

ACKNOWLEDGMENTS

• • • • • • • • • • • • • • • •

Sincere appreciation goes to all the conference participants for their honesty and willingness to address publicly such a painful topic. Randy Fertel and Lou Campomenosi, the cochairs of the conference, did a fantastic job of assembling such a diverse and important representation of views. Their Tulane colleague, David Clinton, provided them valuable assistance. Acknowledgment is gratefully made to the Louisiana Endowment for the Humanities (LEH) and Tulane University for financial support of the conference. Special thanks goes to Michael Sartisky, executive director of the LEH, and to Tulane Provost James Kilroy, who granted permission to publish this report. Appreciation also goes to Yvette Jones, Tulane vice president for finance and operation, and to Louis Barilleaux and Richard Marksbury, the deans of University College at Tulane. Ruth's Chris Steak House made a grant in support of videotaping the conference that was instrumental in making these proceedings possible. Following the conference, Randy Fertel provided further invaluable assistance gathering together the material for this volume. Thanks also goes to Marilyn Young, Gary Hess, and Robert Schulzinger for their constructive editorial suggestions. This book could not have been produced without the help and encouragement of my wife, Helen, and the loving support of my daughter, Hope.

The poetry in this book is reprinted by permission as follows:

"Time on Target" by W. D. Ehrhart is reprinted with permission of the author from W. D. Ehrhart, *To Those Who Have Gone Home Tired* (New York: Thunder's Mouth Press, 1984).

"Interview with a Guy Named Fawkes, U.S. Army" by Walter McDonald is reprinted with permission of the publisher from *Carrying the Darkness: The Poetry of the Vietnam War,* ed. W. D. Ehrhart (Lubbock: Texas Tech University Press, 1989).

"For All My Brothers and Sisters" by Dick Lourie is reprinted with permission of the author from *Carrying the Darkness: The Poetry of the Vietnam War,* ed. W. D. Ehrhart (Lubbock: Texas Tech University Press, 1989).

"Revelation in the Mother Load" by George Evans is reprinted with permission of the author from George Evans, *Sudden Dreams: New and Selected Poems* (Minneapolis: Coffee House Press, 1991). Copyright © 1991 by George Evans.

The Vietnamese love song on p. 82 is a translation by John Balaban and is reprinted with permission of the translator from John Balaban, *Ca Dao Vietnam: A Bilingual Anthology of Vietnamese Folk Poetry* (Greensboro, N.C.: Unicorn Press, 1980).

The Vietnamese song in the epigraph is an extract from a song that Le Ly Hayslip recalls from her childhood and quotes in her memoir, *When Heaven and Earth Changed Places* (New York: Penguin, 1990).

INTRODUCTION

• • • • • • • • • • • • • • • •

What Really Happened?

David L. Anderson

In November 1969 the American public first learned from brief newspaper reports that U.S. army lieutenant William L. Calley had been charged
with multiple murders of Vietnamese civilians at a place called My Lai. At
that time, there were about five hundred thousand U.S. troops in Vietnam.
American combat units had been there for almost five years, and over forty
thousand Americans had been killed in action. The Vietnam War had been
the principal issue in the 1968 election that brought Richard Nixon to the
White House with a promise to find an honorable way to end the war. The
public was tired of and disillusioned with the conflict, and news that U.S.
soldiers might be murderers seemed additional evidence of the liability that
the war had become. After a military court-martial found Calley guilty in
April 1971 of the murder of "at least 22" Vietnamese noncombatants, a
Harris Poll revealed that an incredible 91 percent of its respondents had
followed the trial closely. Among those polled, 36 percent disagreed with
the verdict, 35 percent agreed, and 29 percent were undecided.[1]

The crime in which Calley participated was one of the most horrendous atrocities in the history of U.S. warfare. The initial charges against Calley accused him of personally killing or ordering to be killed 109 civilians on March 16, 1968, but the total killed that day far exceeded that gruesome number. One of the men later described the scene:

> I just killed. I wasn't the only one that did it; a lot of people in the company did it, hung 'em, all types of ways, any type of way you could kill someone that's what they did. That day in My Lai I was personally responsible for killing about twenty-five people. Personally, I don't think beforehand anyone thought that we would kill so many people. I mean we're talking about four to five hundred people. We almost wiped out the whole village, a whole community. I can't forget the magnitude of the number of people that we killed and how they were killed, killed in lots of ways.
>
> Do you realize what it was like killing five hundred people in a matter of four or five hours? It's just like the gas chambers—what Hitler did. You line up fifty people, women, old men, children, and just mow 'em down. And that's the way it was—from twenty-five to fifty to one hundred. Just killed. We just rounded 'em up, me and a couple of guys, just put the M-16 on automatic, and just mowed 'em down.[2]

Although the words *My Lai* and *massacre* will forever be linked in the historical record, the enormity of the evil of that day is scarcely remembered. For many Americans, it is one of a host of unpleasant and uncomfortable images and associations from the Vietnam War that they seek to forget. As the divided public reaction to the Calley verdict also revealed, the explanation of what happened was elusive and has continued to confound those who seek to understand and to ease the psychic pain of the evil and horror of Vietnam. Who was responsible and who was to blame? Time has a way of healing, according to the old adage. Time also erases or blurs memories. Forgetting and healing are not necessarily synonymous.

Some facts about My Lai are generally accepted. On March 16, 1968, troops of Charlie Company, First Battalion, Twentieth Infantry Brigade, Americal Division combat air assaulted a village in South Vietnam's Quang Ngai Province. Known to Americans as My Lai 4, Vietnamese called it Thuan Yen. It was part of a hamlet called Tu Cung, which was part of a

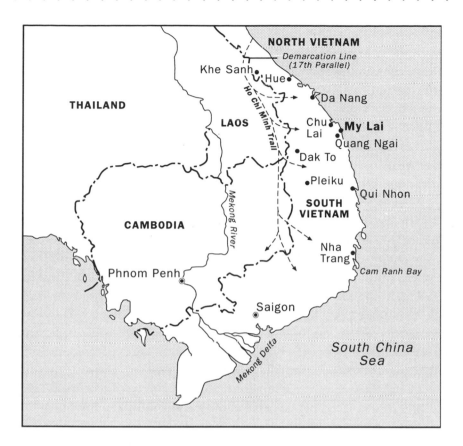

larger village called Son My.[3] In GI slang it was "Pinkville," a name derived from shading on military maps that indicated a densely populated area.

Charlie Company was part of Task Force (TF) Barker, a temporarily assembled strike unit of three infantry companies and an artillery battery commanded by Lieutenant Colonel Frank Barker. TF Barker's mission was to locate and destroy Vietcong main-force combat units in an area that had long been a political and military stronghold for the enemy. Captain Ernest L. Medina commanded Charlie Company and Second Lieutenant William L. "Rusty" Calley commanded the company's First Platoon.

Shortly before 8:00 A.M., helicopters landed the company outside My Lai. Expecting Vietcong resistance, the first and second platoons entered the village with weapons firing. By noon every living thing in My Lai that the troops could find—men, women, children, and livestock—was dead. The total of Vietnamese civilians killed numbered 504, according to North and South Vietnamese sources.[4] The casualties of Charlie Company were one self-inflicted gunshot wound in the foot. The company's report to the division commander, Major General Samuel W. Koster, listed 128 enemy killed in action (KIA) and three weapons captured. Two days later, the division's newsletter proclaimed: "TF Barker Crushes Enemy Stronghold."

What really happened at My Lai? Was it an armed Vietcong village if only three weapons were found? Was it an enemy stronghold if the U.S. troops suffered no casualties from hostile fire? Did anyone from the village fire at all? What orders did Colonel Barker give his officers, and what orders did Captain Medina give his troops? Why did many, but not all, of the men of Charlie Company persist for over three hours in brutalizing and executing all the unarmed, unresisting villagers? The victims included babies in their mothers' arms, young women (some of whom were raped before they were murdered), and elders too feeble to rise from their beds. Why did not someone in command stop the slaughter? Why was there no immediate military investigation of the obvious inconsistencies in the operation? Why did it take a year and a half before the horrible facts of the events at My Lai became public, and then only through the prodding of a conscience-stricken GI, Ron Ridenhour, who was not even present at My Lai? Why was Lieutenant Calley the only person there that day ever to receive any judicial punishment?

There has been no general agreement on the answers to these questions. The U.S. Army eventually investigated the massacre and gathered volumes of testimony and other evidence that detailed the gruesome facts of that March 16. Several criminal prosecutions ensued, but in the courts of law guilty verdicts proved difficult to obtain. Similarly, in the judgment of history, much of the truth about My Lai remains ambiguous. One of the most contentious questions has been whether My Lai was an aberration or an operation. Was the cold-blooded brutality unique or at least an extreme deviation from the admittedly harsh tactics of a counterinsurgency war? Or was it routine or at least close to normal for a war that was conducted with lethal modern weapons among an inscrutable and racially distinct population? Was the atrocity produced by a breakdown of leadership and discipline in one unit, or was it an inevitable and all-too-familiar product of a war that was a bureaucratic abstraction of body counts, attrition strategy, and global deterrence? Does the moral burden fall on a few individuals, on the military and civilian chain of command, or on the entire American way of war? How one answers these questions about the past determines how

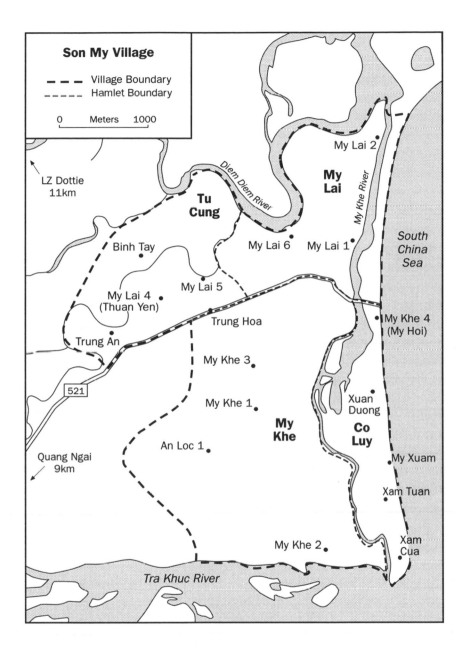

Son My Village

- – – Village Boundary
- - - - Hamlet Boundary

0   Meters   1000

LZ Dottie
11km

Diem Diem River

My Khe River

**Tu
Cung**

**My
Lai**

My Lai 2

South
China
Sea

Binh Tay

My Lai 6   My Lai 1

My Lai 4
(Thuan Yen)

My Lai 5

Trung Hoa

My Khe 4
(My Hoi)

Trung An

521

My Khe 3

My Khe 1

Xuan
Duong

Quang Ngai
9km

An Loc 1

**My
Khe**

**Co
Luy**

My Xuam

Xam Tuan

Xam
Cua

My Khe 2

Tra Khuc River

one lives with the traumatic memories in the present and guards against such disasters in the future.

In examining the My Lai massacre, three explanations emerge. Although they tend to point the finger of blame in three directions, they are complementary and, in combination, help reveal who or what was responsible. One explanation is that a mental breakdown by some individual members of Charlie Company produced this atrocity. The culprit is emotion, ranging from fear, rage, and vengeance on one extreme to no human feeling at all on the other. This interpretation cites mounting psychological pressures on the men. On February 12 a bullet from an unseen sniper had killed Specialist Four Bill Weber. His death was the company's first in Vietnam. Over the next month there were more deaths and terrible wounds from land mines and booby traps, but no face-to-face encounters with enemy troops. The men became increasingly brutal in their treatment of Vietnamese civilians they encountered on their patrols, and the officers tolerated this behavior. On March 15 the company held an emotional memorial service for Sergeant George Cox, a popular squad leader who had been blown apart by a booby trap the previous day. Immediately after the service, Medina briefed the men on the next morning's operation at My Lai. The service and briefing merged into a kind of ritualistic preparation for bloody vengeance. Regardless of what were Medina's specific orders before going into My Lai, the troops were primed to kill, and kill they did. For some the villagers were the unseen enemy that had been killing and maiming their friends for weeks, and for others the victims were scarcely human at all. The soldiers' behavior was so shocking that attention can be misdirected toward them and shifted away from what others were doing.

Poor leadership is a second explanation for the atrocity, and it puts the burden primarily on the company, battalion, and division officers. Medina, Barker, Colonel Oran K. Henderson (the new brigade commander supervising his first combat operation), and Koster are the chief culprits here. Calley himself fits both the first and second explanation, because his rank gave him command responsibility while his inexperience made him susceptible to breakdown. Either from actual orders or from the informal climate in the division, many of the men believed they had license to kill. Ridenhour suspects that the higher officers may purposefully have planned an operation to brutalize the village and others. A similar, somewhat smaller, and never fully prosecuted incident occurred with Bravo Company of TF Barker at the nearby village of My Khe. In this counterterrorism scenario, a brutal attack on a village in a Vietcong-controlled area would be a demonstration to the local people, something like a criminal gang burning out a small business to convince others in the neighborhood to pay protection money. It is likely that Henderson and Koster were in "Charlie-Charlie" (command and control) helicopters over My Lai, and it is certain that Medina and Barker were close by. Did these officers make no move to stop the ground action because it was going according to plan? Even if not planned, Colonel William Eckhardt, who supervised the My Lai prosecutions, notes that Medina quickly knew the men were on a rampage and did nothing to stop it. Medina and those above him may have kept a discreet distance to create plausible deniability later.

A third explanation is that the massacre flowed from what could be called the American way of war in Vietnam. The United States used high technology and vast material resources to inflict maximum suffering and damage on the enemy while minimizing pain and loss to U.S. forces. Military historian Russell Weigley has noted that "war creates a momentum of its own; the use of violence cannot be so nicely controlled and restrained as strategist . . . would have it."[5] The culprit is body count or kill ratio—that is, counting the number of enemy KIA or comparing enemy KIA to American KIA. In a war where the enemy often wore civilian clothes, the bodies were often counted using the "mere gook rule" that "if it's dead and it's Vietnamese, it's VC."[6] Secretary of Defense Robert McNamara's Pentagon devised this war by the numbers, and General William C. Westmoreland, the commander of all forces in Vietnam, tried to implement it through an attrition strategy sometimes labeled "search and destroy." The destruction was accomplished not just by soldiers' firing into villages with M-16s and rocket-propelled grenades (RPGs), but also by artillery, napalm bombs, and B-52 carpet bombing in so-called "free-fire zones." All of this violence was the product of a global strategy to deter the ambitions of America's powerful enemies. How many Vietnamese civilians had to die to prove a point to Moscow and Beijing? What point was being proved? There was no relationship between means and ends.

This same pattern of three causes, which might be characterized as individual, group, and general, is evident in other notorious incidents in American history. For example, in the village of Salem, Massachusetts Bay Colony, in 1692, twenty men and women were executed after being charged with witchcraft. The explanations offered have included the following. (1) Individual: The accusers were mentally ill, and their hysteria spread to others in the community and resulted in irrational behavior. (2) Group: Local magistrates and church leaders used the charges as a pretext to intimidate others in the community who threatened their authority. (3) General: Colonial New Englanders were deeply religious and believed in the reality of witches. Some thirty other people were hanged for witchcraft in other places in New England; Salem's experience was not isolated but represented a particular time and region.

Another example is McCarthyism in the 1950s, in which unsubstantiated allegations of communist sympathies ruined reputations and careers of countless citizens. The explanations include: (1) Individual: Senator Joseph McCarthy himself was psychotic, and his charges triggered irrational fears and hysteria in others. (2) Group: McCarthy's ranting would have gained no credence or audience if cynical politicians had not calculatingly exploited his antics for their own purposes. (3) General: The cold war, Soviet possession of the atomic bomb, and communist success in China were realities that would have generated fear of communism even if there were no McCarthy or those who would manipulate his rhetoric.

In the case of My Lai—as with the Salem witch trials and McCarthyism—the final explanation is a collage of the three factors. Some members of Charlie Company lost their individual moral and rational bearings and committed murder. Private Paul Meadlo, who followed Calley's order to shoot women and small children gathered in an irrigation ditch, later testified:

A: I held my M-16 on them.
Q: Why?
A: Because they might attack.
Q: They were children and babies?
A: Yes.
Q: And they might attack? Children and babies?
A: They might've had a fully loaded grenade on them. The mothers might have throwed them at us.
Q: Babies?
A: Yes.
Q: Were the babies in their mothers' arms?
A: I guess so.
Q: And the babies moved to attack?
A: I expected at any moment they were about to make a counterbalance.[7]

It is difficult to make any sense of such behavior. As Vietnam infantryman and novelist Tim O'Brien has written about GIs in village warfare in Vietnam: "They did not know even the simplest things. . . . They did not know how to feel when they saw villages burning. . . . They did not know good from evil."[8]

Many American combat veterans, however, deeply resented the image of themselves as "baby killers." "I never heard of renegade squads or anything like that," a veteran of the combat-hardened Twenty-fifth Infantry Division later recalled. In his view, "My Lai was bizarre, an unusual aberration. Things like it were strictly for the movies. The average soldier fought hard and well."[9] Historian Eric Bergerud, who interviewed many of the men of the Twenty-fifth Division, concluded: "My Lai was and is an albatross on the shoulder of every Vietnam veteran. . . . It is almost incomprehensible that so many Americans accepted the idea that the insane actions of one perverse junior officer . . . were representative of the entire U.S. Army."[10]

The men immersed in the My Lai mayhem, including Calley, may have been fatally disoriented, but that explanation cannot be used for Medina and his superiors up through the division commander. Regardless of whether Barker and Medina explicitly ordered the men to kill everyone, as some troops later testified, Medina clearly conveyed to the unit that the hostile inhabitants of this village were part of the unseen enemy behind the booby traps and land mines and were to be shown no mercy. In addition, as James William Gibson has described as standard operating procedure in this "techno-war," the "war-managers"—that is, Colonel Henderson, General Koster, and their staffs—would have hovered over the area in their helicopters following and perhaps even directing the action below. The brass had created TF Barker for this purpose, that is, to bloody the elusive Vietcong. They may well have presumed, without knowing or caring about the precise details, that the killing they knew was happening was following the plan. The announced and bogus body count of 123 enemy killed may, in fact, have derived from some earlier planning estimate.

The reporting of the body count points directly to the third cause—the way the war was conducted. While Calley was being tried, the army was already rewriting training manuals to improve teaching the law of land warfare. The military was going to have a lot of retraining to do, however, from the top down. With the My Lai case already uncovered, the lieutenant general who commanded II Field Force (the Saigon area) was still compiling death statistics to determine promotions and decorations, and his forces in the field knew it. Grunts throughout Vietnam may not have been well versed in the Geneva Conventions, but many of them understood the "mere gook rule."[11]

These three considerations are important in trying to obtain some closure as to how this atrocity could have happened, but of equal or even greater long-term significance is the aftermath, including the cover-up, uncovering, trials, and finally the response of the military and the public. The dark secret of March 16 was held within the Americal Division for a year. A complaint by Warrant Officer Hugh C. Thompson, Jr., had been forwarded up the brigade chain of command almost immediately. A helicopter pilot, Thompson was not part of Charlie Company but was in the aviation unit assigned to cover the ground assault on My Lai. Realizing what the ground forces were doing, he landed and rescued the few civilians he could. The actions of Thompson and his crew were a singular and powerful expression of compassion and moral courage amid a scene of human depravity. His formal report of brutal and unprovoked murder of civilians was not investigated or acted upon by brigade or division headquarters. Did the senior officers in charge simply not believe the brash young pilot? Had they become insensitive to violence against civilians? Were they knowingly hiding their own culpability and failure of leadership?

The uncovering began more than a year after the event, when Ron Ridenhour, a recently discharged GI, wrote a letter. He sent copies to the army and to several members of Congress. It asked for a public investigation of "something very black indeed," namely, the possible killing of every man, woman, and child in the village of My Lai. Without this letter, the crimes at My Lai might never have been investigated. Ridenhour had not been in Charlie Company or at My Lai, but he knew several men who were. He had heard them describe that day in chilling detail. His sense of justice and patriotism compelled him to track down other witnesses, to search for more grim facts, and ultimately to speak out. In his letter he quoted Winston Churchill: "A country without a conscience is a country without a soul, and a country without a soul is a country that cannot survive."[12]

Numerous investigations ensued. The Department of the Army Inspector General and the Criminal Investigation Division of the Army determined, largely through interviews with members of Charlie Company and other witnesses such as Thompson and his crew, that the laws of land warfare had been violated. General Westmoreland, who was then Army Chief of Staff, created a special investigation panel headed by Lieutenant General William

R. Peers. With the army's image already damaged by the long and increasingly controversial war in Vietnam, Westmoreland was as concerned about the apparent cover-up by senior officers as he was about the brutality in the village. Peers returned a stunning report that graphically described the carnage and called for the indictment of twenty-eight officers. At the top of Peers's hit list was General Koster, who had moved on to become commandant of West Point, one of the army's most honored assignments.

Naming suspects and getting convictions proved to be very different propositions. Because many months had passed since the crimes, many of those involved were out of the service, and the Nixon administration's Justice Department resisted bringing civilians before military courts-martial. Evidence had been destroyed, and key witnesses either could not or would not remember important details. In addition, military law allowed commanders to review the merits of charges brought against members of their command. As a result of these factors, Koster and several other senior officers escaped the court-martial process entirely. Lieutenant General Jonathan Seaman harshly censured Koster for failing to investigate Thompson's complaint and for ignoring other evidence of wrongdoing. In a nonjudicial action, the former Americal commander was demoted to brigadier general and stripped of his Distinguished Service Medal; he soon retired, his once promising career finished. Although Seaman may have been correct that there was not enough evidence to proceed to open trial, the public-relations impact of his decision was enormous. Since Koster's censure was administered privately, the dropping of the formal charges made it appear that one general was simply protecting another and letting others take the blame and punishment for My Lai.

From the time that Ridenhour wrote his letter, he had feared the military would not pursue the cases. He began trying to get his story to the press but could find no real interest. After the arrest of Calley in September 1969, an investigative reporter in Washington, Seymour Hersh, began to look into the Calley case, not knowing about Ridenhour or the broader investigation. Slowly the story began to come out. Hersh began publishing a series of reports, and he found Ridenhour, who was a fountain of information. On November 20 the *Cleveland Plain Dealer* published photographs of the massacre taken by Ron Haeberle, a combat photographer who had been present. Shortly afterward, Paul Meadlo appeared on the *CBS Evening News*. The press and public had to acknowledge that something horrible had happened at My Lai.

The story became front-page news, but the initial reaction was disquieting. Many Americans simply refused to believe that the allegations could be true, and others accused the accusers of trying to tear down the armed forces. Thirteen members of Charlie Company, including Captain Medina, were eventually charged with murder. All were acquitted or had their charges dropped except for Calley. Colonel Barker had died in Vietnam in a June 1968 helicopter crash. Twelve officers were accused in the cover-up, but only Colonel Henderson stood trial. He was acquitted after several witnesses declared under oath that they could not recall the events about which they were being questioned.

Calley, then, was the only person convicted of My Lai related crimes. A military court of six officers found him guilty of premeditated murder and sentenced him to life imprisonment at hard labor. Responding to public criticism of the verdict and especially the complaint that this one junior officer was being singled out, Nixon as commander-in-chief moved Calley from the stockade at Fort Benning to house arrest and said he would review the case. Privately, Secretary of the Army Stanley Resor and, publicly, Captain Aubrey Daniel, who had prosecuted Calley, took strong issue with the president's action. They argued that the president's interference denigrated the military justice system and that it placed the U.S. government in the position of condoning a crime that, in Resor's words, stood "alone in infamy."[13] After various appeals and reviews, Calley served only four and a half months in the military prison at Fort Leavenworth.

Like Resor and Daniel, many military professionals understood that there was no defense or excuse for the cold-blooded mass murder at My Lai. The U.S. military role in Vietnam ended in 1973, and career officers throughout the Army began to take a hard look at the institution to which they remained loyal. Many of them saw a host of mistakes made in management and organization of the military, and they set out to reform the system and restore its fallen honor. In military staff and command schools and colleges, My Lai and the law of war became important subjects of study.

Answers to disturbing questions about My Lai remained difficult to fashion because the event itself was so painful to recall. For many years Americans sought to repress the entire Vietnam War experience in both their own minds and the nation's collective memory. Vietnam, after all, represented defeat and failure. Immediately after the fall of Saigon to North Vietnamese forces in April 1975, President Gerald Ford and Secretary of State Henry Kissinger urged the public to put Vietnam behind them and not to dwell on

it or think about it. Many Vietnam veterans, tormented by nightmarish rec-
ollections of the fear, rage, and horror that they had been through, wished
to God that they could forget. As Sigmund Freud observed long ago, however, even the most painful memories have a way of reappearing. With the
dedication of the Vietnam Veterans Memorial in 1982, the public amnesia
and the private agonies of many veterans began to be healed. Indeed, the
late 1980s and early 1990s were a time of growing curiosity about the war
as revealed in major motion pictures, poetry, fiction, nonfiction, and hundreds of college courses on the subject.

Yet even as a healthy light of reexamination began to shine on the war
and as many veterans began to feel that the country did care about what
they had been through, dark shadows remained. A sense of alienation and
exploitation continued to haunt some veterans. An unprecedented number
of men and women who had served in Vietnam both in combat and in support suffered severe and ongoing psychological damage. The Veterans Administration (VA) physicians resisted until 1983 recognizing a diagnosis that
specifically related these patients' symptoms to the war. The sufferers experienced anxiety, nightmares, flashbacks, psychic numbing (the inability
to feel strong emotions), aggression, and guilt from either having killed or
having survived when their buddies died. Their behavior included drug and
alcohol abuse, broken marriages, sudden outbursts of violence, and reclusive-
ness. Together these symptoms were given a variety of names, such as battle
fatigue or delayed stress, but finally in 1980, the American Psychiatric
Association settled on *post-traumatic stress disorder* (PTSD). The VA eventually conceded that at least five hundred thousand of the three million who
served in Vietnam suffered from PTSD. Professionals who counsel these
patients estimated in 1990 that the number was more than eight hundred
thousand.

While these veterans struggled individually, the nation struggled collectively with what some conservatives labeled as the "Vietnam syndrome."
Former President Nixon, President Ronald Reagan, and others worried that
public disgust and disenchantment over Vietnam would undermine the
nation's will to defend its international interests with military force. React-
ing to the characterization of Vietnam as a "limited war," other citizens urged
the use of greater U.S. firepower in any future conflict. Sensitive to these
concerns, President George Bush repeatedly chanted, almost as if it were
an exorcism, that his order to invade Iraq in 1991 was not another Vietnam. The U.S. military performed well in the Persian Gulf War, and the

success of Operations Desert Shield and Desert Storm showed that lessons had been learned from Vietnam about keeping a clear balance between objectives and costs. After the swift U.S. victory over Iraq, Bush exclaimed, "By God, we've kicked the Vietnam syndrome once and for all."[14]

Two decades after Hanoi gained de facto control over all of Vietnam, however, the United States remained in denial. It continued to reject diplomatic recognition of the Vietnamese government. It was not until July 11, 1995, that President Bill Clinton announced the extension of full diplomatic recognition to Vietnam by the United States. The issue of accounting for American prisoners of war and missing in action complicated the recognition issue, but the persistent inability of the United States to admit defeat and move on had dramatized how deeply the war had damaged America's self-image.

In the 1950s American culture simply assumed the moral and material superiority of the United States over other nations. The United States had led a great victory over totalitarianism and militarism in World War II, and for the generation of Americans who waged that struggle, right and might had merged. Historians of that generation such as Louis Hartz and Daniel Boorstin wrote that, from its inception, American culture had been uniquely enlightened. Abraham Lincoln had once declared that American democracy was mankind's "last, best hope," and few Americans in the flush of peace and prosperity after World War II would have disputed that proposition.

The children of the 1950s, who composed the postwar "baby boom," did not read Hartz or Boorstin and knew few of Lincoln's speeches, but they breathed the purified air of America's noble self-image. The boys played army or cowboys and Indians. They pretended they were their fathers killing Nazis or Japs. They imitated the heroic exploits portrayed in popular westerns and war movies. In the childhood games, as in the movies, the American GIs or the cowboys (the white Americans) always prevailed over the forces of evil and savagery. For African-American children, their approach was different. Some of their great-grandfathers may have fought Indians, but their fathers had, for the most part, not been allowed to fight the Germans or Japanese. These children wanted the opportunity to prove themselves in combat. The thought that Americans themselves (apart from some stereotyped villains) could be evil simply did not exist for most Americans.

In the 1960s the young men who had fought in World War II had reached positions of national leadership, and the children of the 1950s formed a vast pool of potential military manpower. These leaders and the children of their generation, although usually not their own children, fought a war in South-east Asia. The Vietnam War, which in fact sprawled beyond the borders of Vietnam, began for the leaders and soldiers as a continuation of the nation's presumed role as champion of good and opponent of evil. Before that conflict ended, however, it had delivered some smashing blows to the collective and individual identity of Americans. War is hell, and American soldiers in World War II and Korea, at places such as Omaha Beach, Tarawa, and Chosin Reservoir, knew firsthand what it meant to kill or be killed. But the mayhem of these other wars had some purpose. The enemy usually consisted of uniformed soldiers, and at the end of the battle it was usually obvious who had won or lost. In Vietnam the progress and the results were seldom clear, and often there was no clear-cut way to tell civilian friend from military enemy.

In August 1967, well before My Lai but also well into the U.S. intervention in Vietnam, journalist Jonathan Schell had a conversation with four GIs at Duc Pho, not far from My Lai. "When we got here, we landed on a different planet," one explained. Trying to give his observation historical context, he added: "In Germany and Japan, I guess there was a thread of contact, but even when a Vietnamese guy speaks perfect English I don't know what the hell he's talking about." "No one has any feelings for the Vietnamese," another explained; "They're not people. Therefore, it doesn't matter what you do to them." Schell asked the second GI what he was going to tell people when he returned to the United States. The man responded: "Maybe when I go home I'll just crawl back inside myself, and not say a word. Things are so violent nobody would believe it. And I don't want to die of frustration trying to convince them." Schell had heard this remark—"they wouldn't believe it back home"—many times in Quang Ngai Province. He had pressed a soldier at Chu Lai: "What kind of things, then?" The GI refused to elaborate: "You wouldn't believe it, so I'm not going to tell you. No one's ever going to find out about some things, and after this war is over, and we've all gone home, no one is ever going to know."[15]

Today, we live in an age of historical relativism. Women, minorities, and other ordinary individuals are giving voice to their own histories and expressing open skepticism about the old history that valued consensus and seemed to limit itself to the study of generals, politicians, and intellectually gifted or powerful males. In the cacophony of diverse voices, truth is difficult to discern and cynicism abounds. Can we ever know the truth of the past with certainty? Such reflection can be discouraging and even defeating, if we

allow it. On the other hand, realization that the past has many manifesta-
tions can be liberating. As a recent essay on the nature of history argues,
"since no one can be certain that his or her explanations are definitively right,
everyone must listen to other voices."[16]

Psychologists and historians know that neither memory nor history is
characterized by total recall. Everything about the past cannot be retrieved
and brought into the present. What is retrieved may be only an approxima-
tion or a distortion of the actual past. There are some things that society or
individuals do not want to recall. Memory struggles against forgetting on
several fronts. From bits and pieces, a past is reconstructed in the present
to offer a guide for the future. The process does not stop with listening. "We
cannot meet dogmatism with dogmatism," historian Dan Carter has admon-
ished us, "or simply shrug our shoulders and say there are 'many kinds of
truth.'"[17] We must carefully collect evidence, analyze it, and construct logical arguments. If American political and military leaders and U.S. citizens
are going to face the darkness and heal the wounds of Vietnam—both collectively and individually—they are going to have to confront the war in all
of its reality. The massacre at My Lai is part of that reality, indeed, one of
the most daunting parts of that reality.

NOTES

1. William M. Hammond, *The U.S. Army in Vietnam: Public Affairs: The Military and the Media, 1968–1973* (Washington, D.C.: Government Printing Office,
1996), 254.

2. Quoted in Michael Bilton and Kevin Sim, *Four Hours in My Lai* (New York:
Viking, 1992), 130–31.

3. William R. Peers, *Report of the Department of the Army Review of the Preliminary Investigation into the My Lai Incident,* vol. 1: *The Report of the Investigation*
(Washington, D.C., March 14, 1970), 3-3.

4. Army investigators estimated that over four hundred people were killed in
Son My Village (including the subhamlets of My Lai 4 and My Khe 4) on March
16, 1968. Vietnamese reports at the time indicated about five hundred deaths. The
Son My Memorial at My Lai lists 504 names. See Tim O'Brien, "The Vietnam in
Me," *New York Times Magazine,* 2 October 1994, 54; Peers, *Report,* pp. 2-3, 2-7,
and 2-8.

5. Russell F. Weigley, *The American Way of War: A History of United States
Military Strategy and Policy* (Bloomington: Indiana University Press, 1973), 476.

6. James William Gibson, *The Perfect War: The War We Couldn't Lose and How
We Did* (New York: Vintage Books, 1988), 141.

7. Richard Hammer, *The Court-Martial of Lt. Calley* (New York: Coward, McCann & Geoghegan, 1971), 161–62.

8. Tim O'Brien, *Going after Cacciato* (New York: Delacorte Press, 1978), 272–73.

9. Quoted in Eric M. Bergerud, *Red Thunder, Tropic Lightning: The World of a Combat Division in Vietnam* (New York: Penguin, 1994), 228.

10. Ibid., 220. See also Lewis B. Puller, Jr., *Fortunate Son: The Autobiography of Lewis B. Puller, Jr.* (New York: Grove Weidenfeld, 1991), 257–58.

11. Gibson, *Perfect War,* 179–82.

12. Ridenhour to Secretary of Defense, 29 March 1969, in Peers, *Report,* pp. 1-7-1-11.

13. Hammond, *Military and the Media,* 251.

14. Quoted in George C. Herring, *America's Longest War: The United States and Vietnam, 1950–1975,* 3d ed. (New York: McGraw-Hill, 1996), 311.

15. Jonathan Schell, *The Real War: The Classic Reporting on the Vietnam War* (New York: Pantheon, 1987), 230–31.

16. Joyce Appleby, Lynn Hunt, and Margaret Jacob, *Telling the Truth about History* (New York: Norton, 1994), 11.

17. Dan T. Carter, "The Academy's Crisis of Belief," *Chronicle of Higher Education,* 18 November 1992, A36.

LOOKING INTO THE ABYSS: BEARING WITNESS TO MY LAI AND VIETNAM

Robert Jay Lifton

Bearing witness to history, according to psychiatrist and award-winning author Robert Jay Lifton, liberates us emotionally and mentally. The act of witness is not simply a recounting of an experience, but it is an authenticating of the truth of something that has happened. Furthermore, the individual witness of an event such as My Lai often reveals broader truths about human existence. From his work with Vietnam combat veterans who came to oppose the war and with one veteran who was at My Lai, Lifton developed the concept of atrocity-producing situation. Under certain conditions, otherwise normal individuals are capable of abnormally destructive behavior. The veterans whom Lifton met were suffering pain and alienation. By openly testifying to the absurdity and horror of Vietnam, they were able to regain some emotional feeling and some sense of connection with society. Lifton warns against false witness, that is, misrepresenting or misconstruing what occurred, and he urges that Americans humbly acknowledge that they are no better or worse than other people.

My Lai conveys terrible truths about the Vietnam War that we simply must face. Of course, My Lai in no way conveys the full story of the war. There were, after all, many American acts of the opposite characteristics of decency and courage, but My Lai in its very extremity epitomizes the nature of the American effort in Vietnam. In my work with rap groups organized by the Vietnam Veterans Against the War, I learned what the whole country was soon to learn, namely, that the Vietnam veterans had something very important to tell us. It was something that most people did not want to hear, but which was necessary for us to hear for our own needs as well as theirs. It had to be listened to. The principle was that of looking into the abyss in order to see beyond it. We cannot avoid the abyss; that is our history. We repeat it, if we are ignorant of it and if we cannot confront it. On the other hand, we do not want to be transfixed by it in a continuous mea culpa about American evil. Rather we must assume that Americans are neither better nor worse than any other people. Like other people, we are capable under certain circumstances of taking plunges into evil.

Love for this country requires energetic opposition to such actions. To become angry at My Lai at the time that it was revealed was an act of patriotism of the best kind, as is the thoughtful reflection on the event now. We need to be rigorously concerned not only with the facts of what actually occurred there, but also with the ethical and psychological lessons that we can draw from My Lai. No event has its own lessons that are clearly written. One has to construct them after examining the event. That sounds easy and logical, but it is very difficult to do—all the more so when the event is a highly destructive one performed by oneself or by one's own countrymen.

Bearing witness to history liberates us from numbing and enhances our freedom of the mind and our potential for wise action. The idea of witness seems to have begun as a religious concept, and it has been mainly that. When we try to translate this religious concept into more or less psychological terms, there are certain principles that take hold in relationship to witness or bearing witness. One is the idea of being there, the self being present in an existentialist sense. A second is the recording and confronting of some kind of ultimate matter—a matter of life and death or aspects of pain and suffering. A third is that of transcendence in witness. One is witnessing particular events, but they touch something larger than their own moment, something that has to do with broad human experience. Learning and knowledge come from witness.

In looking at the specific nature of the witness of Vietnam veterans, a few themes are crucial for us to keep in mind and to continue to think about into the future. The first is the atrocity-producing situation. I was able to interview at some length over a number of days a man who had been at My Lai but who had refused to fire or even to pretend to fire. What I learned in those invaluable interviews really taught me the psychological principles that I came to call an atrocity-producing situation. The Vietnam War taught us that one can create a war structure that is psychologically and organizationally primed for atrocity, that is, a situation in which an ordinary person, an average person, is quite capable of walking into and committing atrocities. That occurs because atrocities become the major means of adapting to that situation, and that was very much the situation at My Lai and in much of Vietnam.

At My Lai there were forces pressing toward atrocity. There was basic training, sometimes conducted by Vietnam combat veterans, in which the message instilled was that of random killing in combination with racism. There were policies of counterinsurgency warfare—free-fire zones and search and destroy missions—which encouraged random killing. There was the strange phenomenon of the body count, the enumeration of corpses becoming the only means of registering progress in a war that had no other purpose or meaning, whatever the falsifications of the count. There then took shape a terrible psychological sequence in which there were real deaths in one's unit, as there had been in C Company before My Lai. There were two central deaths—one of a much-beloved sergeant who was a kind of father-figure. There was a fierce sense of anger and grief in the men, and then there was the famous briefing given by Medina, which was a combination of religious ceremony and pep talk about more or less killing everything that was alive. There are many versions of what happened at the briefing, but it was a kind of license to kill. The men had a need to get back at the enemy as an expression of their grief and anger. That need was so great and the structure was so arranged that they could momentarily create the illusion that, in rounding up and killing small children, old people, and women from the villages, they had finally gotten the enemy to stand up and fight. That is the kind of illusion that took shape at My Lai and that can take shape in an atrocity-producing situation. It was not just My Lai; it was Vietnam.

When you study the impact of Hiroshima on America and the way in which the decision to use the atomic bomb was made, you find that it was an atrocity-producing situation. It would have been hard for the average president and the average set of decision makers not to make that decision. If you study Auschwitz, you find that it would have been hard for a person in German employ walking into the Auschwitz situation not to take part in those atrocities. There are many atrocity-producing situations. Vietnam helps us to understand how they can be created and how we can recognize the combinations of ideological, organizational, and psychological structures which lead to ordinary people engaging in slaughter.

There is a relationship between atrocity-producing situation and culpability. As we talked in our rap groups, I raised this idea of the atrocity-producing situation, and a number of the veterans made the point: "Well, we're still responsible for what we did." They were afraid lest that kind of psychological view divest them or anyone from human responsibility. It is a combination of atrocity-producing situation plus culpability. It is a situation in which, although you can describe something psychologically, you are still responsible for your actions. It becomes tragic. People say that Lieutenant Calley was not a person with a highly evolved moral sense. Whether that is true or not, many if not most people could have moved into that situation of Company C and become involved in My Lai, and they would still be responsible for what they did. If you have an atrocity-producing situation in a family where parents abuse their children, they are nonetheless responsible for their actions, even though their own desperation and victimization may have led them to be abusive. Culpability remains an important issue even if there is some understanding of how something happens.

A second witness of Vietnam veterans has to do with the possibility of resisting the atrocity-producing situation. One aspect allowing that to happen was frequent communication. It was understood in Vietnam that this was a very unpopular war and that people back home were hearing things over time about some of the things going on in Vietnam. That communication back and forth became epitomized by the music played in Vietnam. For periods of time in many parts of Vietnam, Country Joe MacDonald's "I-Feel-Like-I'm-Fixing-to-Die Rag," a grim, angry, brilliant statement about the absurdity of dying in Vietnam, was the favorite song of GIs. In that way Vietnam veterans could deepen their testimony about the counterfeit universe of Vietnam, as I came to call it, and relate to the equally counterfeit policies and decisions that brought them there.

Another form of witness is a very radical one. Vietnam veterans testified to the extraordinary phenomenon of combat soldiers opposing and doing much to stop their own war. The Vietnam Veterans Against the War organized the Winter Soldier Investigation in 1971, which dramatically brought the stories of Vietnam veterans to Americans.* Then there was the public theater that rocked this country when the antiwar veterans literally threw their medals in the face of those who had awarded them on the steps of the Capitol—an extraordinary moment. Soldiers in Vietnam, however, helped stop the war to a much greater extent than is still realized. They literally went on strike and refused to fight. There were fraggings (woundings) or even killings of officers who insisted that they fight. It was a kind of sit-down strike in Vietnam, which had as much to do with ending the war as anything else.

There is also false witness. False witness really is a way of ignoring the deepest testimony of Vietnam veterans and seeking to take from Vietnam lessons of more destructiveness, lessons that seek to compensate for or overturn the testimony of Vietnam veterans. Now, one might say that much of the Vietnam War, and certainly My Lai itself, was a form of false witness. Men in combat were witnessing the death of people they loved, of fellow soldiers, and were driven into certain behavior through the constellation of events I mentioned. There is a further and still more malignant kind of false witness, however. It is the Rambo idea of refighting the Vietnam War and winning it this time, or of insisting that we should have used whatever technological weaponry necessary to win that war in an absolute way. That idea would have led directly to the use of nuclear weapons, and has led to the retrospective claim that nuclear weapons should have been used. Then, in order to win this war in Southeast Asia that had so little to do with American interests, we would have had to kill millions or even hundreds of millions of people and perhaps have caused the ultimate destruction of civilization as we know it in order to prevent losing a war that we were otherwise losing. This is false witness.

Another false witness is in the phrase "when men refuse to fight, find robots that will." The reference is to the use of high-technology warfare instead of the use of men. It is nice that men will not be killed, but that is another illusion. When you have a high-technology war, you end up with men and women fighting it and being killed. That is what happened in relation to the high-tech Gulf War. Another lesson from the Gulf War that I

*Much of the Winter Soldier testimony detailed atrocities and war crimes.

would take to be false witness was that of keeping out imagery that might be disturbing to the American public, that is, keeping the press and television cameras from recording dead bodies, civilian casualties, and painful scenes of any kind. That breaks the connection of images between people at home and soldiers fighting the war, which is so crucial for what happened in Vietnam and for the democratic process to reestablish itself. This is a blocking of human truths of war and a preventing of continuous interaction. Instead, the tendency during the Gulf War was to flood the media with seminars on technological marvels, and we were all fascinated by that technology. I take that to be false witness.

Saddam Hussein was not a nice fellow and needed to be stopped or blocked, but much of the impulse to fight the Gulf War was the American leadership's determination to fight that battle in a military way that had much to do with false witness over Vietnam. There was preoccupation with Vietnam War imagery all through the Gulf War: the idea of having a force that would be overwhelmingly powerful so that we would not get into the morass of Vietnam, the repetitious statement that "this will not be another Vietnam," and then, of course, President Bush's triumphal and passionate statement at the end of the war that "by God we've kicked the Vietnam syndrome once and for all." In other words, the Vietnam syndrome for President Bush and for others was a set of images of military frustration and defeat that had produced an unwillingness to go all out to destroy an opponent and a reluctance to involve U.S. troops in faraway conflicts. For George Bush, then, the Vietnam syndrome was equated with American weakness. What we found from the Vietnam veterans in the rap groups, however, was a source of wisdom, not weakness. They found meaning in their war by portraying to the American public its very meaninglessness, and that indeed did require wisdom. My fear is that President Bush and others were seeking to reinstate the good name of war.

Historical memory is never simply factual. Somebody, after all, is doing the remembering, and we must reconstruct any historical experience. There is also group memory, in which some group shares historical memory. Where events are death-dominated, especially when they are relatively recent, as with My Lai and Hiroshima, memory and consciousness are bound up with the psychology of the survivor. In that sense, we are all survivors of Hiroshima; we are also all survivors of Vietnam and survivors of My Lai. The reverberations go through our society, however we may try to block them out, and blocking them out is a mistake. We do better as added survivors,

so to speak, or indirect survivors (it is not the same as being an actual survivor), to confront these issues and to absorb them in all of their detail. This
survivor witness applies to those who are old enough to remember the event,
and for members of younger generations, it continues to be true.

Vietnam bears a very special relationship to American history. In a way it
seems to represent a radical decline in the sense of American world hegemony or leadership and a loss of confidence in American power, especially since it was followed first by Watergate and then by a lot of economic
duress from which we still have not emerged. It can provide us, however,
with much-needed perspective on the American role in the world situation.
A European writer told me some years ago that he liked American writers
and intellectuals better after Vietnam because they had known suffering and
had confronted suffering and tragedy. He was trying to say that experiencing those emotions was a basis for balance and humanity. We have to realize that the American hegemony in the world to which we became so accustomed was strange and aberrant. It evolved at the end of World War II after
we had contributed so much to that important victory. We were dominant
militarily, economically, and also morally because we had defeated fascism.
Scientifically, intellectually, and in almost every other way we had a great
deal of influence and domination. That was not some normal, permanently
ordained state. It was the greatest situation of a single country being dominant that has ever existed. It did not exist before and has not subsequently
existed.

Vietnam can help us to reject our hubris and to accept our own limitations. It can help us see ourselves as no more than a segment of shared human
struggle to overcome mass slaughter and to find sufficient commonality for
alternative patterns, for enhancement, and for continuity of human life. Just
reading the morning papers about the genocides going on in our world makes
all too clear that this is a continuous struggle. There is no moment of resolution. One has to stay with it. The returns are never in in a full sense, but
the witness of Vietnam veterans continues to offer valuable possibilities for
illumination. We should embrace that witness.

EXPERIENCING THE DARKNESS: AN ORAL HISTORY

William G. Eckhardt, Ron Ridenhour, Hugh C. Thompson, Jr.

Hugh Thompson, Ron Ridenhour, and William Eckhardt are three individuals who were touched personally by the events of March 16, 1968, in My Lai. Hugh Thompson was a helicopter pilot assigned to fly air cover for the combat assault on the village. When he realized that the troops on the ground were systematically killing the unresisting villagers, he landed his scout helicopter and tried to stop the carnage, at one point even having his crewmen aim their weapons at the U.S. infantrymen. In recalling the events of that day, he asserts that the My Lai incident was not usual, was not an accident, and was pure premeditated murder. His compelling account provides powerful witness to an unambiguous morality.

Ron Ridenhour describes his military experience beginning when he was drafted in 1967. He relates how he first heard about Pinkville, the GI name for the My Lai area, and about what had happened there. He questioned men in his unit who had participated in or witnessed the killing at My Lai. One of those men, Michael

Bernhardt, said he planned to assassinate all of the officers involved when he got out of the Army. Ridenhour got Bernhardt instead to make a pact with him to tell the truth later about what they knew. Ridenhour ends his reminiscence discussing the writing of his famous letter that triggered the public disclosure of the atrocity.

A military trial lawyer who supervised the prosecutions in the courts-martial of those charged with My Lai offenses, William Eckhardt lauds the citizenship and courage of Thompson and Ridenhour. He recalls how he became physically ill when he first saw the investigative reports. Eckhardt clearly believes that the poor leadership of Medina and Calley caused what happened, but convictions were impossible without evidence. He relates how congressional hearings held by Congressmen L. Mendel Rivers and F. Edward Hebert were purposefully designed to frustrate the prosecution and to intimidate witnesses like Thompson. Under a statute known as the Jencks Act, Thompson's crucial testimony for the prosecution was either prevented from being entered or challenged at the various courts-martial because Hebert refused to make the closed congressional testimony available to the defense. Still, according to Eckhardt, the military learned valuable lessons about maintaining discipline in the field, and in the Gulf War the commanders explicitly warned their troops "no My Lais."

Hugh Thompson

I was a helicopter pilot. That particular morning we were to provide reconnaissance for a ground operation that was going on in My Lai 4, which was better known to us as "Pinkville." It was supposed to be a real big operation. I flew a scout helicopter, which was covered by two gunships. My job was to recon out in front of the friendly forces and draw fire; tell them where the enemy was; and let them take care of it. The village was prepped with artillery prior to the assault. We went in right in front of the "slicks," the troop-carrying helicopters that brought in Charlie Company and Bravo Company. We started making our passes, and I thought it was going to be real hot that day because the first thing we saw was a draft-age male running south out of the village with a weapon. I told my gunner to get him. He tried, but he was a new gunner and missed him. That was the only enemy person I saw that whole day.

We kept flying back and forth, reconning in front and in the rear, and it didn't take very long until we started noticing the large number of bodies everywhere. Everywhere we looked, we saw bodies. These were infants; two-, three-, four-, five-year-olds; women; very old men; but no draft-age people whatsoever. What you look for is draft-age people. Later in some of the interrogations that my crew and I went through, my gunner's big question was, Where were the weapons that day? There wasn't the first weapon captured, to my knowledge, that day. I think the count has been anywhere from two hundred to five hundred bodies, and it was well that many. I think that is a small count, including the three villages that were hit.

We were flying around and saw wounded people. There was one lady on the side of the road, and we knew something was going wrong by then. Larry Colburn, my gunner, motioned for her to stay down. She was kneeling on the side of the road. We hovered around, looking everywhere, and couldn't understand what was going on. We flew back over her a few minutes later. Most of you all have probably seen her picture; she has a coolie hat laying next to her. If you look real close, there is some odd object laying right next to her. That's her brains. It wasn't pretty. We saw another lady who was wounded. We got on the radio, called for some help, and marked her with smoke. A few minutes later up walks a captain. He nudges her with his foot, steps back, and blows her away.

We came across a ditch that had a lot of bodies in it and a lot of movement in it. I landed and asked a sergeant there if he could help them out. There were some wounded people down there who needed help. He said the only way he could help them was to help them out of their misery, I believe. I was shocked, I guess. I thought he was joking; I took it as a joke, I guess. As we took off and broke away from it, my crew chief, I guess it was, said, "My God, he's firing into the ditch." We had asked for help twice, actually three times by then. Every time the people had been killed. We were not helping out these people by asking for help.

Sometime later, we saw some people huddled in a bunker-type deal, and the only thing that I could see at that particular time was a woman, an old man, and a couple of kids standing next to her. We looked over and saw them and looked over there and saw the friendly forces, so I landed the helicopter again. I didn't want there to be any confusion or anything. I really don't know what was going on in my mind then. I walked over to the ground units and said, "Hey, there's some civilians over here in this bunker. Can you get them out?" One said, "Well, we can get them out with a hand grenade." I said, "Just hold your people right here please, I think I can do better." So I walked over to the bunker and motioned for them to come out and that everything was okay.

At that time I didn't know what I was going to do, because there was more than three or four there. There were a lot more than I thought there were. There were about nine or ten or something like that. I had a little problem on my hands now. How was I going to get these people out of this area? They would be dead if I didn't. The Americans just kind of stayed at bay. They didn't interfere. They didn't challenge me or anything. My crew and I were by that time very mad and upset. I don't remember the exact words, but I had told my crew what to do if the Americans started shooting. That didn't happen, so we were okay there. I didn't know what I was going to do with the people now that I had them. I couldn't just leave them there, because there was no doubt in my mind that they would have been killed. I walked back over to the aircraft and kept the people around me. I called a buddy of mine that was flying the low gunship and asked him to do me a favor. I said, "Hey, I got these people down here on the ground. How about landing? I got about nine or ten people here and I can't haul them. You all land and get them out of here." He agreed, which I think was the first time a gunship was ever used for that. He asked, "Where do you want me to take them?" "Away from this place," I said. He could only get about half of them in the first load, so he had to make two different trips. He picked them up and took them about ten miles or so behind the lines and dropped them off. I was sitting on the ground and had only one gunship covering me. That was not the best thing to do, I guess, but I couldn't leave those people there. After he came back and got the rest of them, we took off.

A short while later we went back and made another pass by the ditch. There was still some movement in there. We got out of the aircraft, and Glenn Andreotta, my crew chief, walked down into the ditch. He disappeared for a while. Larry and I were standing by the helicopter. I was on one side covering, and Larry was on the other side covering. A few minutes later Andreotta came back up carrying a little kid, who was covered with blood. We didn't know what we were going to do with this one either, but we all got back in the aircraft and figured we would get him back to the orphanage or hospital at Quang Ngai. We examined him in the aircraft that day, and the kid wasn't even wounded; or we didn't see any wounds, I'll put it that way. All the blood on him was somebody else's. Taking the child to the hospital that day was something I'll never forget. It was a very sad day; it was a very mad day. I was very frustrated and everything. We flew over and dropped the boy off. I told the nun that I don't know what you are going to do, but I don't think that he has any family left.

The question was going through my mind and my crew's mind of how these people got in that ditch. We came up with about three scenarios. One of them was that artillery hit them, but we wiped that out of our minds because every house in Vietnam, I think, had a bunker underneath it. If artillery was coming in, they would go to the bunker. They wouldn't go outside in the open area. Then I said, well, when artillery was coming in, they were trying to leave and a round caught them in the ditch while they were going for cover. I threw that one out of my mind. Then it sunk into me that these people were marched into that ditch and murdered. That was the only explanation that I could come up with. Andreotta had told me that a guy was shooting into the ditch after we had asked for help the first time.

Not just in this matter but on all of our missions, I had an understanding with my crew that we wouldn't do anything stupid if everyone was not in agreement to do it. If we received a couple of rounds, I would ask them if they wanted to stay or go. I do not recall any discussion on how we came to the idea of sitting down to get the people out. There is a lot of that day that's blocked out permanently, I guess.

After the mission that day, I went back to our operations area, which was over at LZ [landing zone] Dottie. I was very upset; I was very mad. I reported to my platoon leader, and I told him that I was not going to be a part of this. He asked what was going on. I said, "It's mass murder out there. They're rounding them up and herding them in ditches and then just shooting them." He said, "Let's go see the operations officer." Then we went to our commander and told him what was going on. I got real close to insubordination toward him. I said something like, "If this damn stuff is what's happening here, you can take these wings right now 'cause they're only sewn on with thread." I said, "I ain't taking part in this." I was ready to quit flying. My commander was very interested, but I don't think that he could believe what I was telling him. He said he would check into it or something like that.

Later that day, sometime in the afternoon, after they had gone through the village, we were back out there again. They were just casually, nonchalantly sitting around smoking and joking with their steel pots off just like nothing had happened. There were five or six hundred bodies less than a quarter of a mile from them, and I just couldn't understand it. Within a day or so—I do not think it was that day, it was probably the next day—we were called up to the command bunker at LZ Dottie. Everybody gave their statements to a full colonel. A full colonel is next to a general, which means he can walk on water. He seemed very interested. I remember him taking notes, and that was it, I do believe.

I don't know if I was called again to report to the commanding general. I think I was, but I can't be positive. Our unit was like sixty miles from head-quarters, and we didn't have contact with these ground people every day. A lot of people don't understand that sixty miles in Vietnam is a long way away. You just don't go there. I guess I assumed something was being done. It wasn't a colonel's position to come down to a W1 [warrant officer] and in-form him of his investigation, that just was unheard of. It seemed like it was just dropped after that.

Later when the story broke publicly and all the investigations started, I was called before the U.S. Senate, the Department of the Army IG, and every one of the court-martial investigations. They appointed Lieutenant General Peers to investigate this. I honestly think the army thought they had a yes-man when they got Lieutenant General Peers and found out, when he released his final report, that he wasn't a yes-man. I think he made a fairly accurate report of what happened that day. I believe too, as everybody says, that there was a cover-up. Everybody that has talked about it says the cover-up started on the ground. In my mind, I'm not real sure that's where the cover-up started. I wouldn't be the least bit surprised if the cover-up started "up" and worked its way back down.

It was probably one of the saddest days of my life. I just could not believe that people could totally lose control like the way it happened. I didn't know anything about that unit then. The only thing I know about the unit is what has been brought out since then. They hadn't been in the country that long. They had only been there, I think, going on their third month. They hadn't supposedly seen that much action. The majority of the casualties that they had taken had been partially self-induced. They had a lot of land-mine in-juries, a little from snipers, but most of their injuries I think had been with land mines. You have the proper way to cross a rice patty. It is much dirtier and takes more effort to go across the rice patty with the leeches and the snakes and the mud. It is a lot easier just to walk right down the dikes. Well, on the dikes is where they put the booby traps, and that is how a lot of their injuries had occurred. They may have had in their minds an invisible enemy that they were trying to get even with that day, I don't know, but I don't see how it could be the people because the people hadn't done anything to them. It's kind of strange. I can't figure out why they snapped. There had been other units there that had been in severe contact or something, but they didn't go out the next day and wipe out a village. I understand that Lieutenant Calley was a joke in the eyes of his men and of Medina. He supposedly worshipped the ground that Medina walked on and wanted to impress him. He may have thought that would impress Captain Medina.

I have heard people say this happened all the time. I don't believe it. I'm not naive. I understand that innocent civilians did get killed in Vietnam. I truly pray to God that My Lai was not an everyday occurrence. I don't know if anybody could keep their sanity if something like that happened all the time. I can see where four or five people get killed or something like that. My Lai was nothing like that. It was no accident whatsoever. It was pure premeditated murder. We were trained better than that, and it was just not something you do.

Ron Ridenhour

I was drafted in March of 1967 and went through basic training and advanced infantry training and parachute training school. That all took about six months, and I arrived in Hawaii assigned to Schofield Barracks in the Eleventh Infantry Brigade in September of 1967. The Eleventh was scheduled to ship out for Vietnam sometime in December. I was assigned to a very small unit with about thirty men, which was to be our brigade long-range reconnaissance patrol [LRRP]* unit. About two weeks before we were scheduled to ship out to Vietnam, our small LRRP detachment was disbanded because the infantry companies were under strength. About half the men, fifteen of the enlisted men, were sent off to Charlie Company, First of the Twentieth, Lieutenant Calley's company or Captain Medina's company, more properly. I was sent elsewhere and eventually became a door gunner on a light observation helicopter. Ironically, I was doing almost exactly the same thing that Hugh was doing at the same time, although we did it with two small ships rather than with the small ship with the two sharks or the two gunships covering. One of our small ships flew very low, about thirty feet off the ground, and the other flew higher in circles to cover it. Our mission was, as his was, to draw fire and then engage whoever fired at us.

We arrived in Vietnam four days before Christmas in 1967. We learned how to stand on the skid of a helicopter while it was flitting and fluttering and dipping and diving around the hedgerows and over tree lines. We practiced how to hold our machine guns and hit things and shoot. We did this for about two weeks, I suppose.

*Pronounced "lurp."

On our first mission we were called to go out and provide what they called light air cover for two infantry companies that were about to sweep through a fairly large village. I would guess it was 100 to 150 homes on Highway One about ten miles south of where we were. Our area of operation was immediately south of Hugh's. We had the southernmost part of I Corps, which was the northernmost part of South Vietnam. On this our first combat mission—our first alleged combat mission—we went out to fly around in this village and to protect the infantry soldiers from an ambush. They got on line, that is, they literally made a line long enough for all the men in the two infantry companies to stretch out in one long line. Then they started to walk through the village. Our job was to fly over the village and to fly behind the village to see if anybody was either trying to ambush them or to flee. And sure enough, after a few minutes here came a young man, military age, running out of the village. There was a trail out to the back end of the village leading off to the mountains to the west. This guy came out of there, and he was running to beat the band. We flew down alongside him, and we were trying to get him to stop. We were waving at him; we were motioning at him. But he was like, "Not me, man, I'm getting out of here"; he was steady trucking on.

After a few minutes of this, the pilot said, "Slow him down. Fire a burst in front of him. Let him know we're serious." So the other door gunner, the crew chief, fired a burst, and instead of firing in front of him, he hit him in the hips. The man went down in a heap, of course. He began to bleed and lay there in his own blood. We were totally freaked out because this was our first mission. We had never fired at anybody in anger before or under combat conditions or anything else. We had shot this guy and did not intend to. So we were pretty upset. The pilot was especially upset, and he got on the radio and called to the officers in the ground company to come help this guy. He was pretty frantic. The pilot was steadily on the radio saying, "Come on! Come on, hurry, this man needs help! This man needs help!" You could hear the infantry officer getting more and more frustrated as he ran. You could hear him running, you could hear him—"(pant, pant) I'm coming! I'm coming! (pant, pant)"—over the radio. It took him about twenty minutes to get there, but finally he broke out on the same trail through the other side of the back end of the village and ran down the trail to the guy. The officer gets there, runs up to him, stops, leans down, looks at him, stands up, pulls out his .45, and cocks it. BOOM! He shoots the guy in the head. He looked up at us, got on his radio, and said, "This man no longer needs any help." Well, that was my introduction to the reality of Vietnam as I saw it.

For four months I did this. I went out and stood on the skids of this helicopter, flew about thirty feet off the ground, and literally had a bird's-eye view. Most of our missions were what we called hunter-killer missions, doing the same thing Hugh was doing. We were going out usually at first light and last light. The catechism was that that was when the VC were on the move, and indeed frequently it was. We would pop up over a tree line or a hedgerow, and there would be two or three guys standing out in a rice field with guns. We would engage them and usually kill one or two of them, but they were well trained and would all run in different directions. Usually some would get away and some would not, but in that entire four-month period of time we only killed thirty-six people, I believe, in that neighborhood. We replaced a unit in that same area which was doing exactly the same thing. They had only been there for eight months before we arrived, and they killed over seven hundred people in eight months. What that said to me, since we were out doing the same thing, exactly the same thing in exactly the same area, was that they were just out there killing a lot of people. They were being a lot less discriminating than we were about who we were engaging. We were looking for people with guns, which is what we were supposed to be doing.

In that four months I guess I witnessed those sorts of events about six or seven times. We would identify somebody, just as Hugh had, who looked suspicious or whatever, and some infantryman would walk up to him and just shoot him. I mean, no provocation. I am not talking about something that is ambiguous. I am talking about murder. I am talking about somebody walking right up, pointing a gun, and, without provocation, pulling the trigger. I oppose that, of course, and so did most of us, but I don't think that we were really quite getting the drift of what was really going on there.

We flew into an area south of our area of operations on a kind of courier mission one day. We flew over a hut, and we could see that there were some guys in there torturing a Vietnamese. They were skinning this guy alive. Atrocities were, I'm afraid, far too common. I thought that it was kind of the way we were fighting the war, but still I was unprepared.

After about four months, I basically got fired from my job in the helicopter company. I couldn't get along with my sergeant. I volunteered then for the division's LRRP team. I hadn't seen my friends from Hawaii who had gone to Charlie Company in probably two months. I hadn't seen them since they had gone off with Task Force Barker and gone up to LZ Dottie, which was I guess about thirty miles north of us along the highway. The first night after I left the aviation company, I ran into a guy whom I had known in Hawaii. He had gone to Charlie Company and had since transferred into the division LRRP company where I was headed. We got a beer and found an empty tent with a table. We sat down and started to tell each other our war stories and get caught up on what we had done and what we had seen since we had last talked to each other.

After a minute or two he said, "Hey man, did you hear what we did at Pinkville?" I knew Pinkville, which was My Lai 4, because we had done some missions up there and it was known as a hot area. "So what'd you do at Pinkville?" He said, "Oh, man, we massacred this whole village." I said, "What?" He said, "Yeah, we massacred this whole village. We just lined them up and killed them." I said, "What do you mean?" He said, "Men, women, and kids, everybody, we killed them all." I said, "Well, how many was that?" He said, "Oh, I don't know, three or four hundred I guess, at least. A lot, everybody we could find. We didn't leave anybody alive; at least we didn't intend to."

It's hard for me to really describe exactly what my reaction was. The language doesn't quite—at least I haven't found a way to capture it, but it was, I guess you would say, an epiphany. It was an instantaneous recognition. There was a collateral determination that this was something too horrible, almost, to comprehend and that I was not going to be a part of it. Just simply having the knowledge, I felt, made me complicit, unless I acted on it.

I started to act on it, and I spent the remainder of my time in Vietnam trying to locate people who had been there. Part of it was easy because I was going straight to the division LRRP company. Four or five people who had been my friends in Hawaii and who had gone to Charlie Company had transferred into the division LRRP company within a week or ten days after the massacre. I was able to talk with them, and two of them were very good friends. In the case of one of them, we were drafted on the same day; we went to basic training together; we were in the same basic training company together; we were in the same advanced infantry battalion together; we both volunteered for special forces together; we were accepted together; and we went to jump school together. We both refused to sign an extension converting us from two-year draftees to four-year enlistees, and so we both ended up being shipped off to Hawaii instead of going on to special-forces school after jump school.

This kid's name was Mike Terry. He was, I thought, one of the finest people I had ever met. He was the all-American boy: wrestler in college, all-state champion, had respect for everybody around him, didn't swear, didn't speak badly of women, and wasn't into a lot of the sort of macho bragging that was going on by a lot of people. He was just a very fine human being. We had talked when we were on our way to Vietnam and after we got there, and I had heard complaints from these guys about Lieutenant Calley, this guy who was their officer, whom they just loathed, whom they thought was incompetent and a whole lot of other things.

I arrived in the LRRP company and began to go out on missions. On my first five missions, four of the six men who were on our team had been at My Lai. I was going out with these guys and gathering information. I would try to get each of them in a one-on-one conversation. I would ask them, "Hey, man, what happened at Pinkville?" And it would be like lancing a boil. I mean, if you asked them, they were compelled to talk. They couldn't stop talking. They were horrified that it had occurred, that they had been there, and, in the instances of all of these men, that they had participated in some way.

The story I had been told about what Mike Terry had done and what my other friend, Billy Doherty, had done was, I thought, stunning and terrifying in a certain way. I didn't ask Mike about it for I guess probably a month. I don't know why, exactly. Just back to the fire base after a four-day mission together, Mike and I went off and found ourselves a bunker to lay up on top of for that night to sleep. We lay down, and I asked him, "Hey, Mike, what happened at Pinkville? Tell me what happened at Pinkville." He told me this terrible story of going in with Lieutenant Calley and sweeping through the village and watching these murders and rapes and everything that was going on and about what happened at the ditch.

About eleven o'clock Mike and Billy sat down within fifteen or twenty feet of the ditch to have their lunch. They took out their C-rations and opened their food and started eating, but they could not really finish it because there was too much noise coming from the ditch. People who are mortally wounded but not yet dead make a lot of noise. People die hard; they do not want to give up life. The people in this ditch were laying there, and those who were still alive were groaning and crying out. Some of them had their limbs flopping spasmodically, which happens to people who are mortally wounded. Sometimes there was a "boom, boom." It must have been a terrible, God-awful racket—a horrifying sound, I'm sure. They couldn't eat, so they stood up. The two of them walked over to the ditch, and they divided up the survivors. They walked down the ditch, one on each side, finishing off all the survivors: "There's one; you take him. Okay. Pow, pow. There's one; you get him. Okay. Pow, pow." Up and down the ditch. When they returned to their food, the ditch was quiet.

A guy whose name was Butch Gruver had told me this story. He had told me about the ditch and about what Mike and Billy had done, but I needed to hear it from them. When I asked them about it they said, "Yeah, yeah, it's all true." Mike told me the story, and it was really a cloudless night. There were a zillion stars out there. After he finished, we just laid there for a couple of minutes. Finally I said, "Mike, Mike, God, Mike, don't you know that was wrong?" He said, "I don't know, man, I don't know, it was just one of them things." He rolled over, and a couple of minutes later I could see he was asleep. We never really talked about it much after that.

I spent the rest of my time looking for people who were not in our company and found about three or four more, I suppose. I was determined to cause an investigation of some kind. I was a kid. I had no idea how to do it, but I knew the first thing I needed was the facts. I went down to the division historical section where they kept an account of all the battles and everything, the official history of the division. There I found the official report that had been released to the press about the battle at My Lai. It reported, I believe, that 128 VC had been killed with force. I found the grid coordinates of the village, the specific date, and a lot of very specific information—the sort of thing that you need to make a persuasive complaint.

The one thing I needed that I didn't have was somebody who had been there, who was a witness but who hadn't participated. I didn't have any reason, necessarily, to believe that my friends would not be honest when they were asked about it. On the other hand, they had participated in this terrible crime, and maybe they wouldn't be honest. I felt I needed somebody that I could count on, and I knew of such a man. His name was Michael Bernhardt, but he was still out in the field. I could never find him because he was simply never available. He was never available because of Captain Medina, or Bernhardt believes that was the reason, I should say. Captain Medina had come to him the night after the massacre and knew that he hadn't participated. Medina knew that he was potentially a troublesome person and threatened him: "Bernhardt, you better keep your mouth shut about this, buddy." And Mike said, "Yes, sir."

Bernhardt stayed out in the field. They wouldn't let him out of the field. He tried to transfer into the LRRP company; they wouldn't let him. He tried to transfer every place; they wouldn't let him. Every time they thought an ambush was coming, they'd send him up to the front of the line, where they thought the ambush was going to be. He walked point in all the dangerous places. In the last four months, he got jungle rot so bad that he could barely walk, and they wouldn't let him out of the field. Finally, with about three weeks to go and without anybody's permission, he just jumped on a resupply chopper as it was lifting off. He went into the infirmary, the aid station, at the Eleventh Brigade headquarters at Duc Pho. The doctor said, "Holy Mackerel, what's wrong with you? I mean, why weren't you here earlier?" Jungle rot is a kind of ulceration that appears on your skin and is caused by a combination of filth and wetness—and some bug, I'm sure. It begins as just a little small open sore, and it just spreads and spreads and spreads and gets bigger and bigger and bigger. Bernhardt had these open wounds all over his legs. He could barely walk.

Two days after he went into the brigade aid station, Bernhardt was at Second Surgical Hospital in Chu Lai, which is where I was then. We were all about ready to DEROS, come home.* We only had a few weeks left in our tours, and most of us were out of the field by then. My friend Pat Keely, who had transferred out of Charlie Company a week before the massacre and knew what I was doing, found out that Bernie was over in the hospital. He came and told me, and we went over there. Pat left us alone, and Bernhardt and I talked. We felt each other out for about thirty minutes, and, when we finally realized that we felt the same way about it, we kind of showed our hands. I asked him what he intended to do, and he had a plan. He knew who all the officers were. He had the chain of command down. When he got out of the service, he was going to go around and assassinate them, one at a time. That was his plan. Now I have to say that I believe he was serious—we were serious people. I said, "Well, you won't get out for a while anyway"—he was an RA, an enlisted volunteer, so he still had some time left to serve—"so why don't we try my plan." I said, "I'm going to get an investigation going." He said, "How?" I said, "I don't know, but somehow. And if I do, will you tell the truth?" He said, "If you tell the truth, I'll tell the truth." I said okay.

---

*DEROS stands for "date eligible for return from overseas." In GI slang, the acronym becomes a verb.

I went home and talked to my friends and my relatives and all of the people who I thought had been my mentors. They all, almost to a person, said, "Shut up. Shut up. This is none of your business. Leave it alone." One person said, "Write a letter and send it to the army. Tell what you know and how you know it." I decided that was half-good advice, that I should do that but that I shouldn't restrict it just to the army. I wrote such a letter, and in the end of March 1969 sent it out to thirty different congressmen and senators. Morris Udall, who was congressman from Arizona—I lived in Arizona at the time—acted on it. He called on the House Armed Services Committee to call on the Pentagon to conduct an investigation, and they did so. The Pentagon responded to my letter less than two weeks later. It was their contention that they had acted independently of Congress, and maybe they did. I have no idea.

While the investigation was going on, I was not a happy camper. The moment when I believe I understood what was going to unfold was after Lieutenant Calley was charged. I had been in contact with an army officer, Colonel William V. Wilson, who was the chief investigator, at least initially, for General Westmoreland. I was calling him several times a week, and basically harassing him. I was certain that the army intended to cover this up and that he would be a willing instrument in that. I misjudged him completely. He was a totally honest and honorable man, and one of the rewarding lessons of this for me was to understand that he did act with honor and pushed this through as hard as he could. But I was convinced that there was going to be a cover-up and kept calling and saying, "You guys are going to cover this up, and I know it, and I'm not letting you get away with this." Finally, in August he told me to cool my jets and that something was about to happen. In early September, he called and said, "We've just charged Lieutenant Calley." I said, "I'm glad to hear that, but what about the rest of the officers. When are you going to charge the rest of the officers?" He said, "I don't know about that. I'll have to get back to you, but we're working on it. I promise you we're working on it."

After a few weeks and no other officers were charged, I became persuaded that the intent was for Lieutenant Calley to take the heat, to be the scapegoat. That was when I began to try actively to get in touch with the press, but I had no idea how to do it. Suddenly, several weeks later, there was Sy Hersh. We connected, and he took off from there. It was Sy's impression also that, until this story became public, the army had absolutely no intent whatsoever to pursue the other officers. I think that was the thing that I was most distressed about. In this entire process, over two years with this issue and this story on the front pages every day, at the end of it, indeed, Lieutenant Calley was the only one convicted.

Within a few years, if you stopped most Americans on the street who were politically conscious and who had observed all of this and paid attention to it and then asked them what My Lai was, they would say: "Well, wasn't that where that lieutenant—what was his name, Kelly, Calley? oh yeah, Calley—went crazy and killed all those people?" My response to that is, not exactly, not at all. It was where an operation occurred and where there were two massacres, and Lieutenant Calley was one of many officers who, albeit too enthusiastically, followed orders. That was my impression, and I just consider that whole period the education of Ron, where I learned something significant and deeply troubling about our society.

William Eckhardt

In my teaching career, I have often used Hugh Thompson and Ron Ridenhour as public examples. Ron's letter is precisely the way that citizens get action when things go awry. An example of something good on that awful day is Hugh Thompson. There are examples of things that happen that are most foul, but often in incidents of human tragedy there are also examples of good. His moral courage knows no bounds. I have said from platform after platform that even Sir Thomas More did not have that much moral courage. My hat goes off to him, and I salute him.

I am an ROTC-DMG [Reserve Officer Training Corps–Distinguished Military Graduate] who decided to be a Regular Army officer. I went to the University of Virginia School of Law and graduated with honors. Within six weeks after I graduated I was in Vietnam. I took the shots to go to Vietnam between final examinations. The largest jurisdiction, court-martial–wise, in the history of the army, was 150,000 in 1966 to 1967, as we were going into Vietnam. There were six of us who did all of the trial work. I saw lots of things as I moved around the country, but I never saw anything like this. There are other incidents that you might know about that I participated in. I defended—I did both sides—the villain in Daniel Lang's book *Casualties of War*. I saw lots of those sorts of incidents as a trial lawyer.

I was in the career course when the My Lai incident broke. It was awful. I was sent down to Atlanta to be the prosecutor of the ground action. The first day I got there, I remember that I looked at these particular files and thought that I was going to throw up. I threw the files against the wall and went and ran about five or six miles. In a telephone call that night, I said, "This is the most horrible thing I've ever seen; it's far worse than I ever thought. We're clearly going to court. There are some cases that there's enough evidence that we can probably, maybe get a conviction, but there's no doubt we're going. The facts are worse than are reported. There are over five hundred. They didn't report to you the sexual abuse, the rapes, the sodomy, the looting." By the way, the enemy gave us a list of the names of those who were in the ditch.

Let me put some things in perspective. The first thing that I saw when I began to look at this evidence was something very strange about Medina's order. Medina was charged initially based on the theory of the government that he had ordered this inexcusable carnage. As I began to read the evidence, a couple of things emerged about the order. There is no doubt that there was a pep talk, and we can talk about the nuances of that and whether it was permissible or not. It is debatable, but there are certain kernels that come out. There was a pep talk. The village was to be burned. The livestock was to be killed. The dead livestock was to be used to poison wells. If it was not military necessity, probably all three of those were wrong, legally and morally. Make no excuse for that. But I am going to hone in right now on the unresisting noncombatants, the people. Everyone said there was a pep talk, but strangely enough, the more I looked, only those who said they received a specific order were the ones who killed. Large numbers of men did not shoot. Large numbers of men simply put their guns down and just did nothing.

I became very concerned about that as I looked at it, and as time progressed, F. Lee Bailey, who defended Captain Medina, requested a polygraph. Polygraphs are made up of two parts: You question someone, and then you test whether their responses are true or false about the best way you know how to do it on a machine. The law is that what they tell you is admissible in court, but the machine is not. We wanted the answers to about sixty-five questions, and we worked for about four days to see what answers we could get. We used the president of the Polygraph Association. He was the most reputable and the best polygraph examiner in the United States, if not in the world. Over a series of weekends, we put Medina on the box as they say, and that is what I need to talk about in relation to the order.

Two questions were pertinent. Medina was truthful in response to this question: "Did you intentionally infer"—note all the connotation to that as to whether he had ordered directly or showed a want to do it or not—"to your men that they were to kill unarmed, unresisting noncombatants?" His answer was no. That was truthful. The next question was what did he know. We did a "peak of tension" test. It is the way, for example, that policemen find dead bodies. Basically, you hook somebody up, and as you move across a map, the person without saying anything reacts. This question was put to him: "Did you know that your men were killing unarmed, unresisting non-combatants?" We listed ninety-minute segments of the day before, the day of, and the day after the massacre. It was flat for the day before, but between seven-thirty and nine in the morning of the massacre, the needle went off the chart, not reacted, went off the chart. It went down and then went off. Medina told us, orally, that he learned about this when he, for the first time, saw a group of bodies at the edge of the village between ten and ten-thirty. The law is that you can use, as we did, that particular statement of time. We couldn't use the polygraph chart, but the government's duty was clear. No one knows what happened, but what probably happened was that this group got out of control and he refused to stop it.

In my mind, knowing this was going on and calculatingly doing nothing about it was murder in the worst sort of way. Evil doesn't come like Darth Vader dressed in black, hissing. Evil comes as a little bird whispering in your ear: "Think about your career. I'm not sure what's going on. We'll muddle through for the next couple of hours. We'll get over the hill, and we'll go on. I mean, after all, I can't call people in and admit that I can't control, I can't do some other thing." In my judgment, the evil comes from that point of view.

Let me turn just a minute to matters prosecutorial in relation to this particular incident. We have a responsibility in this country to prosecute people who violate the law of war. That means those who did it in this entire company. Because the army had covered it up for some two years before it could be investigated, 90 percent of the people that were involved in this incident were then out of the service. If one wanted to do justice, one had to proceed after all violators, not just those who were left in the military. Unfortunately, the method of doing that is controversial. The law as set by the Congress of the United States is that we could have court-martialed those civilians for violation of the law of war. That is the way Congress says you deal with that. We perhaps could have tried them by military commission. We haven't done that very much since Abraham Lincoln and some incidents in Hawaii. Perhaps we could have—and all these options were discussed—tried them in Federal District Court. After all, the rules in courts-martial are just like they are in Federal District Court. We could have used the same rules of evidence and the same law and just tried them in Federal District Court. But the president of the United States and the attorney general determined they could not or would not do that. Therefore, when the government proceeded to prosecute, it could only proceed after the 10 percent who were left in the military. If you are going to give grants of immunity in order to prosecute some poor soldier who killed one or two people, are you to give grants of immunity to someone who killed twenty-five or twenty-six and who raped and did the most horrible sorts of things you can ever imagine?

This was an average company. All sorts of people did not shoot, but nobody would take the next moral step of saying, "Stop it!" We are talking about knowledge here. "Stop it!" That was what just absolutely amazed me.

We're dealing with a company in which the lieutenant, the captain, and the lieutenant colonel had no college education. We went all the way to the brigade before you have a college education. Our society is responsible for the way it controls violence. Once there is a group decision, as the Congress of the United States made, to engage in war, the group is responsible for doing politically what must be done and controlling that violence. It is responsible for the people that we put there to do that. It was a terrible breach by all of us in what we did. To be brutal, if our lieutenants had been of the caliber of Bill Clinton and not Bill Calley, you would not have had a My Lai. It is just that simple.

Which is worse morally: this incident, where you had a group that got out of control and five hundred people died, or a division, and I never saw it go higher, that would cover it up? Justice delayed is justice denied. The politicalization, for example, the rush caused by a two-year statute of limitations on much of this, just knew no bounds. The consequences of not prosecuting the 90 percent who were out of the service are immeasurable.

The military itself, in the glow of publicity, has done a flip-flop. The military currently, I think, would draw and quarter and probably even castrate such violators if it could. That was not necessarily the case at the time because conviction was equal to a slap in the face of the army and perceived as a deliberate attempt to undermine the war effort.

Three quick vignettes. The problem for the government was who sat on the courts-martial. All I wanted was to ensure that they would listen fairly to the facts and that they would obey the rules as the judge gave them. I did some query. We were in the midst of one of these courts-martial, and we had a colonel from the best division of the army, the 101st Airborne Division. I was talking to him, and I said, "Well, what about the law of war?" He looked at me and said, "There's no such thing." We talked a little bit about standard operating procedures, and he said: "Well, they just simply don't apply on the battlefield." This man was nervous because there was lots of press there, so I spent some time, and to make a long story short, went through all that and got none of the answers. I simply turned to the military judge and challenged him for cause. It was instantly granted. I took that transcript to my boss and put it on his desk and said, "God help us all."

On the first day of prosecution, I went to the Fort McPherson Officers' Club that night by myself. At two other tables, the conversation was about how in the world could such a fine, upstanding officer be charged with such a horrible incident. I was sitting there listening. Interesting—that was your jury.

In the case of Sergeant Charles Hutto, his confession said that he received an order, that he killed, that he knew the order was wrong, and that what he did was murder. We presented a prima facie case to a jury. You're darn right we did. I know that because the law of evidence at that time required that you have a prima facie case before you put the confession in, and the confession went in. He was acquitted. Was it because we didn't prove it? I'm not going to knock a jury because they refused to have one sergeant bear the responsibility. I don't know.

What is not generally recognized is that we had a great schism in our government. The Congress of the United States attempted to block the prosecutions. After all, it was not in the interest of the United States to prosecute these people. Congressmen L. Mendel Rivers and F. Edward Hebert held hearings. So did the Senate. There is something called the Jencks Act. It's very simple. If the government has a witness that testifies, I, if I am defending someone, am entitled to look at what that testimony is so I can effectively cross-examine. So, calculatingly setting out to destroy the prosecution, the Congress of the United States held hearings and classified them under congressional classification, not executive classification. They always told us that they were refusing to give those to the government so that they could comply with the Jencks Act. The remedy under the Jencks Act is not to let someone testify at a trial. That was the only issue of constitutional merit in the Calley case that went to Federal Court. The Fifth Circuit in New Orleans split eight to five, if my memory serves me correctly, on that particular issue. It said that it was clear error and regrettable that the Congress did that but that it was harmless. Because there were so many statements available, the defense had not been deprived of their due process rights. It was awful. It compares to the Nixon-tape cases and that sort of thing.

How do you discredit and do everything you can to keep the star witness off the stand? It's that simple, just that simple. If it can be done by congressmen, it can be done by anybody else. During those hearings, Mr. Rivers took Hugh Thompson on the steps of the Capitol and, on national television, browbeat him within an inch of his life. It would make you want to puke.

Thompson

They weren't very happy with me, and they tried to discredit everything I said. They play rough. The damn Jencks Act really teed me off, when I found out what it was. I believe it was really used with Sergeant David Mitchell's case. It was secret testimony in closed hearing. Of course, all you had to do was get in a damn cab, drive by your hotel, pick up a *Washington Post,* and read what you said. Now, I don't understand how they call it "secret testimony." They didn't allow press in that room with the secret testimony. It got out of there somehow, and I sure didn't talk to the press.

Eckhardt

We produced a society at that time in which there was all sorts of pressure not to remember. You don't have to lie, just say you don't remember. Evidence, as in the case of Bravo Company at My Khe, dried up; memories of what were told to reporters early on suddenly were watered down or disappeared; lawyers sent their clients to Canada or to Mexico. When we were trying to receive court orders for fair trials and saying please don't talk to the public, newspaper reporters gave young sergeants ten thousand dollars for interviews. Of course it wasn't very pleasant business.

As a people in this country, we are responsible for educating ourselves in a democracy and knowing what to do. There were only two reporters and two newspapers that wrote anything articulate about this, and that was Homer Bigart for the *New York Times* and Ken Rich for the *Los Angeles Times.* Sound bites don't work very well. There is incredible ignorance, even to this day, over and over and over again about specific facts.

We moved cases as far as they could go. Everything that was done is a matter of record. The military is a great bureaucracy and keeps lots of records.

That's the way you hold people accountable historically as well as currently. We moved as far as one could go down the pike.

When you look at the Medina case, you look at knowledge. There are three things that have to coincide. He had, in sum, command responsibility and a duty to interfere and the ability to do something about it. That ability was radio communication. No doubt about that. The issue is knowledge. Medina never was in the village. It was my opinion professionally at the trial and it still is today that he calculatingly remained out once he knew what was going on, so he didn't have to see. There were the incidents of the woman and the boy at the beginning that were talked about. Both were included in the charges against him. As you know, the jury acquitted. One other bit of information—afterward he was lying in a field with Calley. They had a conversation that included something like, "Goddammit, Calley, how many was it? Was it fifty or was it a hundred?" I thought that was very good because it showed specific knowledge that he knew what went on. If you go with the Medina-order theory, that conversation might have been phrased slightly differently.

What do we get out of all this? You have to stand and say it's wrong! In a democracy you have to take on crimes of atrocities; you have to produce evidence; you have to take it to a tribunal; you have to do something about it. This is the same problem they're having in Bosnia. The important thing is, in my judgment, that this is labeled as wrong. It has been used to teach what is wrong. It has been used to teach the consequences of ill discipline on the battlefield, namely, that you lose wars because of it. It's just that simple. That's what this has been used for. Some days I wondered whether we did more harm than good. The prosecutorial record is absolutely abysmal. The thing that amazes me is that we got so far.

The function of the law is deterrence. This is not an exercise in self-flagellation. We're using history like it needs to be used. You learn from the past to prevent mistakes in the future. That's what My Lai needs to be used for. At least in the Gulf War, I am told, two division commanders had their brigade commanders around them, and the last thing that they said as they went off to do battle was a stern, "No My Lais in this division. You hear me?" We worked long and hard in the military of the United States for that type of statement.

The military has done its duty inculcating the lesson that has to be learned from this. It's almost like losing one's virginity. If someone had told me that as an officer in the United States I needed to stand up and tell my fellow citizens that you do not kill unarmed, unresisting noncombatants and do it over and over again, I would have said you're nuts. That was before My Lai. It is certainly not after. There are twenty years now of how one trains to do that, and it has been done very well. That same sort of human-rights training is going on right now in Peru and Ukraine and Albania in some other ways.

With regard to the legal system, however, things emphatically haven't changed. The system that I described is still the one that is extant. There has been no practical marriage between idealistic international law and practical criminal law, which in our country comes in the Uniform Code of Military Justice. It hasn't been touched since 1950. The law is still that we would court-martial civilians for violation of the law of war. I think that's a tad outdated constitutionally, if not otherwise. Why hasn't it changed? I am infuriated that the judge in this particular case let this go to the jury only on a negligence theory and not on an intentional theory. Negligent homicide at the time was a three-month offense, hardly befitting what happened. We have so civilized our Uniform Code of Military Justice that we don't deal with these sorts of issues. They need to be dealt with. It needs to be clear, not because it is the law, but because it is the very essence of the profession of arms. The law punishes action in everybody else, but in the profession of arms, which deals with dangerous instrumentalities, it punishes soldiers criminally for inaction. Every young sergeant and every lieutenant needs to understand that if things are going awry with matters in which they are professionally competent and they fail to intervene, we're going to try them criminally for that inaction. Maintaining control is the essence of the profession of arms.

There is no excuse for why Calley was the only one convicted, but when one kills some 250 people, one can find sufficient evidence to prove that he killed 22. The issue for others, as in Iran-Contra or what have you, was what did they know and when did they know it. We do not have imputed criminal responsibility. To be culpable, one must knowingly and evilly choose not to do something. I think that's what our tradition requires. Lieutenant Colonel Frank Barker, who was the battalion commander, was dead by the time of the trials. As I have described about Medina, the question of the order shifted from the issue of action to inaction. I saw no evidence that that particular order came from anyone higher than Barker.

That sort of operation is anathema. I stayed in the military and made a career out of it because of what I saw in Vietnam. War brings out the best as well as the worst, and things are, as Harry Summers says, very much a creature of time and place. What I described here today is absolutely anathema. I saw none of that. I consulted on all sorts of other incidents, but nothing, nothing like this. When society unleashes the hounds of hell, it is responsible for controlling it.

After President Nixon commuted Calley's sentence, the final message of the justice system was "politics reigns." Never forget that there are two sides. There is one group that says: "These sorts of things happen. This is routine; the military does this all the time." Then you have the other group over here that says: "Kill, kids, kill. They're Communists, go ahead, kill them." After all, that's what the military is supposed to do, isn't it? It's awful, and to both of them, a pox on both houses! That's why we talk about noncombatants and deal with just war tradition, international law, and all of those things. There's the middle.

On the battlefield, things occur in little pockets. The test was whether someone who had said something to the press was going to say the same thing to us and then say the same thing under oath. It's amazing what happens when people think all they have to say is they don't remember, and if you can't produce it, it's a problem. When you try cases, and I have tried lots of battlefield offenses, you are dealing with hundreds of years of criminal law. When you get in war, society often feels responsible for what happens. In my experience in things that I have tried, the quantum of proof by the government, practical proof, goes up, as probably it should. If someone shoots someone, is it the tragedy that we heard Ron Ridenhour describe about the pilot of the helicopter on his first mission, or is it cold-blooded, premeditated murder? That's the problem.

[*Thompson and Eckhardt respond to a question about whether the citation awarding Thompson the Distinguished Flying Cross stated that his award was for confronting U.S. troops and rescuing Vietnamese civilians during the massacre.*]

Thompson

No, it didn't state it that way. It said something along the order that I set down between some civilians and advancing enemy and rescued them. It wasn't totally wrong. Find out who the enemy was that day. That thing was presented to me a year and a half or something like that after My Lai. It didn't sink in about the date on the award. I didn't put the date together with My Lai. That was the only thing that would have given it away. Other incidents had happened where people had been rescued by my crew with the legitimate enemy there. I really did not put the citation together with March 16 because I had blocked that completely out of my mind.

Eckhardt

This is a man who set his helicopter down, put his guns on Americans, said he would shoot them if they shot another Vietnamese, had his people wade in the ditch in gore up to their hips, took out children, and took them to the hospital. What he did not tell you is he flew back, if I remember correctly, stood in front of people, tears rolling down his cheeks, pounded the table and said: "Notice! Notice! Notice!" You have heard about his courage to testify time after time after time.

Thompson

[*answering a question about how he would respond to the comment in Richard Nixon's book* No More Vietnams *that when Calley, an American soldier, committed an atrocity he got a conviction, but when a Vietcong or North Vietnamese soldier committed an atrocity, he got a commendation*] With our president, I would just tell him he ought to keep the politics out of the military. As far as awarding someone for doing a wrong action, as you indicate they do in Vietnam, they have to live with themselves. I can live with myself.

[*responding to a question about why he reacted differently than did others at My Lai*] I can't answer that. There's nothing special about me. I was raised in a small town in Georgia. You don't have to be a rocket scientist to understand that what was going on wasn't right. Anybody would know that. People that were there knew it wasn't right, and I can't say why they did it. I think that the highest estimate of the bodies that I have ever heard is something like five hundred. I think that's a very conservative estimate. I have heard that one time the commanding general flew over the area that day. I have heard that Colonel Henderson was in the air that day, and, matter of fact, I think that one of my gunships talked to that aircraft when he was trying to get some help. There were large enough clusters of bodies there that, if you were at three thousand feet, you could see them. They should have seen what was going on and at least have had some questions.

Ridenhour

What the record shows in terms of Major General Koster, I believe, is that he and his deputy, Brigadier General Young, flew to LZ Dottie that morning. According to the record, he never flew over the village, but he flew to LZ Dottie. Everybody who was a soldier in Vietnam, certainly everybody who was an infantry soldier in Vietnam, knows that, when there was a lot of shooting going on on the ground and a lot of casualties were being reported, the first thing the general wanted to do was jump in his helicopter and fly out there and get a look at the action. Because Bill Eckhardt was unable to prove that General Koster was there doesn't mean that he wasn't there. Anybody who was in Vietnam knows that, if General Koster was at LZ Dottie that morning, he was over My Lai that morning. There is just no question about it in terms of the reality of what happened. But there is no evidence that he was there, no direct evidence that was usable in court.

REPORTING THE DARKNESS:
THE ROLE OF THE PRESS IN
THE VIETNAM WAR

Warren Bell, David Halberstam, Seymour Hersh,
Ron Ridenhour, Kevin Sim, Kathleen Turner

David Halberstam and Seymour Hersh each won Pulitzer Prizes for Vietnam-related reporting. Halberstam was honored for reporting from Vietnam itself and Hersh for his stories that helped uncover the tragedy of My Lai. Ron Ridenhour, who was instrumental in first exposing the events of My Lai, returned to Vietnam in 1970 as a reporter for *Time* magazine. Kathleen Turner is a professor of communication at Tulane who has made considerable study of the media during the 1960s and particularly of Lyndon Johnson's relations with the press. Kevin Sim is an award-winning documentary film maker whose works include *Four Hours in My Lai,* and Warren Bell is a veteran television journalist and media consultant.

The panelists address three general topics: how reporting on the Vietnam War affected them personally; in what ways today's military reporting is similar to or different from the Vietnam experience, and specific insights on My Lai, particularly those derived from Hersh's and Ridenhour's efforts to get the story to the public. These three discussions overlap, and observations in one area prompt reflections in another. The three reporters candidly examine how their own mounting pessimism about the U.S. conduct of the war shaped their reporting without, in their view, compromising any professional standards. Turner argues that expecting or desiring that reporters be objective is not realistic, and the journalists on the panel agree.

On the issue of contemporary journalism, the panelists worry that a cover-up like that of My Lai is entirely possible today. They note how military and civilian authorities in recent military deployments like the Gulf War have been able to keep reporters away from company- and field-grade officers and enlisted men. War news is managed through the high command.

On My Lai itself, Ridenhour and Hersh explore why the public was unable to understand the moral revulsion they felt about the massacre and the cover-up by senior officers. They also provide reasons for believing that the incident might have been planned and was not just the result of spontaneous rage that got out of control.

Kevin Sim

When you, Mr. Hersh, actually wrote your My Lai story, did you find that the people were running to print it and that the reaction was immediate and as strong as it became?

Seymour Hersh

Yes, it was pretty quick. I went first with the essential story to most of the major media outlets. By that time I had been Eugene McCarthy's press secretary and speech writer in 1968, and in September of 1969 I had the lead article in the *New York Times Magazine*. I had worked for the AP. As press secretary for a guy running for president, I knew every reporter, and I was taken seriously. I still couldn't get a newspaper to run the story. The difficulties of getting it into print were, in retrospect, rather staggering. Like Ron, I should have been more daunted. I should have realized how hard it was, and it was harder than you might think. Once the story got out, it was at first largely through Europe. I wrote five stories, the ones for which I won all the prizes, over five weeks, and we were syndicating them ourselves. Most of the press was picking up on what I was doing. There was some reporting from Vietnam, but the second story was giant in England and Germany. There were parliamentary debates, and we had newspapers then writing stories about debates in London about the story. That was one of the ways it played back. It was a little complicated, but basically I would say within three weeks of the first story it was a cause célèbre.

Sim

But what do you think actually made it as big in America? Was it the press story, or was it the photographs that Haeberle printed, or was it the interview with Meadlo?

Hersh

It was the CBS interview. Paul Meadlo went on CBS. We sold Paul Meadlo, in effect. I do not claim this as the greatest day in my professional life, but I took Paul Meadlo to New York to meet Mike Wallace. I wrote a story, and Wallace did an interview that began: "And what did you do? I went in a village and killed everybody. Women and children too? Yeah. And babies? Oh yeah, and babies too." It was an incredible interview, and that, I think, turned the corner. But it was a pretty big story before that. I think that was the third story I did, and by that time it was out there.

Sim [to Ron Ridenhour]

When the story was broken, there was a furious scandal here, and people were absolutely outraged and there was absolute national clamor for some kind of justice. Why do you think in the way that the story was mediated from that time onwards that somehow that sense of scandal and outrage became diffused?

Ron Ridenhour

When the interviews with Meadlo, with Mike Terry, and with a couple of other guys appeared on national television within a week or two of Sy's first story, it was perfectly clear that these young men were painfully telling the truth. They were telling what they saw and what they witnessed. Then, when it got around to the officers, we discovered that the buck stopped somewhere else—anywhere else. Specifically it stopped with Lieutenant Calley. This entire period of time from my arrival in Vietnam to the end of the various prosecutions of the My Lai war crimes was the education of Ron. I was frankly astonished to see what happened to this story after it was out in the public and under such a bright light for such a long period of time. It was written about and televised and broadcast at great length and in apparent depth and detail. At the end of it, if you asked people what happened at My Lai, they would say: "Oh yeah, isn't that where Lieutenant Calley went crazy and killed all those people?" No, that was not what happened. Lieutenant Calley was one of the people who went crazy and killed a lot of people at My Lai, but this was an operation, not an aberration.

What happened at My Lai was a plan. We have two massacres, remember, on the same day, by two separate companies of the same unit that are only three miles apart.* We have officers, lieutenant colonels, a task force commander, a brigade commander, and the division commander in the air over those villages for significant periods of time, all morning long. You can tell the difference between a child and an adult from five hundred feet or even from a thousand feet in the air from a helicopter. These men knew what was going on down there. It took them four hours to stop it. Well, why is that? How could Captain Medina, for instance, be on the ground in that village for four hours when four hundred people are being shot to death one at a time and not know something is going on? I say it's not possible. He did know what was going on, and so did all the other officers. The fact of the matter was that this was part of a plan. Those men were ordered to go out there and destroy this village. This was an act of counterterrorism, and that fact—I should say what I believe to be a fact, and I think if you examine the evidence it is difficult to draw another conclusion—was completely lost over that two-year period of time. I find it extraordinary. If the question is did the press fail in Vietnam or about Vietnam, I would say that is among the larger of the press' failures—the failure to educate the public and to dig this out and to cause the public to understand what really happened there.

There was a saying in Vietnam among the soldiers—"they're all VC when they're dead"—and that's the way it worked out. That came from body count and kill ratio, and that, again, came from the politicians. It was McNamara and the bean-counter mentality that thought you could measure the success of this war by lining up the bodies end-to-end. That mentality infected the majority of the American military. Company-grade officers didn't devise these strategies; they suffered under them, just as we enlisted men did. Leadership could make a difference, and leadership did make a difference to some units. There were leaders who wouldn't tolerate this type of behavior and who saw how corrupt and evil this notion of body counts and kill

---

*Ridenhour is referring to action on March 16, 1968, by Bravo Company of TF Barker in the village of My Khe near My Lai.

ratios happened to be and refused to tolerate it. In those instances these things didn't occur or, if they did occur, they occurred on a very small scale and there was a quick punishment which set a lesson for other people.

In a large number of instances, however, it was different. Colonel Oran Henderson, the commander of the Eleventh Brigade, went on trial for having covered up the initial investigation after Hugh Thompson made a complaint. When the hearings began on the cover-up, reporters asked Henderson if My Lai was indeed an aberration. He said to them that every brigade commander in Vietnam had a My Lai. I don't think that was true, but I think that it is true that what happened at My Lai was a tactic. It was a tool in the tactical tool kit of military commanders, and they called it counterterrorism. Some chose to use it in some instances, and far more did than we would like to think or admit. I just think that that is true and that the evidence is persuasive.

Hersh

After I wrote the third story, the Meadlo story, it was a huge international incident. On the Sunday after the third story and after Meadlo's interview appeared in every major newspaper, every newspaper that had its own reporter in Vietnam had a dispatch on what the war was like. Some of the stories were just absolutely mind-boggling and maddening. Correspondents who had been in Vietnam in 1965 and 1966 went back to their files. One of these guys was an AP reporter who was with the first group of Marines to go ashore in 1965. Johnson didn't tell anybody they were doing offensive operations. He just said that they were going ashore in defensive positions. This correspondent was attached to this first unit, and he described the murder of a bunch of civilians. On the second day of the war, there were a bunch of Vietnamese civilians in a cave, and he describes somebody shooting in the cave and throwing in a hand grenade—in a Sunday piece! He had been there and seen this four years earlier!

I would echo what Ron said. I wrote a lot about the Peers Report in the second book that I wrote on this incident, called *Cover-Up*. When General Peers began to investigate My Lai and discovered on the same day there had been another massacre by the other unit, that is, Bravo Company, the inference to be drawn obviously was that these guys went out to commit mayhem. The army as an institution simply was unable to cope with that issue. That is what Ron is talking about. All of us were unable to cope with that issue because it's a pretty heavy issue for us to cope with. What was the real day-to-day policy of the war? I know there were a lot of military men flinching at this and saying it depended on the unit commander, etc., but my guess is that the life of Vietnamese wasn't held in very much respect. And that was too bad.

William Eckhardt

Much of the criticism that there was a cover-up is deserved, but we need to be quite fair when we talk about the allegation of the second unit, Bravo Company, at My Khe on March 16, 1968. In that particular allegation the lesson of My Lai is that you do not cover up. You pick up the rug and let the sun shine in. I happen to be the person who was responsible for every bit of the information that came out about that particular unit. The only thing that I can tell you is that I spent tens of thousands of dollars trying to trace down everything that we could trace. I looked at all the information that came out of that particular thing. The investigators went after every particular source we knew that would talk about it.

Hersh

But Peers was able to issue charges against a number of the officers in Bravo Company. As you know, specific charges of criminal conduct were filed. They came up with a specific number of deaths. I think they ended up concluding that somewhere between 90 and 110 people were killed by Bravo Company. Peers found evidence against four or five officers, none of whom stood trial or were held for trial. The only officer found guilty of anything was Calley. So the fact that you did not find people guilty does not necessarily mean something did not happen.

Eckhardt

I understand. What I'm telling you is that the government would have proceeded with charges had it had evidence that would have stood up.

Ridenhour

Are you suggesting that, because you could not establish individual, personal culpability, this incident did not occur?

Eckhardt

No, I'm not saying that, but what was stated here was that there was a cover-up or an attempt to cover up. I think that's not totally accurate. The allegation was that somehow Bravo Company was separate and apart from the tragedy of Charlie Company and that it was covered up by the military institution. That is not accurate.

Ridenhour

I'm not saying that it was separate and apart from Charlie Company. I'm saying that it was exactly the same operation.

Eckhardt

Perhaps I misunderstood Mr. Hersh's comments that somehow there was a separate incident that was over and above what we are talking about. There was certainly a cover-up for a period of time. There is no doubt about that.

Hersh

Ron's letter was dealt with, and we should applaud the military and make the point clearly that Ron's letter did get action.

Eckhardt

It clearly did. It's a classic textbook example of how responsible citizens act and how the government acts.

Hersh

To a point, sir. The point being that there was an internal investigation and the field investigator was brilliant. They went out and began to put the picture together. At some point the enormity in this perversity became clear. At that point, by September of 1969, I will tell you right now there was every intent to minimize this internally. Nobody was going to announce it. By the time I started looking into it, it was under key. In fact, they wanted Calley to cop out. They were putting pressure on Calley to plead to a general charge. If he had done that, it would have all been gone, but he was resisting through his lawyers. When I walked into the picture, the quietus was on it. Believe me.

That doesn't preclude the fact that the army investigated it. After Ron's letter in the spring of 1969, the command in Vietnam sent an officer out from Saigon to investigate. He wrote a report saying that there was nothing to this. It was sent back to the Pentagon in May 1969. Despite having the report and to its credit, the Inspector General's office still decided to take a look at it. When they went back for the second look, every single report in every file was gone. Peers believed that the general officers a year later had conspired to remove all of the files, after it became clear to the general officers that this was a serious issue. That smacks of not just a cover-up of a specific event but an institutional cover-up.

Eckhardt

I agree with you, and that is an absolute moral tragedy. I made my comment because I took your remark to be that the Bravo Company incident was not treated with the same seriousness. That is not the case, and that is what needs to be clearly stated. I wanted the record to be straight on that.

Hersh

I don't think Peers could come to grips with it. I think that he was an honest man but it was just beyond him. I am telling you, however, that it is my belief—there is no evidence and I am just talking about a feeling—that if Calley had copped a plea on a manslaughter charge, they would have closed the case. He was being offered a manslaughter charge in the fall of 1969, or at least that is what his lawyer Judge George Latimer told me.

Eckhardt

As the chief prosecutor of the ground action, I never heard any such discussion of that. One of my heroes is Aubrey Daniel [the captain who was the courtroom prosecutor in the Calley case]. His graceful, articulate taking on of the president of the United States, when the president inappropriately commented after the end of the trial, will always be one of my brighter days. I was responsible for the ground action and conversed with Aubrey Daniel constantly. I knew, as they say, the prosecutorial secrets. I never, ever, ever, ever had any discussion of any such plea-bargaining. I cannot believe that Aubrey Daniel would do that. That would be anathema, and I am quite convinced he did not do it.

In the Calley trial, Medina appeared as a witness and was rather hostilely treated by both sides. He was vigorously cross-examined, and that drama was played out in Calley's trial. The rules of evidence at that time required that the government vouch for the truthfulness of a witness. The United States consistently refused to do anything to vouch for the order of Captain Medina, even at the risk of losing the Calley case. We are talking about a unit war, so we are talking about Medina down, about lieutenants. There is no building of plea-bargaining that way.

Hersh

I can just tell you that it knocked me out when I got into this, sir. It knocked me out that Calley was the one that they came down on.

Eckhardt

If one kills 250 people with his own hands . . .

Hersh

No, sir. He did not. I don't believe that, sir. No offense.

Ridenhour

While this investigation was going on, I suppose that outside of a few people on Capitol Hill I was the only regular citizen who knew that it was in progress. When nobody else was arrested within two or three weeks after Calley's arrest, I decided that I should no longer maintain my promise of silence to the military. I had given it when they first came out in response to my letter and had asked me to please hold my water, as it were, until they had completed their investigation. I had agreed to do that. After Calley was arrested and no other officers were, I began very actively trying to figure out how to get in touch with the press. Of course I was such a neophyte that I had no idea how to do that, and eventually Sy published his story before I was able to get anybody else interested in it. It was only after Sy's first story ran that suddenly every journalist in America was trying to find their own atrocity story from Vietnam. That's when the army seemed to be moved to pursue prosecutions of other officers or even investigations of their culpability. At least that was my perception of it.

Hersh

I'll never forget the night that Ron found me on the phone. He said, "Hey, I started it." I had never heard of him. I was coming at it from a totally different end. I had come in with this story in September to *Life* magazine, and by November, when I had the story, they didn't want it. I later went out to see Ron, after I had broken the first stories. He obviously helped me enormously. He had gone to *Life* magazine himself about four months earlier. I had been talking to the same editor who had gotten the story from Ridenhour. This guy was also getting it from me four or five months later, not telling me about Ron, and also not running the story.

Warren Bell

What we want to try to do is to examine the role of the press in the Indochina conflict and how that role evolved as our experience with that war wore on, and also to identify how that experience has since altered the working relationship between the press and the U.S. military in the subsequent twenty-five years.

David Halberstam

It was an alienating experience at first. I belonged to that very small group of reporters who went there early and who, in the beginning, were more or less "on the team," to use Dean Rusk's phrase. Then, we rather systematically began to write pessimistically. We were not yet "doves." The terms *hawks* and *doves* did not exist, and we weren't fully aware of the scope of the tragedy ahead. We recorded, I think quite accurately, the military side, but we didn't write as well politically. We didn't have good political sources. A journalist is really only as good as his sources, and someone like Ron Ridenhour here is a good example of that. Our military sources were really extraordinary because they were the best young military men of their generation, but the comparable political people that we might have turned to, people who had witnessed what had happened in China and in the French Indochina War, and who would have had the wisdom to see that what was going on in Vietnam had historical antecedents, were not there. They had been driven out during the McCarthy period, when the only way you could get into the State Department's Southeast Asia posts was by showing that you had no experience at all in Asia. When I was there, the ambassador was chosen because he was from NATO. Old China hands whose great expertise was comparable to the expertise of Charles Bohlen and George Kennan and Llewellyn Thompson in Russia, people such as John Paton Davies, John Carter Vincent, and John Stewart Service, were all just wiped out by the McCarthy period. We were never as good in connecting Vietnam to the example of China and to what had happened before with France, and that has haunted me since.

If you look at Neil Sheehan, Peter Arnett, Mal Browne, and the great Charlie Mohr, who was the least known, I think we intuitively understood the limits of technology and of the American presence. To use the phrase of Bernard Fall, we would be walking in the same footsteps as the French although dreaming different dreams. If you ask what was the war's impact upon me, it was personal. It's not much fun to be called a liar by the American ambassador, the American mission, the Defense Department, *Time* magazine, and the Pentagon, and to have the president of the United States ask to have me put out. It was at first an alienating experience. We were impassioned, and we were obsessed.

Hersh [*to Halberstam*]

It's interesting that you guys didn't toe the line as so many military men did. Many military officers covered up the incident in My Lai because of fear. They were afraid of not getting the next promotion, etc. It's as simple as that. It's sort of sad that while all those senior officers looked the other way there were the few reporters who did not.

The thing I am sorriest about in all my coverage was that I used to be mad at the military. Those guys were as much victims as the people they were manhandling. The true villains were the McGeorge Bundys and the McNamaras and the Kennedys and the Johnsons. We were very slow to see and to target the real people. We should have been going after McNamara and the others.

The terrible thing is that things aren't much better now. The press complained about the restrictions during the Gulf War. The military and the civilian leadership has figured out now that there are better ways to handle the press. One of the easiest ways you handle the press is that you make sure the American forces don't lose and that you don't lose anybody. You shoot first. We didn't see much of that in Haiti, but there was one shoot-up in Haiti where we shot first and that was the acceptable principle. In Somalia our forces were certainly very quick to react against anybody, even little children. The extensive use of force in Panama was an outrage. There were four hundred or five hundred civilians killed in that invasion. That is basically murder. I don't see an act of war.

Ridenhour

In Vietnam we would go out in the field and bring back a story and send it to New York, and New York would then rewrite it. Of course New York rewrites everything, that's the way the news magazines work. New York would rewrite it, and when it came back to the reporter in Saigon, it had literally been stood on its head: black was white, white was black. Reporters were having great difficulty with this in Saigon. This went on, I'm sure, throughout the period of time that David was there and far beyond. It was still happening when I got there, although to a greatly diminished degree. You would send in a story. There was somebody in the New York bureau who had been in Saigon and who thought they still knew more about the story than the person on the scene did, and they would write it the way they thought it ought to be. It was very disconcerting. I was a new guy. We had a term for that in Vietnam in the infantry which I won't repeat. I really didn't understand how the world worked. How the *Time* magazine world worked was that, when New York sent your copy back to you turned on its head, you said, "Oh, well, okay," and you went away. Well, I didn't do that. One of my problems there, and some people thought one of my strengths, was that I didn't know what I couldn't do. What I couldn't do was send a cable back to New York saying that I was dissatisfied with this, that they had turned the story on its head, that I didn't like it, and would they please make it right. I was a cherry, as we called them in Vietnam.

Halberstam

How did you get with *Time* magazine, of all publications, in those years? It was their Disneyland.

Ridenhour

It was a quite extraordinary experience. The military was not pleased that I had returned. I don't know why, because I was a rookie. I didn't know what I was doing. But I did know or have some idea of what they were doing, which I suppose was the problem.

I covered a number of stories for *Time* magazine; I covered the invasion of Laos from the field.* There was this enormous animosity toward reporters among a large number of the military officers at that time. Not all of them, but many of the officers felt that they were losing the war and it was the fault of the press, of the reporters. I remember an incident during the invasion of Laos. I had gone out to Khe Sanh, from where the operation was being run, and was walking across a field. It was a hazy morning, and all of a sudden this full-bird colonel appeared out of the mist. He recognized me

*From February 8 to April 6, 1971, the Army of the Republic of Vietnam (ARVN) with heavy U.S. artillery and tactical air support made a bloody and unproductive thrust into Laos.

and the person I was with as reporters. He jumped in our face and cursed us for a few moments and said: "Well you guys have been sticking it in our ass all these years, and now we're going to stick it in yours." He meant that we weren't going to be allowed to cover the invasion of Laos. There was a great deal of animosity between the press and the military in the field at that time.

As for my personal experiences, they were nice enough to pay a lot of attention to me when I got there. As a matter of fact, they ran my picture on the front page of *Stars and Stripes* about once every three months, just to make sure that no soldiers would forget what I looked like and who I was, I'm sure. Coincidentally, it turned out that I was covering the last days of the failed invasion of Laos on the same day that Lieutenant Calley was convicted. That story, of course, was on the Armed Forces Radio stations and also appeared in *Stars and Stripes*. I had gone out to Khe Sanh that morning to do what we called "sights and sounds," to gather a little color for *Time* on the failure of the invasion of Laos. I was, I thought, incognito. I went out there and walked around and talked to soldiers. I asked them their feelings about not only the failure of the invasion of Laos, which we were only supporting, but also about the conviction of Calley. They responded to me, and there were handwritten signs up there in support of Calley, saying "Go Rusty" and "We know you're not guilty" and that sort of thing. These were really littering the entire plain at Khe Sanh.

I did my interviews, and about noon I went out and got on a C-130 transport plane and went back to Danang. It was about a forty-five-minute flight. I was on my way back to Saigon because I had to file that night. I went into the terminal at Danang, which was really a big open barn with enough room for probably a thousand soldiers to sit and wait for their flights to wherever they were going. It was full; there were easily a thousand men in there. I walked in, and all of a sudden it was like "Eyes right!" Everybody in the room, I mean, everybody in the room turned and looked at me. There was this great, enormous wave of hostility that flowed out, and I said to myself, "Whew, I don't like this." I walked over to the little concession stand that they had there to buy a pack of cigarettes, and there on the counter was a stack of *Stars and Stripes*. On the front cover of *Stars and Stripes* was a headline—"Calley Convicted"—and my photograph, covering the entire front page. In the photo I was dressed, amazingly, just exactly as I was dressed at that moment. I have to admit that I thought I needed to find a place to hide, and I did. There was a little press hootch about one hundred meters away, and I stayed in there until my flight came up. The mood, the atmosphere of antagonism, was quite intense.

I'm afraid that the press overall, especially the generation that I was there with, didn't do as nearly good a job as we could have or should have done. I think the earlier generation that David Halberstam was with did a better job. But they had a more difficult problem, I suspect, in that it was awfully hard to get your editors to run the stories that you were witnessing out in the field.

Hersh [*to Halberstam*]

That's the same problem you had.

Halberstam

Well, the *Times* really was pretty good. [*to Ridenhour*] How in God's name did you go for *Time* magazine, which loved the war more than the Pentagon did? Otto Fuerbringer, who was the managing editor then, was the hawk's hawk. He really thought that Johnson and Westmoreland were soft on the war. I wrote about this in some length in a book called *The Powers That Be*. *Time* had a very good bureau that would send back really quite good reporting, and it would just go into the hamburger machine within *Time* in New York. It would just be turned around into inevitable victory. They tell the story of when Otto Fuerbringer finally went to Vietnam. He stood above Cam Ranh Bay, which had just been completed, and he said, "I know how to win the war overnight." Someone said, "What's that, Otto?" He said, "Bring the five top VC generals here, they'll see this, and they'll surrender." I mean, talk about American arrogance and ignorance, it's right there.

The *New York Times* was really quite good. They were uncomfortable with me. It was a generational problem for them. The people who edited the paper were of the World War II generation, in which things like this didn't happen and you could trust generals and public officials. This was a different kind of war and a different kind of world. They were uneasy because I never had sources that I could name. All my sources were unofficial. But I would give them generally quite high marks in terms of what they ran. They were nervous, and they didn't like it. I didn't make friends there, and the foreign desk didn't like me. I was something of a Peck's bad boy. But I really give them good marks. There was a tradition there. I was followed by the great

Charlie Mohr, and Neil Sheehan came back and Johnny Apple and Jack
Langguth. It was a wonderful bureau there that pretty consistently went
against the grain and irritated the Saigon command, as did the CBS bureau.
The *Times* doesn't like encounters like that. It doesn't like being outside
looking in, but if it is a head-on collision, they'll do the right thing.

Hersh

I just remember that I kept on hearing stories about what a pain in the
ass you were. The editors would tell me that.

Halberstam

Well, you should be a pain in the ass. In a time like Vietnam, that's when
it counts. There is no doubt I was very difficult for them. I had jarred nerves.
I was taking too much heat. I'm not easy to deal with anyway; I'm not an
institutional person. Who is being celebrated here today isn't me, however,
but people like Ron Ridenhour. They are pains in the ass, and they do get
listened to. Today Ron Ridenhour could walk through the same hall where
the thousand people shunned him, and they would all turn to say what a
great fellow he is. Bobby Kennedy loved to quote from Emerson: "If one
good man plant himself upon his conscience, the whole world will come
'round him." [*to Ridenhour*] You are that one good man.

Ridenhour

Thank you. That is very generous. In defense of my having gone to work
for *Time* magazine, I would only say that after about six months the bureau
chief began to get cables from New York which would say: "Is Ron Ridenhour still working for you?" He didn't get the message, so after a while the
cables became: "Why is Ron Ridenhour still working for you?"

Kathleen Turner

As a professor of communication, I look at communication as a process
of social influence, particularly in the areas of media, politics, and popular
culture. Complicating the roles of media during Vietnam is our much-
cherished myth that media can be, should be, and at least on occasion are
objective. As human beings we are not objects, so we cannot be objective.
We are subjects, so we must be subjective. The concept of objectivity, as a
matter of fact, came about during the nineteenth century, ironically to sell

more newspapers. Editors such as James Gordon Bennett figured out that, if you removed the language of political opinion from American journals and added more neutral language, then you would offend fewer people and would be able to sell more copies. Yet language is not neutral. Human beings who work within human organizations are constantly making choices—subconscious choices sometimes, to be sure, but nonetheless choices that have to be made about what constitutes a news story, about how to research and write up that story, and about how that story should be connected to the larger social context. We see those decisions being made constantly, not only in the larger context of Vietnam, but also, more specifically, in how My Lai was covered. I am reminded of the story of the three baseball umpires. One said, "I call it as it is." The second one said, "I call it as I see it." The third one said, "Whatever I call it, that's what it is."

There is an additional point concerning the media in Vietnam. Media coverage not only affects the American public, it also affects members of the American government. The members of government do not exist in a hermetically sealed environment. They are very much part of the media environment that we live in. In fact, one might posit that they pay even closer attention to media coverage than your average Jane Doe citizen does because, for them, it is an important conduit of information, perception, and activity. Contemporary American presidents clearly understand that what Elmer Cornwell called "presidential leadership of public opinion" is one of their most important roles. To an amazing extent, members of a presidential administration will conflate public opinion with press opinion. They pay very close attention to news coverage, and they often try to influence it. One classic example is when John Kennedy asked the *New York Times* to withdraw a certain David Halberstam from Saigon because "his stories were casting doubts at home about the wisdom of American policy there." Another classic example is a recollection by Harry McPherson from the Johnson administration. He said he listened to National Security Adviser Walt Rostow's report of what was happening during the Tet Offensive, and to him it was almost hallucinatory compared to what he was seeing on the television screen.

I would argue that Vietnam is at a nexus of critical changes in the media. This confluence accentuated long-standing problems and conditions, including the difficulty of foreign news coverage, the myth of objectivity, and government attention to news reports. I would suggest that there are a number of divisions that have been blamed on Vietnam which, in fact, existed before Vietnam but were exacerbated by the conflict there. There were sharp divisions between government and press, between press and military, between public and government, and between press and public.

Halberstam

I never thought there was such a thing as objectivity. I think all journalism is subjective, but I think the subjectivity can be based upon high professionalism. Any number of people, including authors of the army's own studies of Vietnam reporting, have found that we, in fact, did report on the military quite accurately because there were great sources. Our great problem early on was getting access. That was our big battle. MACV [Military Assistance Command Vietnam] would not let us on the old CH-21 helicopters at first. When the army came in with the UH-1 Huey, Major Ivan Slavich, the first Huey commander, was told to sell army aviation, and from that moment Neil and I and the others could get on any army helicopter we could. With that we had the access, and we could do the job. That was the critical thing. There never was a question of subjectivity. But the interesting thing is that Vietnam was really a rather easy country to cover. It wasn't that hard. It was out there. The fact that the American war did not work didn't take a genius to discover. All you had to do was be reasonably professional. You had to go out and do your job, and you would find the evidence. Actually I thought it was easier than some of the other assignments I had, such as Eastern Europe.

Hersh

On the issue of objectivity, I ended up thinking at the time that McNamara was a psychotic liar. I was working for the AP then, and when a news conference was over the thing to do was to get to the pay phone within nanoseconds faster than the UPI guy and dictate bulletins that summarized what McNamara said. I thought that no matter what I thought about him, I was enough of a journalist and a professional to do the basic story adequately and fairly. Where my subjectivity would come into play would be the next cycle. The next day I would return to the story and try to write a piece showing how what he had said contradicted what he had said, in most cases with him, a few minutes or sometimes days earlier. [*to Halberstam*] Kennedy knew he had it right at some level, don't you think?

Halberstam

There was never any doubt. In 1964 I ran into Kennedy aide Arthur Schlesinger at a party. He said what great coverage I had done in Vietnam, and I said: "Well, that's odd, because the president of the United States had asked the publisher of the *Times* to pull me out." Schlesinger said: "No, no, no. The president used to tell me how he could always find so much more stuff in your stories in the *Times* than he could from his generals and ambassadors." The truth is that Kennedy believed what I was reporting, but he was pissed to read it because there it was—a first-class foreign policy failure on the front page of the *New York Times*. As he got ready for the 1964 campaign, that didn't please him, but he knew it was accurate.

Hersh

That's pretty complicated, actually. He couldn't begin to act on it, because he was in a political situation. His answer then was to blame the press for not being objective. I'm not pleading some sort of case here, but often that's the problem. Journalists, of course, have things they like and don't like, and they do their job. I think it's sad that more journalists aren't angrier today about the restrictions they have to put up with. We're too old now, David, but if we had been in the desert and somebody had told us we couldn't cover the front, we'd have started walking.

Halberstam

The key thing is always access. In the desert war, it was easier to control the access as long as it was a high technology war. Once there was a ground war, there would have been access, but the war was over so quickly. American servicemen are going to be honest with American reporters. If it's a war that works, you'll get stories that say that the war works and this is what is happening. If it does not, you'll get the other. I wouldn't do what I do, and I think most reporters would not, if they didn't believe that they could work out some kind of degree of trust with honest men and women who work for the military. I believe there is trust and honesty on both sides, and it is worth fighting for.

There was never a press struggle in Vietnam. There was a struggle within the military. The Saigon command was reflecting a dishonest and bad policy from Washington. Military reporting is supposed to filter up from the bottom to the top. Washington was pushing the policy down. The people in the field who said it wasn't working were told to salute and report that it was working or otherwise their careers wouldn't go. What was said to be a press struggle was not a press struggle. It was a military struggle between the field and the command.

Ridenhour

When we have a military action now, what you see happening with the press is what the army certainly wished it could have done with the press during Vietnam. The new policy is a direct consequence of the friction between the press coverage and the political needs of high military officers and politicians in Washington. Probably we'll never hear about another My Lai even if there is another one. Part of the reason is, there will be nobody around where it happens.

There was nobody around where My Lai happened actually, but there was a critical difference. I was a citizen soldier. I came in for two years and came out. The people who are in the service now are career soldiers. This bond of brotherhood—the code of silence that people understand when applied to police officers—also applies to soldiers, especially these days and under these circumstances and given our history.

Hersh

Let me give you an example. During the Gulf War there was the horrible incident when a bomb fell in Baghdad through the smokeshaft of an underground bunker, killing more than one hundred people; I don't remember the exact number. They had what amounted to a capitulation committee that met every morning, and clearly what we were targeting was Saddam Hussein personally. Clearly, they were trying to kill the guy every day with the bombs and trying to find out where he was. It really pisses me off no end that this kind of story doesn't get out, because the public should know that. The ease with which they can carry out that kind of a policy and get away with it now is troublesome to me. We have high-tech war and high-tech command, and there is a real problem in access. Some stories make sense. What are you doing dropping a bomb down there, particularly in this day of precision bombing? Clearly they were head-hunting, and people's heads should roll for that. Maybe it will get out and maybe it won't. The point I'm making is that it is a different world today, and I'm not sure that the newspaper editors of today or the television editors today are always up to it.

Walter Boomer

I don't agree with Ron Ridenhour at all when he says, if there were another My Lai, we would probably never know about it. I commanded all the Marines during Desert Shield/Desert Storm, and I welcomed the media into the Marine Corps forces. We got great coverage. The army wasn't particularly happy with that, but we did in fact welcome them into our ranks. I'm not certain that was the case throughout. I will grant him that point. Certainly from my perspective the media were not locked out, and we spent a lot of time trying to convince our young officers that it is to their advantage as an officer on the battlefield to have the media there. It truly is the American way.

Halberstam

[*responding to a question about whether the air war in Vietnam should have been treated as a war crime*] I'm not an expert on war crimes. The anomaly of the Vietnam War is that the nation which lost the war remains more powerful than the one that won. Usually you get war crimes trials only when one nation is much stronger than the other and crushes the other and then forces the other to submit to war crimes trials. There is enough blame to go around on the Vietnam War for all of us. There was enough miscalculation and enough arrogance, cultural and otherwise, to make me feel modest.

The figure who has always irritated me the most is Robert McNamara. I believe his crime is not so much war crimes but the fact that almost two years into the combat commitment he no longer believed that it could be done, but he remained, in the public venue, silent. I believe he is guilty of something even more serious than war crimes—the crime of silence while some thirty or forty thousand young Americans died after he had changed his mind on the war.

QUESTION about whether press coverage would have been different if the Tonkin Gulf Resolution had been a declaration of war.

Halberstam

No. For reporters in Vietnam, our job was to ask, Does it work? Is it working? And it didn't work. There is a wonderful story about Neil Sheehan very early in the war. He was a young kid, twenty-five-years old, and it is 1962. He is with my great predecessor, the sainted Homer Bigart, who won the Pulitzer Prize in World War II and in Korea. The first helicopters have arrived in Vietnam, and they go down to the Seventh Division in My Tho. Neil is very excited because it is going to be a big story. On the first day they have a bit of a small success, and the second day they have no success at all. It is a typical pillow-punching ARVN operation. The third day is the same thing. They drive back to Saigon together, and Neil is mumbling and grumbling and very angry. Homer Bigart, by then in his late fifties, says, "Mr. Sheehan, Mr. Sheehan what's the matter?" Neil sort of grumbles about three days of wasted time and no story. Homer says, "Mr. Sheehan, there is a story. Mr. Sheehan, there's a very good story. It doesn't work, Mr. Sheehan. That's your story." The job of the reporters was to cover whether it worked or not. American combat troops could fight bravely. Read a heartbreaking book like *We Were Soldiers Once . . . and Young* by Harold G. Moore and Joseph L. Galloway. It's the best book of combat I have read about Vietnam. We could fight bravely, and then we would be gone and the VC and the NVA would keep coming.

Ridenhour

I think that it wouldn't have changed the way the war was conducted. If you changed the way the war was conducted, you would have had different coverage. As long as you have the same war, you have the same coverage. I don't think a declaration of war would have made it a different war.

QUESTION: Then it is impossible for a journalist to give "aid and comfort" to the enemy?

Ridenhour

Whoa. You mean that if our military is conducting an illegal, immoral, vicious, and savage war, and we report that to the American people in a democracy, that makes us traitors? Is that the implication?

RESPONSE: No, not at all. Not at all. That's not the issue. You said that the coverage would have been no different.

Ridenhour

I said that if the war had been different, then the coverage would have been different. A declaration of war would not have, in my judgment, made the conduct of the war any different. So therefore you would have had the same coverage.

Hersh

There would have been more people with the notion that this reporting was aid and comfort. The criticism of the press would have been much more polarized. It would have been much tougher to do what David was doing because of people who would have said you were giving aid and comfort. During World War II and the Korean War, things were much cleaner. We always thought the bad guys, the Germans and the Japanese, fought wars very badly. It was hard to think that "they" are "us." That was what Vietnam was teaching us, and nobody wanted to see that. That would have been very tough. Declaring war would have taken some guts though; it was a political step Johnson didn't want to take. The real failure of courage was in Washington, and the real hypocrisy was in Washington all along on this one.

Ridenhour

[*responding to a question about whether enlisted men as well as officers gave him "friction" as a reporter*] You find honest people in the most unlikely places. You have to be open to the possibility that they're there and they're honest. At the time I thought that the officer corps of the American military was a very unlikely place to find an honest man. I stand corrected in that. I met many who were fair and honest and who saw that our policy there was deeply flawed. Most of the enlisted men I met were really easy to get along with. It had only been eighteen months since I had been there as a soldier for one thing. I had long hair, I had a beard. Their attitude was, "Cool, man, hey, come on in, sit down," and they would tell me what was going on. They were very valuable sources to me. Every once in a while I would run into an officer who had a bad attitude about me in particular. It hadn't been long since I'd been an enlisted man, and since I was no longer an enlisted man, I was kind of happy for the opportunity to engage one of those fellows.

QUESTION: Do you believe the access that the media has during wartime jeopardizes certain military operations? What responsibility does the American media have to protect the American national security?

Hersh

In the case of Desert Storm, everybody was kept in Saudi Arabia, and the news consisted of formal, televised briefings by the briefing officers from the joint command there. That's very troublesome. In Vietnam they used to call those briefings the "five o'clock follies." You get a certain amount of "spin" on all that. A senior officer briefing you and presenting other officers. You're getting access to the top command, General H. Norman Schwarzkopf and others, but given your druthers you would much rather roll around with some of the majors, lieutenant colonels, and captains and find out what's really going on. You weren't able to get that kind of access. To back up what Ron says, an astonishing number of military men do believe that stuff about duty, honor, and country and really are very willing to be honest, particularly if they see something wrong. You weren't able to get to them, and I think that's a big problem.

Richard Nixon was much more of a national security threat to the United States than any reporter I know. I'm not worried about the press being that much of a danger to the national security. It seems our leaders have been much more of a danger. Reporters, by and large, are a little foolish and stupid about things, but most of us have a reasonably good sense of what national security is. Also, I have backing me up something called the Constitution. Nowhere in the Constitution is there any talk of anything about barring the press's access. There is nothing, whether I get it legally and honorably or any other way, that I am barred from publishing. There is no constraint in the United States.

COMMENT from audience: There is aid and comfort to the enemy. It is constituted as treason.

Hersh

There is always treason, but there is nothing that bars me from publishing something. Treason is a subjective standard. There is no objective standard for treason. If I'm publishing something in the belief that what I'm doing is helping my country, it's going to be hard to convict me of treason. In the Pentagon Papers case, Daniel Ellsberg's defense was that he was doing a public service.* I used to tell the military guys that it's your job to keep it secret and my job to find it out. I believe that very much. We would have been much better off letting reporters go out to the units in the Gulf War. If it's a just war and it makes sense, it's going to be reflected in the coverage.

To go back to the My Lai case, the security about My Lai wasn't designed for operational security but political security. You get a lot of abuses. There

---

*A former Defense Department official, Ellsberg leaked a secret Pentagon history of Vietnam decision-making to the *New York Times* in 1971.

was something wrong with that war. I used to always say to myself that there wasn't a kid doing dope in 1965 in Haight-Ashbury in San Francisco that didn't know we were going to lose the war. I don't know why people in Washington didn't know that. It was the strangest thing. There wasn't anybody on the street in the middle sixties that didn't know we were losers and that the other guys simply had something we did not have. It was the strangest phenomenon. I cannot get over how we got into that. I'm actually writing a book now about the early sixties, and one of the things I'm looking into is President Kennedy. I've been working at it for a couple of years, really for thirty. Obviously I'm a little fixated on McNamara. McNamara was an amanuensis; he was a factotum of somebody called Kennedy, who I don't think we understand very much about. One of the things that has always interested me is that some of the great words that came out of Vietnam— nation building, counterinsurgency, strategic hamlet, fortified hamlet, green berets—started big time in 1961. I don't think we paid enough attention to it. Those people who think we were going to get out after 1964 are really kidding themselves.

CARRYING THE DARKNESS: LITERARY APPROACHES TO ATROCITY

John Balaban, W. D. Ehrhart, Wayne Karlin, Basil Paquet

John Balaban, Wayne Karlin, and Basil Paquet are authors of poetry, fiction, and nonfiction that powerfully depict the agony and atrocity of the Vietnam War. All are sensitive artists who were profoundly influenced by their personal experiences in Vietnam. Each has labored to communicate his own witness through his writing. John Balaban volunteered for alternative service in Vietnam as a conscientious objector and spent much time caring for war-injured children. Reality for him is that more civilians died in Vietnam than combatants. The atrocity of Vietnam was not just My Lai but daily destruction of the civilian population. How does one write about cluster bombs, napalm, white phosphorous, and free-fire zones and translate this madness and mayhem into something alive and sensible to people who were not there? Balaban finds that one way to humanize Vietnam for

American readers is to write down and translate the folk poetry that has been trans-mitted orally throughout countless generations of rural Vietnamese.

Wayne Karlin recounts that he went into the Marines as a high school dropout and served in Vietnam as a helicopter door gunner. His experiences changed him. One of his first attempts to write about Vietnam was a short story about GIs killing a rat. It was a parable to represent atrocities that he could not express. Healing needs to be defined carefully. For him the real victims of the war were Vietnamese like those in the ditch at My Lai and the families that survived them. Healing can-not come from denial but must come through admission, punishment, and expia-tion. Writing about atrocity troubles him. Atrocity inspires the writer's art, but the writer must not exploit it.

Basil Paquet, who served as a medic in Vietnam and who is a poet and editor of poetry and fiction, also sees atrocity as a particular challenge for writers. For the artist, the subject may be a personal catharsis, a political statement, or an aesthetic expression. The difficulty comes, as it does with art in general, in con-necting the artist and the audience. He cites as examples his own experience with publishing anthologies of Vietnam War literature and the differing reactions to these volumes by readers and critics. In response to audience questions, the panelists discuss the "moral density" of Vietnam literature, the "moral fog" in the discus-sion of PTSD (who are the victims?), how remembering Vietnam is different from remembering other American wars, and how healing for Americans can come from doing something today for the Vietnamese.

W. D. Ehrhart, poet, editor, and Marine Corps veteran of Vietnam, is the moderator. He begins by reading two poems from *Carrying the Darkness: The Poetry of the Vietnam War*, which Ehrhart edited. They deal with atrocity in one form or another. The first is by Walter McDonald. It is called "In-terview With a Guy Named Fawkes, U.S. Army."

> —you tell them this—
> tell them shove it, they're
> not here, tell them kiss
> my rear when they piss about
> women and kids in shacks
> we fire on. damn.
> they fire on us.
> hell yes, it's war
> they sent us for.

what did they know back where
not even in their granddam's days
did any damn red rockets glare.
don't tell me
how chips fall.
those are The Enemy:
waste them all.

The next poem is by Dick Lourie. It is called "For All My Brothers and Sisters."

this is not easy to write about   it involves
the ignorant peasants shot by the A-
merican soldiers   these peasants were so
ignorant they had no names   so primitive
in nature they were all indistinguishable
from one another   so like dumb animals
their language was babbling nonsense   and when
they died all you could remember was their
gestures   clinging together in the ditch

W. D. Ehrhart

It seems to me those two poems really frame the poles of what happened, not just at My Lai, but all over Indochina for a very long period of time.

John Balaban

I went to Vietnam in 1967. I was in graduate school at Harvard. The war was going on at an extraordinary level, and it was hard to stay in graduate school just reading the newspaper and watching TV. I think my political views then were antiwar, but they were not very thought out. They were just reflex. It was at a time when the United States said very little officially about what was happening to the Vietnamese in the conduct of the war, but the newspapers seemed to be onto something about that. We now know that more civilians died in that war than combatants on either side. Nearly a million South Vietnamese soldiers died, and something more than a million North Vietnamese soldiers died. Something like two million, perhaps, civilians died in the North and South. No one really knew this then; no one was really trying to gather any kinds of facts.

I volunteered to go as a conscientious objector. My first job was to teach linguistics and English at a Vietnamese university. That job got cut short by the Tet Offensive, when the university was bombed flat. What I saw during the Tet Offensive was so horrific that I volunteered with some other friends with the group I worked for to help out in the province hospital. It was a scene like that famous Atlanta railyard scene in *Gone with the Wind,* just a sea of mangled people lying in the hallways and corridors of the hospital. There were no doctors; nobody was doing anything. The staff had left, so we stayed. For the first time, I suppose, for all my political sentiments, I understood what a genocidal war really is in a way that I had no way of comprehending. It was just an overwhelming event, but it did make me come back again to Vietnam to work for a group called the Committee of Responsibility to Save War-Burned and War-Injured Children. I was their field representative for a year or so. This was still doing alternative service to the military.

My job, as one of my friends said, was with "the burned baby business." Literally we were chartered by the Ministry of Health in South Vietnam to evacuate civilians who were children and who were specifically war injured. We weren't allowed to take any others out. We had hospitals in the United States that agreed to take these long-term and difficult reconstructive cases. I took referrals from doctors and helped American doctors who had volunteered to do this work get around the country.

My sense of the horror of that war was the atrocity upon the Vietnamese. It wasn't the single incident of My Lai but a daily incident as the war simply progressed day from day from day. It grew and grew in me. As someone who had gone to Vietnam after having studied with John Barth and Robert Lowell and who had a sense of a literary future for himself, I wondered: How do you write about this incomprehensible destruction that is here? It seemed to be a destruction unlike any that I had been prepared to write about from anything I had read before. I knew the axioms of Dante, for instance, that the proper subjects of poetry are love, virtue, and war. But how do you write about that war with its cluster bombs and white phosphorus and napalm? How do you write about people who in fact were noncombatants but simply happened to be in the way, or about villages that were, because they were in a free-strike zone, fair game for anything that might be dropped upon them? That, I think, is the central difficulty for anybody who has tried to write anything about Vietnam. How do you translate madness and mayhem on a scale that is just not reducible to anything offered up in literature before? How do you reduce it to something alive and sensible to people who have not been there?

I've tried this in a number of ways. Different genres offered different properties. I've written a novel, and I've written a memoir and a good deal of poetry. In 1971–1972 it occurred to me that, in poems like the ones that Bill just read, the general sense of the Vietnamese is nonhuman or barbarian. I thought that, more effectively than doing the hospital work, which maybe brought a few hundred children to the United States for care and maybe a few hundred more to better care in Vietnam, I could use the knowledge of Vietnamese that I had. I could speak it, and since I was trained as a poet, I could do something there too. Maybe the thing that I could do properly was just translate. Let Vietnamese, in other words, speak for themselves in the vast literary tradition that they have held for so many years.

I went back in 1971 to 1972 with a tape recorder and saw myself simply as the vehicle by which Vietnamese could gain a voice in this country that would render them human to Americans. Possibly, in that process, that voice would encourage Americans to stop the war. It sounds naive and simple to me now, and it certainly was then. But I went out in the countryside with a tape recorder and walked up to people who were farmers and to women who were often sewing. I remember one old woman who was working an old Singer pedal sewing machine on a little pyloned house over the Mekong River. I would ask these people to sing me their favorite poem, and they did.

All the folk poetry of Vietnam—the *ca dao* of Vietnam—has been handed down by word of mouth at least for a thousand years. It's probably a tradition that's even longer but datable for a thousand years. There is so much habitual thinking in poetic form in Vietnam among people who cannot read or write as well as among the literary poets of the country that this was not an unlikely proposition. It immediately says something about the humanity of the Vietnamese. I walked up to them a perfect stranger—an American, no less, with a recorder in his book bag—and said, "Sing me your favorite poem." They must have been very suspicious of what I was doing. For hours I taped people who knew poems by heart. They knew the poems from childhood. That became a last way that I was able to somehow overcome the atrocity of the war, by simply providing something else that existed within the context of that atrocity—the long-standing humane and literary tradition of the Vietnamese.

I'll give you a sense [sung in Vietnamese] of that folk poetry from my book *Ca Dao Vietnam: A Bilingual Anthology of Vietnamese Folk Poetry.* This is actually a love song. The English translation is:

> Stepping into the field, sadness fills my deep heart.
> Bundling rice sheaves, tears dart in two streaks.
> Who made me miss the ferry's leaving?
> Who made the shallow creek that parts both sides?

Someone has gone away, someone has been left behind. It's probably a woman because she's bundling rice sheaves, and she's wondering what created this river that separates her from her lover. All Vietnamese poems—peasant tradition especially—are highly structured. Every syllable is counted. The word-pitch upon each syllable is regulated, and rhymes are tucked in in a particular way. Since Vietnamese is a tonal language, the result is actually, in the word-pitch of the line, a suggestion of a melody. The melody then becomes actualized in song. That's how the poems are transmitted.

Wayne Karlin

Kien coaxed himself: "I must write!"
Collar up, coat wrapped securely around him, he paced the quiet Hanoi streets night after night making promises to himself, dreaming up slogans to pull his thoughts into line.
"I must write! It's going to be like smashing granite with fists, like turning myself inside out and exposing all my secrets to the outside world.
"I must write! To rid myself of these devils, to put my tormented soul finally to rest instead of letting it float in a pool of shame and sorrow."

That is from a novel by Bao Ninh, *The Sorrow of War: A Novel of North Vietnam.* Bao Ninh was a member of a brigade of People's Army forces that went south in 1969. Out of five hundred people, he is one of the ten who survived, and he's become a novelist since then. The anguish that he voices in that passage in the novel is parallel to what got many of us writing about war and atrocity. Atrocity has a central place in all the serious narratives about Vietnam.

I went to the war as a high school dropout. I went into the Marine Corps and served time as a helicopter gunner. I came back and started going to school. The first story I ever wrote and got published was actually published by Basil. We were putting together an anthology at that time. It was a story about a group of GIs who were very frustrated by the war. The place where they're living is infested with rats. They try and try and try to exterminate these rats, and the rats keep frustrating them. Finally one day they find a rat that they can trap. The reason they can trap this rat is that it is a mother rat protecting her babies. They proceed to kill all the rats by sticking a wire through their throats and then trying to drown her in a bucket. As she keeps coming up for air, they spray her with deodorant and light it like a little flamethrower. They're just obsessed, and she just will not die. She will not die. Then finally she does. It was based on a real incident.

What had I felt as a writer? Why did that story come out and no others? I had seen many worse things in the war. I wanted that small atrocity to stand for all of the atrocities. I wanted it to stand for the things that I could not express in words at that time. There were pictures of the real incident. There were pictures of remembering a coffle of prisoners held by Nung mercenaries who had been wired together with a wire punctured through their cheeks in order to control them. It was a top layer of many things that I could not otherwise express except through literature.

I think I was representative of many of the people who came out as writers of the war and put it into words. Peter Taylor, I believe, has said that good fiction takes what everybody knows but nobody has put yet into words. I think we felt—and still do in many ways—that we came back from the war to an atmosphere that prevented our experience from coming out. It was as if our own experience—the thing that had changed us from what we were into people who looked at the world with completely different eyes—meant that we could no longer look at ourselves, our country, and all of the beliefs that we had grown up with with the same eyes. It was an atmosphere that negated all that and said it isn't true. It said: "No, you shouldn't look at it this way. Here are the models that already exist; you should look at what you did and what happened through these lenses." We knew this wasn't true. As writers we had to have the ability—and maybe it is the part of our nature that makes us writers—to avoid that kind of convenient wishful thinking and to find stories that would allow our readers to see the truth.

I'm not sure what "healing" means. Because we are writers, language is important to us; the definition of words is very important to us. I almost feel that the word "healing" as it relates to My Lai has been ill-defined, or not defined in a way that is useful, if there is going to be something good that comes out of reexamining My Lai. Healing, it seems to me, involves doing what we saw we had to do as writers. Good writing has to say: "Here is the truth. Here is the horror. Here are the real victims. Here are the real victims of war and the real victims of My Lai."

The real trauma victims of My Lai were the Vietnamese at the bottom of that ditch and the family and relatives who survived them. As soldiers, we were all very much complicit to one degree or another in that kind of crime. I don't think we can afford, however, to take that experience now, and to look at the people who did that killing, and define healing as healing their trauma. To define healing, we need to look at what this was and ask what do we do with it now. Literature can be healing in that sense. If you want to look at something like My Lai as being a morally ambiguous action, this gets us nowhere. Healing involves admission of crime, and then it involves doing something about it. It involves punishment and expiation.

Let me read you a poem by a friend of mine, George Evans:

> How tired I am of hearing about that war,
>   which one should struggle
>   to keep the nightmare of, suffer from rather than forget.
>   I don't want to heal, and I'm sick of those who do.
>   Such things end in license.

I think it's one of the clearest statements by a writer of what writers have to say. We cannot allow the healing to be a kind of denial in itself.

The depiction of atrocity in literature becomes complicated. It's one of the things Basil and I have talked about often. We worked on a book of short stories back in 1973, when the war was still going on. We were publishing stories by veterans. It was some of the first fiction to come out of the war. As artists, we were very conscious of doing something truly as a work of art, in the sense that art can move and change people. It can become an experience for people that they will live through, and therefore it will change them in the ways that the artist became changed. At the same time we were conscious that this process could become something that has its own pleasures. It becomes its own way of life and becomes a way of living, and in this way we become part of the exploitation. If we talk about the literature of the Vietnam War, that is something we need to look at also. We have to be careful not to become vultures.

I go through agony about this all the time, in a personal sense, as a writer. I write about terrible things, and I think that I have no choice but to write about terrible things. I think I would have been a writer whatever my situation, but what I was handed was Vietnam. Now as a writer I have to write about that. As a result of writing about those terrible things, my books make money and all the rest of it. That bothers the hell out of me, and I think that is always the dilemma as artists. As a writer, I put things into beautiful language. For it to affect you, it has to go into beautiful and effective language. As Tim O'Brien said about writing a war story, to do that is itself almost a disservice. I don't have an answer to that. I'm bringing up where I think we are as artists.

Basil Paquet

What does writing about atrocity represent in terms of a challenge to the writer? There is a series of challenges there, not the least of which is what set of aesthetics you use to approach the issue. I'd like to talk about it from a couple of different angles. One is as a writer myself, as a poet and a novelist. But maybe more important for this discussion is to talk about it as an editor of the works of other writers in the early days when Jan Barry and Larry Rottmann and I started First Casualty Press.

The particular challenge at that time in dealing with writing coming out of the war, both poetry and prose, was that we were dealing with writers who oftentimes were struggling to write for their own personal reasons. That is to say, they were trying to express themselves and deal with their own personal demons. For many of them writing was a cathartic act. They were attempting an act of healing—through whatever definitions you want to approach healing. As an editor and as an artist, I would say that for the three of us our approach was really quite different. Bill Ehrhart could probably attest to that as he struggled against his editors from time to time. Our purpose was political, as well as aesthetic, and we had no separation in our minds of the aesthetics of editing those works and the politics of them. We were trying to get works—both poetry and fiction—coming out of the war and bring them to the attention of the public. We believed that, to the extent that those works accurately reflected the minute particulars of the war as well as larger events such as atrocities, they would raise the awareness of the public in general. While we were happy if it had a cathartic effect for the writers, it was frankly not our intention or purpose. We were struggling with our own demons as well, but we were pretty clear in terms of what our purposes were. That probably gave us a chance to sleep at night in ways that other writers did not because we had that to hold onto in terms of clarity of purpose.

The first book that the press published was a book of poetry. It was an anthology called *Winning Hearts and Minds* [1972]. When it came out, it was extremely well reviewed, and we published four editions of the book. There was something like over thirty-five thousand copies distributed throughout the United States. For a book of poetry that is quite extraordinary. If you sell eight hundred books of poetry, that's not a bad job, so thirty-five thousand is pretty damn good. It's deeply disturbing still, even from this moment in time, however, to understand why the book was so successful. It wasn't successful in the ways that we intended it to be successful. I raise this issue because I think it speaks directly to the challenges to the artist of how the hell you deal with these things. We intended for the book's particular poems to have a cumulative effect that would depict the war in terms of its brutality and its atrocity and that would have some political intent and content. The thing that the book's reviewers most admired about it was—in separate poems as well as collectively—the lyric voice of these beautiful, young poet Americans who could depict their war experience. It took me a little while to understand what was going on. We had a set of writers trying to depict the war and trying to depict atrocities, brutality, criminality, and some of their own circumstances in terms of being brutalized themselves. This remains a great challenge to me and a great mystery that we could have made such a good book that would have done so well and been so widely distributed and yet be so incredibly misunderstood in terms of its aesthetic and in terms of its purpose.

The second book that we published was a book of short stories. Wayne, Larry Rottmann, and I pulled the book together, and it was called *Free Fire Zone* [1973]. Given the experience of the first book, we set out with a little stronger intent, and it was an interesting cut at the prose versus the poetry. There was no lyric voice to hide behind. Largely, people who were writing prose were writing in third person. They weren't writing personal confessionals. They were a set of writers creating characters and trying to picture the war with some sense of verisimilitude—whatever the aesthetic. Whether the work was naturalistic or abstract, a collage or a parable—as in one of Wayne's short stories—there was a brutal accuracy to the depiction of life there. I think it was probably one of the most successful books about Vietnam capturing what U.S. soldiers did to the Vietnamese people—and to all people in Indochina because the war spread quite beyond Vietnam alone. That book was roundly and soundly condemned. The reviewers viewed it as a tragic fall, I think, for the editors and for First Casualty Press because they had strayed from the beauty of *Winning Hearts and Minds*. This was very, very hard to take. They also viewed the works as largely confessional, and, while there was an element to that, it wasn't what that work was about.

Those two issues and those two books raise central challenges to the artist about how you write about war and how you write about atrocity. In both those books I thought the artists were enormously successful in terms of their working out a way to write about war and atrocity. They wrote about the great difficulty they had created for a people who they, in their own minds, had gone to liberate and ended up oppressing and murdering. What magnificent failures they were. As works of art as well as politics, the books didn't accomplish a lot in terms of getting to the public that we were writing to. That remains a challenge for writers who are trying to write about Vietnam and the Indochina war. I'm sure there are parallel situations for other writers writing about other parallel situations in the world. It's difficult to have art work in a way that you can direct it towards an audience, make a connection with that audience, fight your own demons, and have that art serve all the gods you worship. It's an enormously difficult thing. Some writers, I think, have done a lot better job than others, but it's an enormously difficult struggle.

QUESTION from female audience member: What do you say to people who say that you had to be there to understand?

Paquet

I don't think that's a good approach for a writer to take. I don't think you would be very successful taking that tack in terms of creating a work of art. One of the principal differences in the literature coming out of World War II, the Korean War—little of it that there was—and the Vietnam War or Indochina war was the struggle of the artist to somehow include issues about women and children. It's one thing to write about set-piece battles or a war that takes place in terms of campaigns with set armies. There is some of that clearly in the Vietnam War in terms of people who fought against NVA regulars or whatever. For many soldiers, however, the great struggle was to write about circumstances in which they were fighting. Fighting is a funny word.

You were murdering women and children; you were burning down villages; and they were very much a part of your war. That's pretty different than a lot of the literature, such as the classics like *The Naked and the Dead* or whatever. It's a real challenge to the writer coming out of Vietnam to include those circumstances about how you relate to women, children, and old people, as well as to other soldiers. Film, poetry, fiction, and theater are replete with material in terms of the relationship of women and children to the circumstances of the war, and much of that art gives voice to that.

Karlin

As a writer, one of the things that I hate is being told that I cannot write in a voice that doesn't reflect my own particular experience or that I cannot write as a woman, a child, or a person of a different race, culture, and so on. I don't accept that in any sense. Writing is art, which is imaginatively putting yourself into the point of view of people other than yourself and creating situations and so on. There is no point in writing if we feel that you can't share the experiences.

Balaban

I don't know that there is an exclusiveness to the male experience which says that no one else can understand or that says only I am the true understander of what happened. I think it's a literary trope. It's only "I have come back to tell you all." It's the person who has seen something unique. It's not a class, race, or gender separation. It's the sense of an individual isolated so thoroughly that he believes only he has come to any kind of revelation about an incident which perhaps no one else has actually even seen. Or if others have seen it, they haven't seen it the way that person believes they have. That voice excludes even other people who might have been around him at the time. I think it's the sense of one action so unimaginable and of pressures upon the individual so vast that you have this sense of exclusivity that comes out of it. Part of it, I think, is a literary trope. It's a way of attracting audience attention.

Ehrhart

The very fact of the writing itself means the author is trying to put you there and is trying to share that experience. You're never going to do it completely, but the writing itself makes clear that the writer believes that this can be a shared experience, no matter what anybody is saying in the writing.

QUESTION about whether war lends itself to a greater eloquence than other experiences.

Paquet

No. It is a transforming experience. It is not transforming in that way.

Ehrhart

I think that war is a kind of experience that causes some people—many people—to reflect very deeply and to think very hard about what is going on around them. There are other experiences that draw forth that kind of eloquence. One can find it in Frank DeFord's book about his daughter's dying. This guy is a sports writer for *Sports Illustrated,* and he wrote this book about his kid who died of, I think, leukemia or something. It is just beautiful writing.

QUESTION about how tension between memory and reality affects writing.

Balaban

This was all twenty years or more ago, and we were a lot younger. We were just out of college or just out of high school. What happened to us then was part of an incredibly formative period when our adult natures were really being formed. I had a friend who said, "I grew up in Vietnam," and he meant that literally. There were just simply extraordinary events that they took in or partly took in. That they were partly taken in means that over the years they were also taken in in your memory. These very vivid events, which for me are as real as all of us in the room, stay with you. You think about them. You're at a dinner table having conversation with family or friends and something will come forward. The danger of it for me is the fear of becoming a kind of beer-bellied legionnaire bore. Your impulse is to say, "Oh, that reminds me of . . ." *Of course* it reminds you of something in Vietnam, because that's your telling experience. So I bite my tongue all the time for fear of embarrassing myself that way.

A lot of conversations that occur around me bring me back to Vietnam, or things that happened in Vietnam are simply staying with me. Part of that seems to me unfortunate, but part of it is that I think I still learn from things. I simply turn them around in different ways. I've written poems, fiction, and nonfiction about the same event and each time learned something different from that event. It still happens for me. I hope that I'm not obsessed with it, and that I'm not morbidly chasing my tail on this topic. That would be too bad. Nothing good could issue from that.

Paquet

The issue for me about difference between work that came out of the Vietnam War and poetry that came out of World War I or World War II is the moral density of the work that came out of Vietnam. The tension to me is how you depict those things and have it reflect that kind of moral density. Some of the artists seem to go, in terms of their aesthetic choices, in almost the exact opposite direction of density. They choose minimalist approaches, as in the poem by Walter McDonald that Bill Ehrhart read. For me the central issue is around tension, and some of the greatness of the poetry is the issue of moral density. Moral density is, in itself, almost contradictory because the morality of it is at times so clear.

In the discussion of post-traumatic stress disorder, for example, there is what I would refer to as a moral fog. We talk about post-traumatic stress disorder and include people from the Trojan War, the Civil War, World War II, and Vietnam. I don't have any difficulty with people talking in clinical terms about what happens to a soldier who has been in a traumatic situation. My degree of difficulty here comes in our failure to differentiate who is a victim and who is an oppressor, and what trauma is to those different parties. If you were a soldier in a set battle, I have no doubt about how stressful that could be and how that can affect you for the rest of your life. I have a great deal of sympathy for someone who suffers that way. I have a great deal of sympathy for anybody who suffers from any form of post-traumatic stress disorder. But for the clinicians, I would simply ask what is to be cured. There is a big difference between somebody who is in a battle zone, deprived of sleep, and in great fear going through a war, and the person who gunned down innocent women and children in an irrigation ditch. What could "cure" mean for those two different people, both suffering from post-traumatic stress disorder? If I am the person who gunned down the villagers in the ditch, what does "curing me" mean? Does it mean I get by that morally? Does it mean I get a chance not to feel guilty again? I would hope not. What I would call the moral fog is identifying a whole lot of people who were suffering because they were feeling a great deal of guilt about what they did and who ought to feel guilty and culpable about it. I would draw a very sharp line of distinction between those people and lots of soldiers in Vietnam and other wars who were suffering from more classical descriptions of battle fatigue or shell shock or exhaustion or whatever. I find the inability of our medical people to deal with that to be symptomatic of our society's inability to deal with it.

Paquet

[*responding to a follow-up question asking for other examples of this moral fog*] We've heard it said that there were moments of "lapse" for the Americans in Vietnam and that My Lai was one of them. I would turn attention to the air war in Laos. By what stretch of semantics would you describe that in terms of a brief moral lapse? If My Lai was genocide but was not representative, then what do you call an air war against an entire people in which the only Americans present were reconnaissance troops who would be able to report on how effective we were at eradicating an entire population?

Balaban

[*responding to a question about how one faces both the pain of one's own PTSD and the knowledge that the Vietnamese are victims*] The victims are the Vietnamese. Obviously a good number of Americans came back in pain, and that pain may indeed be lifelong and maybe should be lifelong, as expressed in that George Evans poem that Wayne read. But the Vietnamese are still there, and the same villages are still there. There are a number of Americans who have done remarkable things. Vets on their own have built clinics in Vietnam, and it seems to me that there is a way of healing oneself. If you were a soldier who has done something that sticks with you in a destroying way, one advice would be to reinvolve yourself with Vietnam—go back and do something good there. It's not out of any American's reach to do that. If it's only writing and saying you will tithe a part of your monthly salary to a hospital in Vietnam, that is a healing step. It's certainly a step that the Vietnamese can appreciate too.

[*responding to a question about whether Vietnamese poetry is a healing thing for them as his poetry is for him*] Two aspects come out of every Vietnamese poem, whether it is sung by peasants or written by literary scholars. One is a love of verbal play—a love of music and intricate verbal play. The other is a sense of community, a sense of belonging to a cultural stream that crosses geographical miniboundaries within Vietnam and goes way back in time. Indeed, when I recorded I thought that I was recording a dying tradition. I thought the social fabric of Vietnam would have been so destroyed that the poetry would have been one of the quickest things to go. People in the cities have radio and television, and they've learned to read and write. They don't need an oral transmission. I think that's the reason many people I spoke to in Saigon didn't know the poetry—especially the younger people. Everyone with a root in any Vietnamese country home knows that poetry, and it's really very hard to find any country person who doesn't know something by heart. It certainly is at the heart of Vietnamese consciousness. So much so that, when Vietnamese courts wanted to understand the sensibility or the sense of political fervor or interest among the local population, they would send people out into the countryside to collect that poetry. It's the way that Confucius, Kong Fuzi [K'ung Fu-tzu], was supposed to have collected the *Book of Songs,* the *Shi jing* [*Shih ching*], and created the Music Bureau in ancient China. The idea was a kind of Harris Poll of the time. Indeed, you can find in the folk poetry an expression of popular sentiment. Since the end of the war, there have been lots and lots of books published in Vietnam of the kind I did in 1974. Some books are very specialized—just the poetry of a certain province in the Mekong Delta, or the poetry of children in a certain area. The Vietnamese are very much interested in that poetry in ways ranging from ethnography to just celebration of folkloric life.

QUESTION about the interest of publishers today in books about Vietnam.

Ehrhart

The problem is you can't go to the supermarket and pick out a publisher. Everybody here can tell you about rejection after rejection after rejection after rejection, consistently over a period of twenty-some years. And the same thing is still heard, regardless of all those books. All those books have made every editor jaundiced. Oh, there are all those books about Vietnam. Before, it was "Nobody wants to hear about it." Now, it's "Look at all these books about it—not another book about Vietnam." It's a difficult business.

Karlin

The books about Vietnam that are coming out in such quantities are combat narratives. That's always a good seller, but it says nothing new.

When First Casualty Press first came out, Basil and Larry and Jan had shopped that manuscript around to about forty publishers, all of whom said people are not going to be interested in this. When I decided to do the anthology of fiction by American and modern Vietnamese writers, I was working through an agent who does my novels. She started taking the proposal around. The language of the editors was exactly the same language that we had experienced twenty years before. People are not going to be interested. One editor actually said that, if this were more immediate, meaning if the stories were actually combat stories from both sides, we would be interested in doing this. The people doing it now are Curbstone, who are about three miles down the road from where we did First Casualty Press. It's a small, nonprofit alternate press, just as we were. I went up there, and I hadn't been back there since we did First Casualty Press. It was a sort of defeated sense of déjà vu. I'm happy they're doing this, and they're good people for doing it—but good God.

Paquet

Having flashbacks?

Karlin

[*responding to a question about sexual imagery in literature about Vietnam*] I don't remember where this quote comes from or who said it, but it certainly reflected a real feeling among GIs. The quote was that "we were the system's women." I say this being totally conscious of what is going into that remark— the denigration that is going into that remark. It's a sense of being used for a purpose other than what you feel your personal self is—in that sense being violated and raped. I think that a lot of the sexual imagery in the war comes from our sense, on the one hand, of being the perpetrator and, on the other hand, being the victim also.

WHAT KIND OF WAR WAS THE VIETNAM WAR?

George C. Herring

Examinations of My Lai and of the Vietnam War in general often lead to the question of whether this conflict was, indeed, a different kind of war. Highly regarded for his critical and nonideological analyses of the American war in Vietnam, George Herring provides a useful historical perspective on facing the darkness of My Lai and Vietnam. He raises a number of questions about the distinctive nature of the war and about its impact on the individual American soldier and the American nation. A host of frustrations—including guerrilla warfare, booby traps, limited warfare, poor relations with the South Vietnamese, and declining morale—led many American soldiers and citizens to decide that the war was without meaning or purpose. The war challenged America's self-image, especially the notions of invincibility and moral rectitude.

Many soldiers were troubled that what they were doing did not square with their notions of America's proper role in the world. My Lai was particularly troubling in this regard, according to Herring, not because it was typical, but because it raised the most basic questions about the U.S. role in Vietnam and about Americans themselves. It was the sort of thing Americans were presumed not to do. If My Lai was what the war had become, then many Americans decided they wanted no more of it.

What did we encounter when we arrived in Vietnam in force? Those Americans who fought in Vietnam, at least in the early stages of the war, were very much products of the cold-war culture and generally accepted its major tenets. These members of the baby-boom generation were younger on the average by seven years than the GIs of World War II. They were raised on tales of American heroes and heroism in the Second World War, fed to them in a steady diet of John Wayne and Audie Murphy movies. They were driven to enlist by fears of the communist menace and inspired to serve by the militant rhetoric of John Kennedy, among others. At least at the beginning, they went to war willingly, even eagerly, certain of the rightness of their cause and expecting gratitude from Americans back home and from the Vietnamese that they went forth to save from communism.

The war they found in Vietnam was quite unlike their images of what war was about or the vision that drew them there in the first place. It is extraordinarily difficult to generalize about the experience of the war in Vietnam. It made a great deal of difference when one served, what one did, and where one was. There were huge differences, for example, between being an advisor in 1962 or a combat infantryman in 1968, between being with the First Cav in the Highlands in 1965, with the marines along the DMZ at Tet in 1968, or what was called a REMF [rear echelon mother fucker] in Saigon at any time.

This much conceded, there are generalizations that can be made and that distinguish this conflict from others. By the time Americans were in Vietnam in large numbers, the war had already been raging for nearly twenty years—first as a nationalist struggle on the part of Vietnamese revolutionaries against French colonialism, subsequently as a determined effort on the part of Vietnamese revolutionaries, north and south, to unify the country arbitrarily divided by the 1954 Geneva Conference. By 1965, National Liberation Front insurgents had mounted a full-scale revolution in South Vietnam that threatened to bring down the American-backed Saigon government. North Vietnam had fully committed itself to the southern insurgency, dispatching men and supplies and then sizable detachments of its own army along the fabled Ho Chi Minh Trail into the South.

During this stage of the war—at least, for America's adversaries—it was a war that was as much political as it was military: a war waged fiercely and relentlessly in the villages of southern Vietnam; a war where winning the support of the people and undermining the Saigon government were the most important goals; a war where political reforms, propaganda, coercion, and terror—rather than guns, tanks, and planes—were the essential weapons.

That type of war posed extremely difficult challenges for Americans. It was fought in a climate and on a terrain that were singularly inhospitable: thick jungles, foreboding swamps and paddies, and rugged mountains. The heat could "kill a man, bake his brains, or wring the sweat from him until he died of exhaustion," Philip Caputo tells us in *A Rumor of War* (1978). "It was as if the sun and the land itself were in league with the Vietcong," Caputo goes on to say, "wearing us down, driving us mad, killing us." The climate and terrain were so harsh that one GI proposed that the national flower of Vietnam should be an enormous thorn.

More important, perhaps, was the formless yet lethal nature of guerrilla warfare in Vietnam. It was a war without distinct battle lines or fixed objectives, where traditional concepts of victory and defeat were blurred. It was, Caputo writes, "a formless war against a formless enemy who evaporated into the morning jungle mists only to materialize in some unexpected place."

The danger was nowhere and everywhere. "We'd be expecting a huge firefight and end up picking our nose," one GI wrote. "And then one day we'd be walking along daydreaming and—BOOM—they'd spring an ambush." As many as one fourth of the total U.S. casualties in Vietnam came from mines and booby traps, an omnipresent reality that was both terrifying and demoralizing.

Schooled in the conventional warfare of World War II and Korea, Americans found this type of war particularly difficult to fight. There was always the gnawing question, first raised by no less a personage than President John Kennedy: How can we tell if we are winning? It is a pretty important question in war, and a question that Americans repeatedly asked themselves. The only answer that could be devised was the notorious body count, as grim and corrupting as it was unreliable as an index of success. For many GIs, a strategy of attrition and the body count came, in time, to represent killing for the sake of killing. "Aimless, that's what it is," one of Tim O'Brien's GIs laments in *Going after Cacciato* (1978), "a bunch of kids trying to pin the tail on the Asian donkey. But no fuckin tail. No fuckin donkey."

It was a limited war in both ends and means. The United States never set out to win this war in the conventional sense, in part for fear that winning might provoke a larger war, even the nuclear war that our intervention there was prepared to fend off. Also, at least at the beginning in 1965, winning seemed both unnecessary and counterproductive. The Johnson administration sought rather to apply just enough military pressure to get North Vietnam to accept a permanent division of the country at the seventeenth parallel. "I'm going up old Ho Chi Minh's leg an inch at a time," LBJ proclaimed in his inimitable way in 1965. Consequently, the United States did not mobilize its vast resources and fought under often restrictive rules of engagement.

The result was extremely frustrating for those who managed the war, for those who supported it, and especially for those who fought it. It was especially frustrating for those in the field who were not supposed to fire unless fired upon, who were not supposed to pursue the enemy into sanctuaries in Laos and Cambodia, and who sometimes felt they were fighting with one hand tied behind their backs. It was even more frustrating after 1968 when the United States stopped the bombing of North Vietnam and began withdrawing its troops even while the war raged on. If "you're going to commit troops, you don't just leave them out there hanging to dry," a marine complained. "You can't be playing by some weird rules you make up as you go along."

At least in its initial stages, it was a peoples' war, with the people rather than territory as the primary objective. But Americans as individuals or as a nation could never really bridge the vast cultural gap that separated them from all Vietnamese. Not knowing the language or the culture, they could not know what the people were thinking. "Maybe the dinks got things mixed up," one of O'Brien's bewildered GIs comments after a seemingly friendly farmer bows and smiles and points the Americans straight into a mine field. "Maybe the gooks cry when they're happy and smile when they're sad." Recalling the emotionless response of a group of peasants when their homes were destroyed by an American company, Caputo notes that they did nothing, "and I hated them for it. Their apparent indifference made me feel indifferent." The cultural gap led to a questioning of goals and produced a great deal of moral confusion among those fighting the war and those at home.

Indeed, ironically and tragically, America's allies—the South Vietnamese—became the target of much of the anger and frustration that built up during the war. In the early years, many U.S. advisers had developed close attachments to the Vietnamese, living with them, sharing their food, and imbibing their culture. In the aftermath of the U.S. buildup, some Americans continued to work closely and effectively with their Vietnamese ally. This was especially true at the lower levels and in combat situations, where a shared danger naturally drew disparate peoples together.

As the American presence became more pervasive, however, suspicion and resentment increased. The two peoples approached each other with colossal ignorance. "My time in Vietnam is the memory of ignorance," a GI later conceded. "I didn't know the language. I knew nothing about the aims of the people—whether they were for or against the war." For the Americans, indeed, the elemental task of distinguishing friend from foe became a sometimes impossible challenge. "What we need is some kind of litmus paper that turns red when it's near a communist," one U.S. officer, half-jokingly, half-seriously, commented to journalist Malcolm Browne.*

Although fighting in a common cause, the two peoples grew increasingly suspicious and resentful of each other. The more the Americans assumed the burden of the fighting after 1965, the more they demeaned the martial abilities of their ally. Although the South Vietnamese army had been relegated to pacification duty as the direct result of a U.S. policy decision, it became an object of ridicule. Its attack mode was best depicted, according to a standard American joke, by the statue of a seated soldier in the national military cemetery. "They have too few Nathan Hales," an American adviser complained. "They want to make babies during and after the conflict. They do not equate their dying for their country as a necessity for the future."

The South Vietnamese people became an object of scorn and fear. Their seeming indifference, while Americans were dying in the field, provoked hatred. Americans expressed contempt for the consumer culture that they had done so much to create in South Vietnam and from which they saw the Vietnamese profiting. "The war has brought out all the venality imaginable in these people," one GI observed with obvious disgust.

The villagers were more baffling and infuriating to many soldiers than their Vietcong enemies. At least the guerrillas were a known quantity, hidden, for the most part, and entirely lethal. The villagers, by contrast, lived out in the open, but their loyalties were obscure. While the war raged all around them, they went on with their lives, tending their crops and livestock

*Quoted in *The New Face of War* (Indianapolis: Bobbs-Merrill, 1968), 46.

and raising their families. Their role remained a mystery to most Americans. They seemed not to support the government of South Vietnam or the United States. But it was not clear to what extent they supported the revolution.

Their unerring ability to avoid the mines and booby traps that killed and maimed Americans led to charges of collusion. The people were "treacherous," one soldier commented. "They say 'GI number one' when we're in the village, but at night the dirty little rats are VC." They came to be viewed as the cause and embodiment of all the war's contradiction and confusion. "In Vietnam you identify every gook with the enemy. . . . If it weren't for the Vietnamese you wouldn't be here."

The actual experience of warfare in Vietnam thus sharply contradicted the explanations GIs had been given for their service. Told they were there to help the people of South Vietnam, they found indifference or antagonism. Told they were there to prevent the spread of communism, they found that support of the revolution flourished throughout the country. Told they were there to protect the villagers from aggression, they destroyed villages and terrorized civilians.

Many Americans thus came to perceive the war as without meaning or purpose. Those who thought the United States was right to be in Vietnam were angered that it was not doing what was necessary to win. Those who questioned the purpose of the war were bothered by the senselessness of trying to fight it. "It don't mean nothin'" became a common saying among GIs, and they responded in different ways. Some simply did their job and blocked out questions of purpose and right or wrong. Others found ways to shirk or resist. Some accepted the war on its own terms and found an outlet in the violence that was sometimes unleashed against the people of South Vietnam.

As with so many other areas of the war, the Tet Offensive of January and February 1968 aggravated attitudes already well developed. Tet further delegitimized the South Vietnamese government in the eyes of many Americans. The ease with which the Vietcong had penetrated the very centers of U.S.–South Vietnamese power raised profound questions about the viability of the Saigon government. The street execution of a Vietcong captive by the Saigon police chief—an event brought home to Americans dramatically by television cameras—signified even to White House officials that we were "involved up to our necks in a war among very alien peoples with whom we shared few values."

For their part, American servicemen manifested more openly after Tet the accumulated frustrations of fighting a war they could not win in an increasingly hostile environment, and the savagery of the combat at Tet inflamed anti-Vietnamese feelings. A gallows-humor solution to the Vietnam problem that went around the firebases and bars typified a growing attitude among GIs: "What you do is load all the friendlies onto ships and take them out to the South China Sea. Then you bomb the country flat. Then you sink the ships."

As the morale of the U.S. Army disintegrated under the surreal conditions of the war after Tet, Americans increasingly vented their frustration on Vietnamese. Soldiers fired weapons at civilians, hurled rocks and cans at villagers, and drove their vehicles in life-threatening ways. "Many armies have dealt harshly with enemy populations," the journalist Jonathan Schell observed in 1970, "but ours certainly is one of the first to deal so harshly with its allies."* Without exonerating the Americans, Schell sought to put their behavior in perspective. They had been sent to protect the South Vietnamese from communism only to find that their help was not wanted or appreciated. Unable to tell friend from foe, they came to regard the entire population as the enemy and began to make war "against the people they were supposed to be saving who didn't want to be saved."

That America would eventually fail in Vietnam seems now, from the vantage point of twenty years, to have been likely if not inevitable. The balance of forces was stacked against us, and success, as we defined it, was probably beyond our reach. In southern Vietnam we attempted a truly formidable undertaking on the basis of a very weak foundation. The country to which we first committed ourselves in 1954 was a country in name only. It lacked most of the essential ingredients for nationhood. Indeed, had we looked all over the world, we could hardly have found a less promising place for an experiment in nation building.

For nearly twenty years, we struggled to establish a viable nation in the face of internal insurgency and external invasion. But we could never find leaders capable of mobilizing the disparate population of southern Vietnam. The fact that we had to look for them is in itself telling. We launched a vast array of ambitious and expensive programs to promote sound government,

---

*Jonathan Schell, *Observing the Nixon Years: "Notes and Comments" from the New Yorker on the Vietnam War and the Watergate Crisis, 1969–1975* (New York: Pantheon, 1989), 61.

win the hearts and minds of the people (WHAM—the acronym of the age), and wage war against the Vietcong. When our client state was on the verge of collapse in 1965, we put in our own military forces. But the rapid collapse of South Vietnam after our military withdrawal in 1973 suggests how little we really accomplished.

From beginning to end, we also drastically underestimated the strength and determination of our adversary. I do not wish to imply here that the North Vietnamese and NLF were some kind of superpeople. They made colossal blunders and miscalculations themselves. They paid an enormous price for their victory. They have shown a far greater capacity for war-making than for nation-building.

In terms of the balance of forces of this war, however, they had distinct advantages. They were tightly mobilized and regimented and fanatically committed to their goals. They skillfully applied a strategy of protracted war, perceiving that the Americans, like the French, would become impatient and, if they bled long enough, would weary of the war. "You will kill ten of our men," Ho Chi Minh said, "but we will kill one of yours, and in the end it is you who will tire." The comment was made to a French official in 1946, but could serve as a commentary on the American war as well.

The circumstances of the war thus posed a dilemma that we never really understood, much less resolved. Success would probably have required the physical annihilation of North Vietnam, but given our limited goals this seemed excessive. Destruction of the North also held out the serious threat of Soviet and Chinese intervention and a much larger war, even possibly a nuclear war. This larger context makes the Vietnam War and the Gulf War totally different. The only other way to win was to establish a politically viable South Vietnam, but given the weak foundation of the Saigon regime and the U.S.-Vietnamese cultural gap, not to mention the strength of the internal revolution, that goal was probably beyond our capability. To put it charitably, looking back with the wonderful hindsight of twenty to thirty years, we probably placed ourselves in a classic no-win situation.

The outcome of the war was itself, of course, traumatic, far and away the most traumatic of all the wars the United States has participated in. For many who had fought in Vietnam, for some who had supported the war, and even for some who opposed it, the end in April 1975 came hard. "I grieved," an army officer told me. "I grieved as though I had lost a member of my own family." For those who had lost children, it was especially painful. "Now it's all gone down the drain and it hurts," a Pennsylvanian said of his son.

"What did he die for?" The fall of South Vietnam came at the very time Americans were preparing to celebrate the bicentennial of their nation's birth, and the irony was painfully obvious. "The high hopes and wishful idealism with which the American nation had been born had not been destroyed," *Newsweek* observed, "but they had been chastened by the failure of America to work its will in Indochina."

Indeed, looked at from the larger perspective, Vietnam, as perhaps no other event in our history, forced us as individuals and as a nation to confront a set of beliefs about ourselves that formed a basic part of the American mythology of the American character. This goes a long way toward explaining why the war has caused such pain and helps to explain why we have had such difficulty coming to grips with it.

The idea of American exceptionalism holds that we are a people apart, a nation different from other nations. The first of its components, which might be labeled the myth of American benevolence, holds that in our dealings with other people we have in general acted kindly and generously. We have not been exploitative or imperialistic like our European brethren. When we have used force, we have done so in the pursuit of noble goals.

For many Americans, to be sure, the war in Vietnam remained from beginning to end, in the words of former president Ronald Reagan, a "noble cause." But for many others, there was enormous confusion, uncertainty, or outright revulsion. It was a perplexing war, where the old standards did not seem to apply and where we did not seem to be playing our traditional role. This caused great problems. We had to look at ourselves in a way we never had before. This is where My Lai fit in very powerfully. It raised in the most tragic way basic questions about our role in Vietnam—indeed, most important, about ourselves. It was the sort of thing Americans did not do according to the national mythology. If that was what the war was doing to us, many concluded in an interesting spin that was being put on it, then they wanted no part of it. So that revelation, twenty-five years ago, was a powerful force toward moving even those who supported the war into trying to liquidate it.

Was My Lai an aberration, uncharacteristic of the war and the way it was waged, or was it exactly the opposite, emblematic and symptomatic of U.S. conduct of the war? It was not typical in any sense. Certainly in terms of scale and magnitude, it was not typical. The burning of villages and the victimization of civilians did take place from the early stages on. One can go back to Cam Ne, the village that Morley Safer's CBS crew filmed being destroyed by marines in August 1965. To Lyndon Johnson's eyes at least, it was an infamous episode. One can probably find examples even earlier than Cam Ne. In terms of its scale, certainly My Lai was not typical at all, but the complexity of the relationship with Vietnamese civilians was very typical. The relationship with civilians does mark this war as distinct and different from many other wars we fought, but not from all. One can look at the Philippine war in the early part of the twentieth century and find some rough parallels there in terms of the kind of war it was and the way that Americans dealt with civilians. One can find some parallels in what might loosely be called pacification efforts in Central America in the early part of the century. What is important is the sort of attitude that developed toward Vietnamese civilians that came out of this dynamic of war. It tells us a side of ourselves that we don't like to hear. It's not something that squares with who we think we are.

By the late 1960s Vietnam had become much more than a country or a war for Americans. It became, and remains, a metaphor for what America was or should be. To be sure, many continued to feel throughout the war that the United States was doing the right thing. Others, however, went backward from Vietnam to rediscover a pattern of wrongdoing deeply entrenched in American history. One of my favorite examples is a Jules Feiffer cartoon from the late 1960s or early 1970s. A fellow is commenting, "When I went to school, I learned George Washington never told a lie, slaves were happy on the plantation, the men who opened the west were giants, and we won every war because God was on our side." But he goes on to say, "Where my kid goes to school, he learned George Washington was a slave-owner, the slaves hated slavery, the men who opened the west committed genocide, and the wars we won were victories for U.S. imperialism. No wonder my kid's not an American. They're teaching him some other country's history."

Vietnam also challenged the notion of American invincibility, the conviction that we could do anything we set our minds to: The difficult we do tomorrow, the impossible may take awhile. This view was seemingly confirmed by our spectacular growth as a nation, our unparalleled record of success in peace and war. This attitude was an important factor in our involvement in Vietnam. At each step along the way, policymakers plunged ahead certain that the United States—as it always had—would eventually succeed. When it did not, it came as a rude shock to the national psyche. We were so accustomed to success that we had come to take it for granted.

Failure came hard, especially when our armies were never really defeated and when we were frustrated by a small, presumably backward, and—perhaps worse—Oriental enemy.

In the aftermath of war, therefore, we concocted various myths to explain the otherwise inexplicable. The national will was subverted, it was said, by a hostile media and antiwar movement. We failed because we did not use our power wisely or decisively. The civilians put restrictions on the military that made it impossible to win. Hence came the classic statement of Rambo, upon being given his mission to return to Vietnam and go the second round singlehandedly: "Sir, do we get to win this time?" A simpleminded line, to be sure, but one rich in national mythology.

For twenty years we continued to treat Vietnam as an enemy, displacing our anger and perhaps some of our guilt by turning against the Vietnamese, accusing them of various crimes, holding them accountable for all our MIAs. We stubbornly refused to make peace, journalist Joseph Galloway observed, even as we "mourned the fact that somehow the war wouldn't go away and leave us alone." Embittered and trapped in denial, we were unable to see, as Galloway put it, that "peace is made, not found." Full normalization of relations with Vietnam is the indispensable and long-overdue step to begin the process of putting an end to America's longest war. By doing that, we begin to come to terms with the Vietnamese, and maybe we begin as well to come to terms with ourselves.

6

ATROCITIES IN HISTORICAL PERSPECTIVE

Stephen E. Ambrose

Atrocity is a part of war that must be faced, noted military and political historian Stephen Ambrose maintains. Individual and collective responsibility for atrocity is difficult to determine. There are several cases of potential and actual atrocities in American military history. Famous explorer Captain Meriwether Lewis ordered some Indians killed if they did not return his dog. The dog was returned and the Indians spared. On other occasions, however, scores of Native American men, women, and children at such places as Sand Creek (1864) and Wounded Knee (1890) were wiped out. U.S. troops tortured enemy prisoners in the Philippines in 1899–1902, and on June 10, 1944, an officer in the 101st Airborne Division murdered twelve German POWs who were under guard by a roadside in France.

How could My Lai happen? In Ambrose's view, the origins begin with politicians who kept the war going too long on what he terms "the strategic defensive." He also blames civilians in the Pentagon for the body count, which encouraged troops to fight to kill and not to obtain surrender. Overall he sees atrocity as an aberration in American military history. Many officers did not lose control in the Indian wars, he notes, and many platoon leaders in Vietnam similarly did not lose control.

We have a painful task—to examine a side of war that is awfully hard to face up to but is always there. When you put eighteen-, nineteen-, twenty-year-old kids in a foreign country with weapons in their hands, sometimes things happen that you really wish had never happened. It is a reality that stretches across time and across continents. It is a universal of war. Do not think that My Lai was an exception or an aberration when you consider war from the time of the ancient Greeks up to the present. Atrocity is a part of war that needs to be faced and discussed. It is not our job as historians to condemn or judge. It is our job to describe, to try to explain, and, even more so, to try to understand.

In the case of My Lai, it comes down to the question of who is responsible. Is it one guy? Is it a bad platoon leader who was inadequately trained all of his life, both by the army and by his society? Was it that he just couldn't handle the responsibility, and he broke? Maybe it's as simple as that. I know an awful lot of Vietnam War veterans who would take very extreme action if they could get Lieutenant Calley in their hands. They blame him for besmirching their reputation and the reputation of the United States Army and the reputation of the American armed forces in Vietnam. Then there are others who say, "No, no, you can't blame Calley. What you need to do is to look at the U.S. Army as a whole, the army as an institution, the way the army was fighting that war, and the things that Westmoreland was demanding from his platoon leaders. There's the explanation for what happened in Vietnam." The problem here is that you have the whole U.S. Army going berserk. Then others would argue, "No, no, the army is but a reflection of the society. Although it is one of the greatest of all of our glories in this republic that the army is a reflection of the society, it was American society that made this happen. The racism that permeates all levels of American society is where you look for the cause of what happened at My Lai. It is America's sense of exceptionalism, America's self-appointed task of cleansing the world, and on and on and on that made My Lai happen." In this view, responsibility rests with the society as a whole.

I would like to take a slightly different perspective on what happened at My Lai and begin with some reminders of other American soldiers, in other situations, in other countries, at other times. The first thing that those of us who have never been in combat have to recognize is that no one who has never been in combat has a right to judge. I have never had other men shoot at me. I have never had to shoot at other men, but I have spent my life interviewing people who did both. Combat is the most extreme experience a human being can go through. There is little in civilian life to compare to it, and for the vast majority of people this combat business is all very mysterious. Most people in human history do not go through combat. It depends on when you were born. If you were born between 1890 and 1900 and you were white, you were almost certainly going to be in combat. If you were born in the 1830s and were white in Europe, you almost certainly were not going to be in combat. And so it goes. For most people, combat is an experience they don't have. Could I stand up to the rigors of combat? Could I kill? Could I charge an enemy who is trying to kill me? Would I be brave? Would I be cowardly? Would I hide? Would I lead? Very few men get to answer those questions. Always keep that in mind when you are dealing with things that happened in and immediately after combat.

There is nothing worse than combat. What do you threaten the combat soldier with if he does not stay in the line? Are you going to throw him into the stockade? It is warm in the stockade. They give you hot food. You got a bed, and nobody is shooting at you. And you know damn well the president is going to give a blanket pardon when the war is over. They stay in the line because they are doing their duty. They stay in the line even more so because their buddies to the right and to the left of them are counting on them. One of the things that went wrong in Vietnam was that sense of comradeship was awfully hard to build up when you were rotating constantly and you weren't shipping over as units. Divisions didn't train together, go over together, and fight together, and thus that comradeship wasn't present.

Most of us see war through the movies. In the movies a man gets shot, and he dies. He never knew what hit him, and the C.O. can write home to the widow or to the family, "He was doing great and everything was going fine. Then he got one right through the middle of the eyes. He never knew what hit him, and he was gone." Well, it doesn't happen like that. That is not what takes place. What happens to men in combat is that they see their buddy with his brains oozing out of a hole in his head. It hasn't killed him, and he's begging for water and begging for a cigarette and begging for morphine simultaneously. They see a man trying to stuff his guts back into his stomach. They see a man carrying his left arm in his right hand. They see men who have lost their manhood to a piece of shrapnel. They see farm boys who have lost a leg. None of these guys are dead. They all have to be dealt with. They have to be comforted, they have to have some kind of medical assistance, and they are there. If they all died the way they do in Darryl Zanuck's movies, war would be a lot less horrible than it is, and you would see a lot less atrocities.

Another feature of war in general and of the combat experience, which seems to apply to My Lai, is that very seldom in war do you see your enemy. In the nineteenth century that wasn't so true. Surely General Meade's troops saw George Pickett's men coming across that open ground at Gettysburg. Of course they did, but later the range of the weaponry increased. Rifled bullets came in approximately in the late nineteenth century, and so the distance at which the killing took place increased. Artillery got more accurate, and then there was the coming of the airplane. In the twentieth century, men at war very seldom see their enemy. I know a guy who went through World War II, and twice in eight months he saw and aimed and fired at an enemy. Most casualties in twentieth-century war don't come as a result of someone that you can see firing at you. They come as a result of booby traps or snipers. They come as a result of that invention of the devil—the land mine. As an aside, if there is any weapon that I would ban it would be the land mine—ban it just like gas warfare. It's not that effective militarily, and it leaves problems that are still in Vietnam today. In fact, in France today they are still digging up World War I mines and still losing farmers to them. In combat you are always afraid, you are always enraged, and you are very often seeking revenge.

Now I want to go into some case studies of the United States Army. Some of these did not end up in massacres and others did. The first one comes from a book that I've written with my wife, a biography of Meriwether Lewis.* That topic is a long way away from My Lai, but I think you'll find that there are some very genuine connections.

The sentinel detected an old Indian trying to sneak into the expedition's camp site. The soldier threatened the intruder with his rifle and, Lewis writes, "gave the fellow a few stripes with a switch and sent him off." So the men's tempers were running very high, just like Lewis's. Never before had they whipped an Indian, but never before had they been so provoked. One party of warriors tried to wrest a tomahawk from Private John Colter, but they

*Undaunted Courage: Meriwether Lewis, Thomas Jefferson, and the Opening of the American West (New York: Simon & Schuster, 1996), 345–47.

had picked the wrong man. Colter was the original mountain man and the discoverer of Yellowstone National Park. "He retained it," Lewis dryly recorded. Still, as the expedition worked its way up river, whether dragging the canoes through the rapids or portaging them, the Indians were always there, ready to grab anything left unguarded for one instant. There are various accounts of their stealing knives, kettles, and other things.

In the evening three Indians stole Lewis's dog Seaman, a wonderful black Newfoundland. That sent Lewis into a rage. He called together three men and snapped out his order: "Follow and find those thieves, and if they make the least resistance or difficulty in surrendering my dog, shoot 'em." I want to tell you, Meriwether Lewis in my mind was one of the greatest soldiers the United States Army ever produced. Here he is sending men out with orders to shoot those sons of bitches if they do not give his dog back. He was under direct orders from the president to avoid hostilities with the Indians if at all possible. He wanted to build a trading empire with these Indians, but this was how provoked he was. Fortunately for him, when the Indians realized they were being pursued, they let Seaman go and fled. Lewis was ready to kill to get his dog back, but the Indians weren't ready to die for Seaman.

Back at camp, meanwhile, an Indian stole an ax, got caught, and, after a tussle, gave it up and fled. Lewis told a bunch hanging out at the camp that "if they make any further attempts to steal our property or insult our men we should put them to instant death." After several days and several more thefts, his pent up fury burst forth. He caught a man stealing, cursed him, beat him severely, and then "made the men kick him out of camp." His blood was up. He informed the Indians standing around "that I would shoot the first of them that attempted to steal an article from us, that we were not afraid to fight them, that I had it in my power at that moment to kill them all and set fire to their homes."

The next morning the Indians stole a saddle. Lewis's blood rose past the danger point. He swore he would either get the saddle back or he would burn their houses. "They have vexed me in such a manner by such repeated acts of villainy that I am quite determined to treat them with every severity. Their defenseless state pleads forgiveness so far as respects their lives." He ordered a thorough search of the village and marched there himself to burn the place down if he didn't get that saddle back.

That was the closest Lewis came to applying the principle of collective guilt. Fortunately, the men found the stolen goods hidden in a corner of one of the houses before Lewis reached the village. He had been wonderfully lucky. Had those goods not been recovered, he might have given the order to put the houses to the torch. The resulting conflagration would have been a gross overreaction, unpardonably unjust, and a permanent blot on his honor. It would have turned every Chinookan village on the lower Columbia against the Americans, and thus made impossible the fulfillment of the plan Lewis was developing for a cross-continent American-run trading empire. He had a lot at stake, but he had been ready to allow his anger to override his judgment. He had come close to being out of control.

Flashing forward to after the Civil War, the United States Army has been unjustly maligned for its record in the wars with the Plains Indians. It is accused of starting most, if not all, the wars, and then of blundering once hostilities broke out and committing various atrocities. The army was badly served by its political masters, however. It was given conflicting orders and hardly ever knew from one month to the next what the policy of the government might be. It was poorly equipped and inadequately supplied. It was the clear duty of the army to protect the advancing frontier and the transcontinental railroads, and the Indians were in the way. They had to be removed. There were two ways to do this: drag them onto reservations or bribe them. The government never made the bribe attractive enough, so the army got the dirty job of removing them. In the process, though the army contributed its share of blunders, stupidity, and cruelty, and initiated its share of hostilities and atrocities, it also fought with great skill and bravery.

Near dawn on November 28, 1868, Major General George Armstrong Custer led his Seventh Cavalry to a Cheyenne encampment on the banks of the Washita River in what is now Oklahoma.* The village contained some young men who had been guilty of hitting some frontier outposts, were probably guilty of some murders, and were certainly guilty of some theft. Custer was acting under orders from Major General Philip H. Sheridan to wipe them out. He attacked at first light with the band playing "Garry Owen." Warriors rushed from their tepees, confused, disorganized, unbelieving. Custer's men shot them down. Some Indians managed to get their weapons and fled to the safety of the river, where they stood waist-deep in freezing water behind the protecting bank of the river and started returning fire. Others managed to get into some nearby timber and began to fight. But that first

---

*The following account is from Stephen E. Ambrose, *Crazy Horse and Custer: The Parallel Lives of Two American Warriors* (Garden City, N.Y.: Doubleday, 1975), 291–94.

assault was overwhelming, and Custer had control of the village. His men were shooting anything that moved.

Many of the troopers had been fruitlessly chasing Indians for two years, and they poured out their frustrations. Everyone was extremely tense after the night-long approach to the village, and the indiscriminate killing relieved the tension. In any event, the soldiers said later, it was hard to tell warriors from squaws, especially because a few of the squaws had taken up weapons and were fighting back. So were Indian boys of ten years of age. The troopers shot them all down. Still, according to George Bird Grinnell, who got his information from the Indians, "practically all the women and children who were killed were shot while hiding in the brush or trying to run away." Within an hour, probably less, resistance was minimal. A few warriors kept up a sporadic firing from the banks of the river, but for all practical purposes the battle was over. Looking around, Custer could see dead Indians everywhere, 117 of them, their blood bright on the snow. He was in possession of fifty-one lodges and a herd of nearly nine hundred ponies. He burned the village, destroying several hundred pounds of tobacco, enormous quantities of meat, more than one thousand buffalo robes, and so on. Before leaving Custer detailed four of his ten companies and ordered the men to shoot the ponies. Within minutes, more than eight hundred ponies lay on the ground neighing and kicking in their death throes.

At Sand Creek in Colorado, six hundred to seven hundred Cheyenne gathered in November 1864 to camp for the winter. Without warning or provocation, volunteer soldiers commanded by Colonel John Chivington charged the camp and brutally murdered and mutilated about a third of the Cheyenne, mostly women and children. In the Philippines from 1899 to 1902, U.S. troops waged a bloody conflict with Filipinos—they called them "gooks"—who were resisting American colonization. Torture of captives and destruction of villages, including the killing of all inhabitants, punctuated the American conduct of the war.

The incident that came to most people's minds when My Lai was revealed, however, was the massacre at Wounded Knee in December 1890. These Indians, Big Foot's band, were Oglala Sioux. They had been out on the prairie engaging in the Ghost Dance, which was a religious phenomenon that swept through the Plains Indian tribes in the late 1880s. A very high proportion of the Indians west of the Mississippi River were participating in this Ghost Dance, which they believed, if continued long enough, would bring back the buffalo and their old way of life and make the whites disappear. It caused great consternation and even panic among the whites in the areas where these Indians were dancing and in the War Department of the U.S. government. So the orders went out to the army to round up these dancers and bring them back into the reservation, where they could be watched.

A detachment from Custer's old regiment, the Seventh Cavalry, rounded up Big Foot and his band of Sioux up in the Badlands in Dakota and was bringing them back to the reservation near Crawford, Nebraska. They were camped overnight at a place called Wounded Knee. In the morning the colonel in command, James W. Forsyth decided to disarm the Indians before proceeding on. It was a foolish decision to make. They were causing no trouble. They were moving exactly as ordered, and they were badly outnumbered and very heavily outweaponed by the white soldiers. Forsyth took it in his head to disarm them, however, before proceeding on. This process of disarmament stirred emotions on both sides. The Indians refused to produce what weapons they had, which they had hidden in blankets and in their tepees and so on. The soldiers were now inside the tepees throwing off the blankets and digging under other material, looking for weapons. They had entered these Indians' homes and were carrying out an indiscriminate search, which we may assume was leaving behind a lot of damaged goods and chaos. Tempers rose. A medicine man named Yellow Bird pranced about performing incantations and calling for resistance. There was a scuffle between a soldier and an Indian, and a shot rang out.

God, how many atrocities in the world's history have started with "a shot rang out"? And nobody knows who fired it. It is not just atrocities either; think about Lexington and the origins of the American Revolution. Who shot first? We do not know at Wounded Knee whether a soldier shot or whether an Indian shot. Anyway, a shot rang out. Instantly the young Indian men threw off their blankets, pulled out their rifles, and sent a volley towards the nearest formation of soldiers, or so the soldiers reported. The Indians told a different story, which is also typical of atrocities. In a murderous face-to-face melee, Indians and soldiers shot, stabbed, and clubbed one another. Women and children scattered in panic as bullets laced the tepees. The close range action ended abruptly, and the combatants broke from the council square. On the hilltop the artillery jerked their lanyards. A storm of exploding shells leveled the village. At least 150 and perhaps 300 Sioux, about half women and children, died. Twenty-five soldiers were killed, many by friendly fire.

Later testimony showed conclusively that the troops, with several exceptions, had made efforts to avoid harming noncombatants, but a lot of questions were raised as to how strenuous those efforts were. The testimony also supported Forsyth's placement of his units for the task of disarming the Indians, although here the judgments were less persuasive, especially in light of Major General Nelson Miles's repeated injunctions to his subordinates never to let their units mix with Indians, friendly or not. In other words, don't go into the village and don't go into the tepees and don't try to carry out searches in there. Keep a distance and be always aware that the possibility of hostilities exists. Forsyth got off, although Miles branded him guilty of incompetence, inexperience, and irresponsibility, and basically his career came to an end.

Let me give one example from World War II before going on to Vietnam. This happened in the 506th Parachute Infantry Regiment of the 101st Airborne Division on the tenth day of June in 1944. Captain Spears was walking back to his command post and came by a ditch that a bunch of German POWs were digging with one sergeant guarding them. Spears had been in four days of combat and probably had not slept in all that time. He had seen buddies killed, and he had killed and had been slightly wounded. Spears stopped at this group of twelve German soldiers who were all in this ditch digging. He jumped into the ditch with them, pulled out his Luckies, and shook the pack. With each one of them saying *"danke, danke, danke, danke, bitte, bitte, bitte, bitte,"* they all got cigarettes. Then he pulled out his Ronson lighter and lit it up for each one of these twelve men. They were inhaling the first cigarette and the first nicotine they had probably had since the sixth of June. They were really sucking it in and really feeling it good. Spears got back up on the outside of the trench, took his carbine off of his shoulder, and shot them, all twelve of them, in the coldest of cold blood, while the sergeant looked on horrified. Spears walked on to complete his mission for that day, went on to become company commander, stayed in the army, and had a very good career there. It just happened. He just broke. He just lost all control in this most cold-blooded of ways. It seems like an entirely irrational act. Those are some of the examples of atrocities in history that I wanted to make sure were a part of the reflections on what happened at My Lai.

My Lai was the single most shocking thing to come out of the Vietnam War for me. I had a very, very hard time watching those young men on television describing to Mike Wallace what they had done at My Lai. I was a student of military history. I was teaching at the Naval War College. I had spent eight years with General Eisenhower, and it was beyond my understanding that American boys could do this. Now, atrocities were certainly not beyond my understanding. I had been studying the Second World War. The Japanese and the German and some American atrocities I knew about, but My Lai and the way it was presented on television just shook me to my roots. I have spent a lot of time since trying to understand how this could happen—how American boys could do what SS boys did, how Boy Scouts could do what the Nazi Youth did. How did that happen?

What happened at My Lai in one way was a logical development from what happened in the Second World War. In the Second World War, the civilian became a legitimate target. This was a new thing, and it was very deliberately done at the highest levels by the German government, by the British government, and by the American government. In the period 1939 to 1941, Franklin Roosevelt took the lead in denouncing the bombing of cities and renouncing any attempt to turn a civilian into a target. He called on the nations of the world to treat the bombing of cities as they had the use of poison gas, that is, to make it a war crime and eliminate it. Then we got into the war, and Roosevelt became the most enthusiastic advocate of strategic bombing. By late 1944 and 1945, he was pushing General Hap Arnold, the air force chief, to burn Japanese cities to the ground. He wanted Arnold to go in there with high incendiary bombs and napalm and burn down their homes built of sticks and wood. I see a direct link from there to My Lai.

It seems to me that the fundamental problem in Vietnam from the military's point of view was that they were trying to win a war on the strategic defensive. This was an army that had a tradition from World War II that you go after the enemy. You go to his homeland, and you force an unconditional surrender. This is the kind of an army these guys had been brought up in. They had not quite achieved that in Korea and yet they had achieved a very great deal in Korea. Vietnam was certainly the kind of action that any World War II commander would have taken one look at and said, "We go for Hanoi."

There was, however, the fear that the Chinese would enter, a hangover from the Korean War. We did cross into North Korea. We almost liberated North Korea in the late fall and early winter of 1950, and what happened was that we brought these Chinese hordes down on us. Later we presumed that the Chinese would never allow us to invade and hold North Vietnam. We didn't want to get in a war with the Chinese army, so we weren't going to invade North Vietnam. We weren't going to take Hanoi. That decision was made, and whether they were right about what the Chinese might have done or not, I don't know, but after having decided that we weren't going to go over to the offensive, every effort should have been made, and was not, to shut that war down right then, on whatever terms we could get. It's a lot easier to say now than it was to see how to do it then. The Americans should also have abandoned this fiction that worked altogether to the advantage of the North Vietnamese, and altogether to our disadvantage, that this was a war in South Vietnam, and that Laos and Cambodia were neutrals. The arguments for not going into North Vietnam were very strong and were persuasive to the president.

Because Westmoreland was on a strategic defensive, those above him either agreed to or suggested to him the idea of body count. Using the body count as a way to measure progress in the war was a terrible idea, and it had all kinds of awful repercussions. In the first place, what does body count mean in war? It means that the soldier has fought until you had to kill him. There never came a point in the enemy's experience in which he threw down his weapon and threw up his arms and said "I'm yours, I quit, I surrender." If you had to kill him, he never said that. That means that he was being fed well enough to stay in the line. That means that enough ammunition was reaching him. That means that his morale was high enough that he continued to fight until you had to kill him. You want to measure progress in a war by how the enemy soldiers react, and you count POWs. You count how many guys are coming in with their hands up in surrender. Those are guys that are demoralized. Those are guys that are out of ammunition. Those are guys who are not being fed. When you have the enemy in that situation, you are making progress. When the situation is that you cannot dispose of an enemy until you have killed him, you have the opposite of progress. Also, and let us say it out loud, the problem with the body count above all else was that every body counted as long as it was dead and Vietnamese. In far too many cases, promotions depended on the body count that was reported.

Some people have asked: Wasn't it true that the American army over there had just given up on the war, and that they were all on drugs, and that there was no discipline left? First of all, that is very badly exaggerated. Insofar as it is true, you have to remember that in February 1968 Lyndon Johnson decided we were going to retreat. He refused Westy's request for reinforcements to follow up the Tet victory, and in fact they began drawing down in the summer of 1968. Nixon won in the fall of 1968, and shortly after taking office, he announced publicly we were getting out of there. We were retreating. In effect he was saying, "We can't win this war, and my aim is to turn it over to the Vietnamese and pray God that they'll hold on until I get reelected." That left the young men in Vietnam, the soldiers, fighting a rearguard action. Who the hell wants to be the last man killed in a retreat? Insofar as there was a breakdown in discipline in Vietnam, and there was, it happened because of a political decision made in Washington, not because of what was happening in the field.

Lieutenant Calley lost control, as did his men. Meriwether Lewis did not, although he came awfully close. Forsyth lost control. Chivington lost control. And Custer certainly lost control, if he ever had it. There were hundreds of other officers in the wars against the Plains Indian tribes of the latter part of the nineteenth century who never did lose control, although they were as provoked as Lewis had been, or Forsyth or Custer or Chivington. There were hundreds and hundreds of platoon leaders in Vietnam who were as provoked as Calley, as scared, and as poorly trained, and who were leading kids fresh out of the high schools of America who were inadequately trained, and they never lost control. One of the things that stands out about My Lai to me and makes it not only possible for me to live with it but to be once again proud of the institution that I have spent most of my life studying, the United States Army, was that the army investigated this itself and made that investigation public, and did its best to punish the perpetrators of this outrage. I defy you to name any other army in the world that would do that.

COMMENT from audience member: The army did not investigate My Lai until they had to investigate. They conspicuously did not investigate and covered up immediately after the event, although there was knowledge in the units. This is a considerable blemish. The official army investigation did not begin until the spring of 1969. One very brave colonel [William V. Wilson of the U.S. Army Inspector General's office] risked any future promotion by going around and interviewing everybody. In other cases, we did investigate, and I participated in prosecutions. Our army was probably "better" than others in that respect, but that's hardly an excuse.

I would submit for discussion that Lieutenant Calley did not lose control; Lieutenant Calley knew exactly what he was doing. He was not in a frenzy, so "lost control" is a fuzzy term that I don't think works here. After the exposure and after the trial, there never was any excuse made on his part. There was no loss of control. He was in control, and that's the terrible thing about it.

Perhaps there were atrocities and problems with fighting the war because of the rotation question. If I'm not mistaken, in the case of Lieutenant Calley's platoon and his company, they came over as a unit. The brigade came as a whole unit, and I submit that that was the problem. I was in a situation where I was rotating, and you blended in. Certain things would not have happened perhaps in the rotating unit. It can go either way, so you cannot use rotation as an excuse. You have to be careful of that, but this has been discussed in the literature quite a bit. There were many things wrong with the rotation system, but that is not an explanation for that massacre.

David Halberstam

On the question you raised about quantifying and body count, I remember an anecdote of McNamara at I Corps at Danang in November 1965. He was getting a briefing from a marine colonel. If you knew how to listen in those days, it was quite a pessimistic briefing, and McNamara clearly was edgy. The colonel was saying that the enemy had a great capacity to replenish, to keep coming. McNamara was uneasy and started asking constant questions, which were all numerical, all quantifiable. The marine colonel, being very bright, quickly broke the code and started talking nothing but numbers. McNamara began to smile and smile and smile. Later that day, all he could talk about was the marine colonel: "That marine colonel is one of the finest young officers I've met. Get him up there." Of course, everyone in the army or the marines is going to know what is wanted, what is rewarded in a briefing, and what you get ahead with. Very quickly the word went out to "give numbers." Later that day Sander Vanocour, my colleague who then was at NBC and who was at the briefing, went to McNamara and said, "Mr. Secretary, that did not sound like a very good briefing. It sounds to me like it's a bottomless pit." McNamara, with the arrogance that came out of that civilian leadership, said "Mr. Vanocour, every pit has its bottom."

Harry Summers

I was a battalion operations officer in the First Infantry Division. We got a requirement down to have the rifle companies report the number of incoming rounds by caliber, because someone in Washington dreamed up that, if they could compute the number of incoming rounds, they could compute the ammunition supply rate of the North Vietnamese. Of course, when you get down to the rifle company, what figure do you want? We can give you any figure that you want because this is absolutely ludicrous, but some clerk in Washington thought that it was possible. That's an idea of the degree to which the statisticians had taken over the Clausewitzian prosecution of the war.

By the time of My Lai, it was obvious that victory wasn't in sight. When I was in Vietnam for my first tour in 1966–1967, we really thought we could win it, but by the time of My Lai, it was obvious that you were fighting for nothing. That lack of objective more than anything else undermined morale, undermined discipline, and undermined the entire situation.

THE LAW OF WAR:
THE CASE OF MY LAI

Walter E. Boomer, David Clinton, David Halberstam, Hays Parks, Harry G. Summers, Jr.

David Halberstam as a war correspondent and Harry Summers, Walter Boomer, and Hays Parks as infantry officers all observed firsthand how the U.S. military forces conducted themselves in Vietnam. Although none of them witnessed My Lai itself, all had a wide range of experiences that enables them to put the My Lai atrocity in the context of how soldiers are supposed to behave during wartime. Political scientist David Clinton specializes in the study of international relations. Both through formal treaties and unilateral declarations, the U.S. government subscribes to the international law of war, which is a body of both law and custom intended to lessen and control the extreme destructiveness of modern warfare. The application of the law of war to specific cases, especially in an irregular con- flict like Vietnam involving regular military forces, guerrillas, and civilians, can be difficult, but in general U.S. troops are to observe "the laws of humanity and the dictates of the public conscience."

Halberstam argues that civilian leaders in Washington, especially Secretary of Defense Robert McNamara, relied too much on high-technology warfare and statistics, most notably the body count. The result was a disproportionate use of American firepower that produced a high number of Vietnamese deaths. The three military officers agree that the notion of body count was destructive not only to the Vietnamese people but to the integrity and discipline of the U.S. military. Indeed, they contend that many officers grew bitter about the pressure to kill or to lie about killing just to produce the appearance of success. Recalling their experiences as young officers, military leaders during Operation Desert Storm were determined not to repeat the mistake of measuring success by piling up enemy bodies.

The editor of *Vietnam* magazine and author of many books on military strategy, Summers reminds us that there are many Vietnam stories. How individual soldiers perceived Vietnam depended upon where they were and when they were there. In the case of My Lai, he sees the problem as what he terms the "command climate." There was a lack of leadership throughout the Americal Division, but he holds Medina and Calley specifically responsible for what happened in the village. Summers believes that My Lai was an aberration.

A young rifle company commander when he went to Vietnam, Boomer commanded the U.S. Marines in Operations Desert Shield and Desert Storm and was assistant commandant of the Marine Corps before his retirement in 1994. He recalls that he had no doubt when he was in Vietnam that killing innocent civilians was wrong morally and legally, and he views atrocities as a question of small-unit leadership. In Operation Desert Storm, there was not a single atrocity by Marines during the taking of twenty-two thousand Iraqi prisoners.

Hays Parks was a marine infantry officer and prosecutor in Vietnam and is now an international lawyer in the Office of the Judge Advocate General of the Army. He insists that the shooting of unarmed civilians was not tolerated in Vietnam and that soldiers were prosecuted for murder. He cites the impeccable discipline of the U.S. troops in Operation Desert Storm. At My Lai, he views the problem as lack of cohesion in Charlie Company and Medina's and Calley's tolerance of misconduct: "Calley did not deserve to be in the U.S. military."

David Clinton

Since war has existed, attempts at regulating and limiting the violence of war have existed through the medium of law and through other forms. In one sense, the job of instituting these standards ought to be easy, since they accord with standards that we're taught throughout our lives. Things like defining the limitations of military necessity or proportionality or observing the protection of noncombatants have a resonance in phrases that we use often in civilian life, such as "innocent bystander." In another sense, maintaining these standards is very difficult given the special stresses and strains of combat. Looking at the case of My Lai, what were the standards governing the protection of the innocent that were in force at that time and how were those standards communicated all the way down the line? What happened in this incident that caused the system to break down? Should we be surprised that there weren't more My Lais given the character of this war and all wars?

David Halberstam

When the United States committed its ground troops to Vietnam in 1965, the McNamara Defense Department and particularly the secretary of defense himself had a limitless belief in the uses of technology. An equation was set in motion that assumed that we didn't want to and were unable to match an Asian nation on its indigenous soil man-for-man and that consequently we would depend on our superior technology. That it would be an unpopular war was probably not quite so obvious, although anybody who had studied the French experience there from 1946 to 1954 would have had a sense of it. Also unclear at the outset was the eventual impact upon the army or the prospect that one day you would have a Calley as a commander, instead of the extraordinary young men who were the officers in the first years there.

It wasn't the United States Army that wanted to go there. There was no rush from the military to go there. I think the top army officers were always a little uneasy. The roots of that war are in the McCarthy period. After Harry Truman defeated Thomas Dewey in 1948, which was five Democratic wins in a row, the Republicans feared that they were a permanent minority party. They needed an issue, and they seized upon the issue of subversion—McCarthyism—and the Democrats' loss of China. They claimed that the Democrats were soft on communism—men as tough as Truman and Dean Acheson were labeled as soft on the communists. None of these Republicans, mind you, wanted to send American troops to China, but that toughness got into the bloodstream. In the mid-1960s, when Johnson made his decision to escalate in Vietnam, it really wasn't about the efficiency of the war—whether it could be done or not—but about his own fear of the domestic political equation if he lost Vietnam. There was a failure to understand how the size, the terrain, and the nighttime could swallow up a force as large as five hundred thousand men and deflect our technology.

In fact, technology proved inadequate, and those miscalculations began to surface later in the war. The results included frustration among the men who were there, the turning of the country back home—domestic America—against the war, and the sending of men like Calley, who weren't normally going to be platoon leaders. There's a moment in the Medina trial that illustrates what had happened. The snobbish novelist Mary McCarthy was covering the trial for the *New York Review of Books*—then a most snobbish publication—and she made fun of Medina's language, his poor English, in one of his answers. The writer Gloria Emerson scolded McCarthy in an article. Emerson pointed out that it wasn't the sons of Harvard and Yale and Princeton who fought that war—and it wasn't! In fact, the school I went to, Harvard, probably had as many Pulitzer Prize winners there as it had combat dead, or damn close to it.

There were, for every Calley, extraordinary young American officers who were brave and selfless, protected their men, and treated those around them on both sides with ultimate decency. There is a sense that that which happened at My Lai was an aberration. There is a sense also that it was not an aberration, given the McNamarian decision to use that much technology in a country like this, in a war like this, and to insist on quantification: body count, body count, body count; not weapons count but body count. I can remember my friend John Paul Vann telling me about a particular American officer with the Ninth Division who had gone through the Mekong Delta, in Vann's exact words that I still remember, "like a butcher."

Harry Summers

As the editor of *Vietnam* magazine since its inception, one of the things that I have found is that there is not one truth about Vietnam; there are at least a million. Vietnam is probably the most time- and space-sensitive war we have ever fought. It really mattered where you were and when you were there. When word of My Lai first broke, I thought that it was an antiwar propaganda scheme, and I came to this with some experience. I served thirty-eight years on active duty as an infantryman, enlisted and officer. I am a veteran of the Korean War, 1950–1951, as a squad leader in a rifle company in the Twenty-first Infantry Regiment. In the Vietnam War in 1966–1967, I was a captain, the operations officer of a rifle battalion—First Battalion,

Second Infantry, First Division. I later returned to Vietnam in 1974–1975. So I've seen a little bit of war. My Lai was so far beyond my experience that actually I could not believe it. Unfortunately it was all too true. Later in my career I served in the office of the army chief of staff, where I read the original Peers Report, the official investigation of My Lai by Lieutenant General William Peers. I found that My Lai was worse in reality than it was reported in the media. It was one of the few cases where the media account wasn't nearly as striking as the report of the investigation itself.

How could My Lai happen? Peers asked that question in his report. The army investigators thought that this was, by happenstance, a bunch of losers, that there were a bunch of thugs in this company who had come together by accident of assignment. They started looking into that, however, and found out that the company was above average. It had more high school graduates, more people who had attended college, and more college graduates than an average rifle company. So that didn't wash. The only variable that they could find was leadership, and it comes down to that.

A military unit has a personality. Most sailors know that ships have personalities—everybody knows that who has been to sea—but so do rifle companies, infantry battalions, and infantry divisions. My Lai could not have happened in the First Infantry Division (the Big Red One) in 1966–1967. For one thing, General William E. DePuy, the division commander, knew very well the Vietcong tactic of trying to draw friendly fire on villages, shrines, and temples. If an artillery round landed within a hundred yards of a shrine or temple, the battalion commander could count on being relieved. Not only that, in my battalion the battalion commander had been an adviser, spoke Vietnamese, and had a very warm feeling toward the Vietnamese people. Two of the three rifle company commanders spoke Vietnamese and had been advisers. What I'm trying to get across is that the command climate in that unit was what protected it from these kinds of atrocities. The command climate is set by the commander—in this case General DePuy, and, more to the point, by the battalion commander and the company commanders. The command climate in that unit was so strong that My Lai couldn't have happened.

There was a study done at the beginning of World War II by a clinical psychologist who looked at the First Infantry Division and a National Guard division going ashore in North Africa side by side. They had the same mix of people, that is, the same number of draftees, regular army people, and national guardsmen, and yet the National Guard division had three times the battle fatigue casualties—what we now call PTSD—than did the First Infantry Division. The only difference he could find was regimental tradition. I mean, you just did not do this in the Sixteenth Infantry, which traced its legacy back for many years. I think that same thing was true to some degree in Vietnam.

The Americal Division was not the First Infantry Division, to put it mildly. It was a paste-up unit put together by brigades that wouldn't normally serve together. There was a devastating piece in the *New Yorker* about the commanding general of the division, General Koster. He was such a hard-nose and the staff was so terrified of him that they were afraid to approach him with a problem. When My Lai broke they thought, "My God, the last thing we want to do is have the old man find out about it." In keeping it from him—almost with poetic justice—they destroyed him. You can see problems as you go down the ranks to Medina, the company commander, and to Calley, the platoon leader.

I used to lecture at Fort Leavenworth and in the local colleges in Kansas around Fort Leavenworth during the period when My Lai first broke. I expressed my feeling, which was shared by most of my contemporaries, that what they ought to have done with Calley and Medina was to have hung them, then drawn and quartered them, and put their remains at the gates of Fort Benning, at the Infantry School, as a reminder to those who pass under it of what an infantry officer ought to be. I got an enormous reaction from the promilitary and the antimilitary people. The promilitary would say, "Poor Calley, he's just being made a victim by the antiwar movement." The antiwar movement said, "Everybody's doing it, so why blame Calley?" The bastard fell through the cracks, and he got away with it.

In Oliver Stone's movie *Platoon,* an atrocity takes place, and the platoon leader is another Calley. At first, it sort of confirms the idea of the antiwar movement that everybody did it, so therefore there was no particular penalty attached to it. The conflict in the movie is set up, however, by the company commander who says, "I'm going to dig into this, and, if this was a murder, I'm going to take him to court martial." That sets up the conflict between the two sergeants and ends up with the death of one of them. So Oliver Stone, who was a combat infantryman in Vietnam and won a bronze star, has a much deeper movie than it may appear on the surface.

In my mind and I think in the minds of most of the people who have my experience, My Lai was an aberration, and we should have punished it most severely. General Peers himself said that it was a breakdown in the military justice system that the people were not brought to justice and were not held to account. There was much more kindness in Vietnam than there were atrocities and much more good works than there were evil deeds.

Walter Boomer

I was twenty-eight years old when I entered Vietnam as a rifle company commander. When I entered Vietnam there was absolutely no doubt in my mind that killing innocent women and children was not only morally wrong, from what I had been taught as a child, but that, if I did this, under the law of land warfare, which I understood very well, I would be convicted by court-martial. No doubt. There was no doubt in my mind, and I believe that there was no doubt in the mind of anyone I served with. Vietnam was a place, however, that could become and did become conducive to atrocity situations. Perhaps all war is that way, and it is for that reason that the role of leadership becomes so critically important.

The company that I took into Vietnam had already been there and had been returned to Okinawa to be refitted and to get some rest. I picked them up and took them back into Vietnam as their company commander, and I stayed with them for the rest of my tour. We hadn't been there very long when the battalion surgeon, a navy doctor, called me from the battalion command post and said, "May I come back to see you? I have something you need to know." I said, "Of course, come on back." He got in his jeep and drove back, and he said to me, "Do you know, Walt, that some of your men, after being in battle, and after having killed an enemy, are cutting off the ears of the dead enemy?" I said, "No, doctor, I didn't know that, but thank you very much." That evening before it got dark I gathered the company around. I don't remember exactly what I told them, except that it was wrong; it wasn't something that they could go home and look their families in the eye and be proud of; it was against the law and morally reprehensible; and stop it; just stop it. To my knowledge it didn't occur again. That's one reason why a unit in combat has officers.

During Operation Desert Storm, we didn't have an atrocity on the Marine Corps side during the three-day attack into Kuwait—not a single one. You say, Well, so what? The so-what is that in my estimation about 75 percent of the Iraqis wanted to give up and about 25 percent wanted to fight and did. So what you had was the young infantryman again placed right in the middle of an ambiguous situation. He was scared to death. He was absolutely convinced that chemical weapons were going to be used against him.

There had been talk, more than talk, about biological warfare and anthrax. He had two significant mine fields to cross. In the middle of all of this there was one group of people who wanted to kill him, and, on the other hand, there were a tremendous number of others who wanted to give up. To their credit, the marines took in the group that wanted to surrender, and we captured twenty-two thousand Iraqi prisoners in the marine area alone. The other 25 percent were dealt with as they needed to be dealt with. Were our troops in Desert Storm better educated and better trained, and did they better understand the law of land warfare than did those of us who were in Vietnam? I submit to you that for the most part, as Colonel Summers just said, the vast majority in Vietnam knew right from wrong and tried their best in a very, very brutal, uncompromising situation, to give it their best day after day.

Hays Parks

These are my personal views and do not represent the views of my present employer, the Department of the Army. I was in Vietnam in two capacities: as an infantry officer and as a senior prosecuting attorney for the First Marine Division. I prosecuted Marine Corps cases in which marines did murder people. We were doing our job. Crime of some sort in war is something that happens all the time, and we tend to forget that there were crimes in previous conflicts. During World War II, in the United States and in Europe, the United States Army tried, convicted, and executed 146 United States Army soldiers for rape or murder, plus one for desertion. We convicted a number of others who received life sentences. Crimes are not something unique to Vietnam.

There were some things that did make Vietnam unique and difficult. We were—I hate to use the phrase—literally fighting for the hearts and minds of the people. The difficulty was—if you understand communist revolutionary warfare—you cannot win the hearts and minds of the people unless you can guarantee them twenty-four-hour-a-day security. Lacking that, they were terrified. If someone comes into your home and says I'll kill your mother unless you plant this booby trap, you're going to plant the booby trap. Having our marines and soldiers understand that was a very important part of leadership. You've heard or read about people who were at My Lai saying, "We couldn't tell one from the other." We did make those distinctions. We didn't engage people who were carrying out perfectly friendly acts. We didn't shoot disarmed people. That was just the kind of thing that we would not tolerate. The other thing that I think was unique to Vietnam was the small-unit tactics. We placed a great deal of responsibility in the hands of some very young men.

What did we do in Vietnam to prevent other My Lais? First, we did explain to our troops why we were there. We did explain to them the necessity for distinction between unarmed civilians, noncombatants, and those people who were, in fact, shooting at us. This was something that was emphasized over and over and over again. I agree completely with General Boomer's perception. There was no doubt in my mind that you didn't do anything to innocent civilians, and if you did do something to them, you would be punished for it and should be. There was also effective leadership at all levels. There was a recognition of the need for discipline at all levels, particularly because of the complexity of the situation in which we were operating.

I'll give you two very quick examples of that. One officer, who was a young second lieutenant in Vietnam in 1965 when the marines first started operating there, found himself in his first combat action, his first firefight. As the firefight ended, he burst through a hedgerow, and standing to one side was one of his marine riflemen with his rifle at the head of an old woman. The lieutenant later said, "Frankly, I froze. I wasn't sure what to do. I didn't know what to say." About that time his gunnery sergeant came through the hedgerow right behind him and said very quickly, "Knock it off! Marines don't do that." He said that set the tone for the conduct of that unit from that time on. As General Boomer pointed out, that's all that needs to be said. In another circumstance, a company had been attacked during the night by a Vietcong force and had defeated the attack. They were collecting the bodies of the Vietcong dead and lining them up on the road before they were to be buried. Some Marines chose to lay down among them and have some "cute" pictures taken. When the company commander saw that, he immediately ordered them to stop it, and he said, "Look at it the other way. How would you feel if Vietcong laid dead marines out on a road and acted up around the bodies?" That was the type of intolerance that you saw at so many levels.

I was in Airborne School at Fort Benning at the time of Lieutenant Calley's trial. I found it interesting that every night there would be two dozen of us sitting at the bar in our uniforms that very clearly indicated we were Vietnam veterans. None of us had any tolerance for what Lieutenant Calley did at My Lai or for what the United States Army did at My Lai. The media at that time, however, would go over to Officer Candidate School and ask young men, who had just joined the army and who hadn't even been to Vietnam and who hadn't been in combat, how you could deal with this complex situation. We could have given them the answer if they had asked us. I think the things that did happen, in most cases, led to a report, an investigation, and, if a crime had occurred, a prosecution of that offense. The Marine Corps has written a monograph on this, detailing all the Marine Corps cases. I've tried for ten years to get the army to write the same type of monograph, because I think it's a story that needs to be told—that from the very day that we went into Vietnam those types of acts were going to be reported, investigated, and prosecuted.

The thing that happened was what I would call personnel check-kiting. To take a play on the bumper sticker that you see on some people's cars— "Can I pay my Visa with my MasterCard?"—we were robbing Peter to pay Paul in order to meet the personnel requirements in Vietnam. The My Lai unit didn't come into Vietnam as a cohesive unit. It left Hawaii as a numbered unit, but in fact it had gone through 200 percent personnel turbulence in the three months prior to its deployment. The people really didn't know each other, and that lack of cohesion, I think, was a very important thing. It goes back to what Colonel Summers said about the command climate. You had a certain disorganization. You need leadership, and this unit didn't have it.

The Peers Report points out that, in the months preceding the My Lai incident, Charlie Company, First of the Twentieth, hadn't been heavily engaged in combat. I think that the Peers Committee said they had five killed in action. That's not a heavy load considering that this was during the 1968 Tet Offensive period. That's not many casualties if you think about it. The brigade commander who preceded Colonel Henderson, however, had a reputation for letting a lot of things slide, and Captain Medina did too. There was tolerance of a lot of misconduct by the soldiers.

Lieutenant Calley didn't deserve to be in the United States military, much less to be an officer in the United States military. It's unfortunate that you had this personnel-kiting, check-kiting type of scheme. When you had a leadership breakdown at the brigade, task force, company, and platoon level, My Lai occurred. Had there been any strength in leadership at any one of those levels in expressing the intolerance that certainly was my experience in Vietnam, My Lai would not have occurred. So it was an unfortunate combination of failure at all those levels.

The Marine Corps had a similar, smaller incident in which sixteen South Vietnamese civilians were murdered in 1970. This was in part a product of taking marines from the Third Marine Division, which was basically engaged with North Vietnamese forces, and moving them into an area where we were engaged with Vietcong with a lot of civilians in the area. The people who engaged in that particular operation unfortunately were Third Marine Division forces who had not, I think, been properly reindoctrinated for that area. The offenses were reported and investigated, and these people were brought to trial and convicted.

Did we uncover all the offenses in Vietnam? No, I'm sure we didn't. The uniform crime statistics that the FBI puts out each year and other investigations assume that we probably detect approximately half of the murders that occur in the United States. Of those people who commit an act of murder in the United States, less than one tenth of them will actually go to prison. If the military is a cross-section of America, we're probably a cross-section in our ability to detect all crimes and to investigate and prosecute them. Did we actually investigate all these offenses? Yes, we did. In fact, I was prosecuting a case in 1968 and 1969 and, at the time we took the people to trial, we informed the Danang press center, where we had members of the media. Their response was, Why should we bother to come watch your trial? You're doing what you are supposed to do. This was not a newsworthy event.

I do believe that (a) we had only one My Lai incident in a very difficult and complex war because of the leadership that was exercised in other commands and (b) My Lai occurred because of this fundamental breakdown at all levels of command in this particular unit.

Clinton

It seems that all four panelists agree in pointing to the importance of leadership in preventing such incidents as this, but there may be some differences in emphasis among the four. It seems that Colonel Summers, General Boomer, and Colonel Parks think that the safeguards were pretty strong against incidents like My Lai and that was why this aberration was not widely repeated. I'm not sure that Mr. Halberstam left the same impression.

Halberstam

There was a disproportionate use of technology in certain instances. The Ninth Division was a particular one where you might, as I think John Paul Vann told me, have sometimes four or five hundred bodies and maybe thirty weapons. It was in the equation of that war. I don't want to diminish the bravery and the individual character of so many young men who were thrown into situations far beyond anything that should have happened to them in this foreign country, but the central equation coming down from the Defense Department and from Mr. McNamara was that our superior technology would be used. It was the body count, not the weapon count, that was disproportionate. We were going to a foreign country where our only superiority was our weaponry. We had absolute military superiority. The other side had absolute political superiority, which allowed them to keep coming and to keep recruiting. Essentially, we were fighting the birthrate of a nation. There was an inevitability of disproportionate killing there.

Summers

Michael Howard, one of our better military historians, has pointed out that, with the beginning of the industrial age, we get the kind of firepower technology and reliance on technology that Mr. Halberstam is talking about. We saw it in Korea. A *Time* reporter in Korea said that the Americans expend bullets the way the Chinese expend men, and I thought, thank God, I'm on the right side of that equation. In one battle alone, the X Corps fired twenty-seven Liberty Ship-loads of 105mm howitzer ammunition in two weeks to stop the Chinese advance. Certainly one of the valid criticisms of the Vietnam War, which John Paul Vann made so well as recounted in Neil Sheehan's book *Bright Shining Lie,* is the indiscriminate use of firepower. But if you're looking at it as an American mother, you would probably say, thank God. We take 47,000 killed in action in Vietnam and another 10,000 killed by accident and disease. The South Vietnamese take 240,000 killed; General Giap admits to 500,000 killed. It gives at least a reason why there was this reliance on firepower.

As Michael Howard said, the industrial age really changed the equation in terms of technology, but he went on to say that, if Vietnam taught us nothing else, it taught us that we have to learn to fight at the level of the agrarian age. As an infantryman, I can say that was certainly true, because someone with a sharp stick could still kill you. Even in the computer age he can still kill you. That was part of the anomaly of Vietnam. Yes, we were in a technological age, but much of the fighting was still done at the level of the agrarian age. That, I think, is not readily apparent. Still, the greater atrocity, and I agree with Dave Halberstam here, was the indiscriminate use of firepower.

Boomer

I agree completely with David Halberstam. This whole thing of body count was barbaric. It was driven from Washington. It affected deeply those of us who were in Vietnam and left much bitterness in our hearts. Those of us who were leading the forces in Desert Storm were so adverse to such a thing that we ended up having no idea what enemy casualties totaled during that operation. We were absolutely dedicated to the proposition that we weren't going to go into Desert Storm and fight it under the same kinds of rules that we, as youngsters, had been forced to fight under in Vietnam. We fought the Vietnam War, for the most part, with great stupidity.

[Audience member reads from the transcript of the Winter Soldier Investigation and notes how it contradicts what panelists said about atrocity being the exception in Vietnam. He says it is a myth that My Lai was an aberration.*]

Parks

Rather than respond to it line by line, I would commend to you the two chapters in Guenter Lewy's book *America in Vietnam* published in 1978. Lewy went through the Winter Soldier Investigation and the actions taken by the Department of Defense to examine the claims and statements that were made during that investigation. Not one single person who testified there was willing to talk to criminal investigators to ascertain if these events in fact occurred. What was equally interesting, however, was that, in many cases, they found that an individual would get up and say, "My name is Private Joe Schmuckatella, and I was in First Marine Division in 1968, and this is what I saw." As it turned out, as they traced down Private Joe Schmuckatella, they found that this person was not Private Joe Schmuckatella but in fact a high school classmate of his, and Joe Schmuckatella had never been to Detroit and didn't know what the Winter Soldier Investigation was all about. In other cases they found that these individuals who claimed to have been there (a) had never been in the military or (b) had never been to Vietnam, one or the other. So, yes, these things have been responded to, and, rather than dignify this further, I would commend to you those chapters in Guenter Lewy's book.

COMMENT from audience member: None of that is true, sir.

*The Winter Soldier Investigation was a three-day hearing in February 1971 conducted in Detroit by the Vietnam Veterans Against the War. It was an explicit expression by some veterans who believed that Calley was a scapegoat for high civilian and military officials who purposefully had designed tactics of terror and mass destruction. The speakers in Detroit testified that atrocities were commonplace and condoned, and they offered graphic details.

Summers

Oh, boy.

COMMENT from audience member: Guenter Lewy lied. That is not true.

Summers

Everybody lies but you.

QUESTION from different audience member: Who fed off the body count? Was it the military or the press? Who was picking up on the body count? Do you want to know why My Lai happened? It was because you're drilled. I have seen soldiers given two- or three-day passes, in-country R&R, for a kill. That happened all the time. I think that General Boomer indicated at one point that it was Washington that was pounding it down on you. I'd like to hear you all talk a little bit about who really got that body-count ball rolling.

Summers

I was in a rifle company in the Korean War. We took about 400 percent casualties. To me Vietnam, in a lot of respects, was a walk in the woods. Be that as it may, nobody ever asked us how many Chinese we killed, and we killed a lot of them. We were there during the Chinese Spring Offensive in 1951, where they hit a three-division front with twenty-some divisions. When I went into Vietnam with the First Infantry Division in 1966, there was no emphasis on body count. Of course, they wanted to know if you recovered bodies. They had categories, such as confirmed, that is, a report that there was an actual body in the field. After that, however, the Ninth Division became almost the epitome of the insistence on body count. It had an effect beyond belief in terms of lowering the ethical standards of everybody involved, because if you didn't have a body count, God help you. It really began to undermine the entire integrity of the force. We saw the result of that when somebody asked General Schwarzkopf in the Gulf about body count and he went up like a sky rocket.

After the Vietnam War, the Army War College did a professionalism study. General Westmoreland found to his horror that the majority of the senior officers at the War College, and these were the guys that had been battalion commanders in Vietnam, were saying that they had never been in an honest army. They had been forced to lie; their integrity had been compromised. They went on and on, and all of them seemed to zero in on body count as the root or virus that drove all this.

It began innocently enough. When we couldn't measure the war as we did in World War II with lines moving on the map, some bright statistician in McNamara's Defense Department—and they were all statisticians—said that the unit of measure would be body count. Ironically, in the Korean War the Senate blasted General MacArthur among other things for the number of enemy soldiers he killed. They said that wasn't the American way of war. We shouldn't measure things in terms of soldiers killed, but then we took that very same measure and used it in Vietnam. Not only did we compromise the integrity of the army, we turned off the American people. We kept drilling on how many people we killed, killed, killed, and it turned out to be totally counterproductive. It was a bad policy from start to finish. Mr. Halberstam can probably answer better than I, but I think it started innocently enough and then just got out of hand.

Halberstam

We in the press disliked the body count in particular because we thought that it was pathologically dishonest. The numbers were constantly inflated. They were padded lies. In those days advisers passed them on from South Vietnamese units. There was no real validation. We thought that it was extraordinarily dishonest and inflated, and we fought it. The early press corps certainly didn't emphasize it, but it became a way of proving yourself if you were a young and ambitious officer. Officers began to break the code of what the McNamara people wanted, which was numbers, numbers, numbers. It became clear that that was part of the ticket to get ahead.

Boomer

One of the ways, of course, that we solved it was we just lied about it. You're absolutely right, David, it was inflated. The pressure was on in the beginning, but then pretty soon you began to figure it out, so you just lied. Nobody had the guts to come out and really check and see what you had done. Anyhow, you're out there by yourself. So, in the end, maybe it didn't make as much difference.

Summers

One of the great ironies of the war, though, came out in that famous in-

terview with North Vietnamese General Vo Nguyen Giap by the Italian journalist in which Giap admits that his forces probably had five hundred thousand killed in the course of the war. He almost validated the body count
figures.

Parks

From a historical perspective, part of the dilemma was in the very early
days of the Vietnam War when South Vietnamese and/or U.S. forces engaged Vietcong forces. After the battle the Vietcong would drag their dead
off the battlefield. There was an attempt to do some extrapolation of the
number of bodies found, number of wounded found, and number of weapons found and to put that into some sort of a "wag," as we would call it,
which in proper parlance is a "guess." It simply became a very, very bad,
made-up formula that people then simply began to make worse.

QUESTION: What was the state of law-of-war training in the army and the
marines during the early 1960s?

Summers

I think in the army, at least in basic training, you got a smattering of the
law of war. You don't shoot prisoners; you don't do this; and you don't do
that, according to the Geneva Conventions. I'm not sure how much attention people paid to it, but at least it was presented. The real safeguard against
this was in the unit itself and what the unit commander would tolerate and
the command climate that he established. That was much stronger than any
regulation. Of course, in Vietnam they gave everybody a little card that you
were supposed to carry in your wallet with the rules of land warfare on it. Now,
how many troops carried it and how many ever read it is another story. The
real answer to this, at least in my estimation as an infantryman in two wars, is
the climate your commander sets, what he will tolerate and what he will not
tolerate. That's far more important than the written regulations. Still, if you
go back and look at the curriculum of the war colleges, the staff colleges, and
basic training, you'll find some instruction on the law of land warfare.

Boomer

It probably wasn't as good as it should have been, but I recall from the
day that I first entered the Marine Corps we had classes on this and discus-

sions on it. There was some training. What should have happened, of course, was that it should have been intensified on the order of perhaps a hundred before we went into Vietnam. It wasn't, but there was training.

Parks

I can speak from having gone through the training in those days as a lieutenant. Yes, we were receiving the training, and we received it in a lot of different ways. You had to learn, for example, the basic procedures for handling a prisoner of war, and you practiced those. Jones, Smith is your prisoner of war; how do you do it? You learned how to handle that and that you don't shoot the person. Every single base and every single school had a Vietnamese village, and you practiced different ways of clearing the village. You held a country fair; you moved the civilians outside. You weren't specifically getting law-of-war training in every case, but you were getting training on how you handle noncombatants. I would point out, however, that both in the Peers Report and in some of the other reports at the time, there was a finding that the army was getting complaints at General Westmoreland's level that training in the law of war in some units was too academic and abstract. As a result that training suffered. I would also point out that cards were put out on how to behave in Vietnam, but the German Wermacht during World War II also had a paper pay record with some rules on the back that they kept in their pockets. Having the mere rules isn't sufficient. You have to have the leadership to back them up, and that was what Colonel Summers was talking about.

[*Question from audience member leads to discussion of Project 100,000.**]

Summers

Project 100,000 was a great social experiment. We were going to take these Category IV people, Category IV being the lowest intelligence levels on the scale, and we were going to sort of rehabilitate them by bringing them into the military. It was an absolute disaster. We found a 100 percent corre-

---

*The Department of Defense initiated Project 100,000 in 1967. Through a lowering of mental and physical standards for induction, thousands of the nation's poorest, least educated, and most disadvantaged youth who had previously failed preinduction tests began to obtain what the Pentagon termed "the opportunities and obligations of military service."

lation between these IQ levels and indiscipline, AWOL, drug use, and right down the scale. Project 100,000 was a disaster both for the people involved and for the military.

Parks

Let me add, though, that the number of Project 100,000 people in the My Lai unit, Charlie Company, First of the Twentieth, was smaller than in most units, and in fact the average educational level and high school graduate number in that unit was higher than usual. So you come back once again to the basic leadership issue.

8

• • • • • • • • • • • • • • • •

INDIVIDUALS AND THE TRAUMA OF WAR

Robert Jay Lifton, Patience Mason, Jonathan Shay, Karin Thompson

Hundreds of thousands of Vietnam veterans suffer from what is now termed post-traumatic stress disorder (PTSD). Studies show that this condition is most prevalent among those soldiers who participated in heavy combat and among those who participated in or witnessed atrocities or wanton violence such as Charlie Company experienced at My Lai. Vietnamese civilians who died as a result of the U.S. military presence in their country were obvious victims of the war, but so too were many of the men who pulled the triggers and in the same moment had their own lives destroyed. Many who have PTSD manifest severe personality changes, including agonizing grief, tormenting guilt, suicidal longings, violent outbursts, severe depression, isolation, and a feeling of meaninglessness.

The author of *Recovering from the War: A Woman's Guide to Helping Your Vet, Your Family, and Yourself,* Patience Mason is the wife of Bob Mason. Bob was a helicopter pilot and is a victim of PTSD who himself has written two widely read memoirs, *Chickenhawk* and *Chickenhawk: Back in the World.* Patience relates how the struggles with PTSD that she went through with Bob led her into understanding the importance of listening to the veteran. Jonathan Shay, Karin Thompson, and Robert Jay Lifton are mental health professionals who share their insights into the disorder gained from their work with PTSD sufferers. These four voices address the interconnection of war, death, atrocity, survivor guilt, moral guilt, psychic pain, and healing. What applies to individual veterans in struggling with their personal pain also applies in a generic sense to all of society's contending with painful memories like My Lai.

Patience Mason

Living with somebody who has post-traumatic stress disorder is very difficult. I know that because, when my husband Bob got back from Vietnam in 1966, he couldn't sleep. He is 5'10" but weighed only 119 pounds. He looked like he had been in Buchenwald. They told him that he would be over this in a couple of months. He didn't get over it. He got worse. After about a year, he found that if he drank he could sleep, and he had to drink more and more. Eventually he got grounded from flying because he was having anxiety attacks and chest pains. In doing my later research for *Recovering from the War,* I heard his condition described as "soldier's heart." It was known since 1871 in Civil War soldiers.

The American Psychiatric Association was going through a lot of denial. In 1968 they came out with a book called *Diagnostic and Statistical Manual II* (DSM-II). They dropped the category that they had before, called "gross stress reaction." If you had been through a gross-enough stress, you could have problems with it. They now said that anybody who had any problems with a gross stress, like combat in Vietnam, for more than six months after they got back from Vietnam had been defective before they went. One reason why so many Vietnam veterans had problems then and still have problems is because they got mistreated. Instead of getting help, they got pills and were told, "Get out of here, you were screwed up before you went." That happened to my husband. The local VA gave him all the Valium he could eat. At the time he was drinking a quart of whiskey every day and smoking all the pot he could get his hands on. That just kept him down to wired.

He thought he was just innately defective, and I thought this was all my fault. I thought that, if I was a good enough wife, he wouldn't be having these problems. So I tried to find a solution by reading self-help books and trying to learn how to listen and stuff like that. It wasn't until 1980 that we got a pamphlet that the Disabled American Veterans wrote and published. It was about the effects of the war on Vietnam veterans. I read through this pamphlet, and it described my life. The veteran had depression. Bob was often so depressed that he could hardly move. He could always put on a good act for other people, but he was a very depressed person. He would go into rages. He was isolated. At the time, we were living in the woods in a cabin that he built by hand on ten acres. It was the story of my life. I cried all the way through it.

Then *Chickenhawk* came out, and Bob got a lot of praise for it. At the same time, he also went to jail because he had smuggled some pot into the country as a crew man [on a sailboat from Colombia]. He served his time. He was one of the few people in the prison who actually said that he was guilty of what he was there for. Everybody else would say, "I was framed." Not Bob, but that's another story. While he was in there, I went on a book tour for him. I talked to a lot of veterans. I found that I was really interested in that. Afterward we visited some guys in a real prison, Raiford, up in north central Florida. They asked him to come talk to them, and he did. When we were leaving, they said to me, "I wish you could talk to my wife." I realized I could talk to their wives if I wrote a book.

At first I thought I would write a book about my own experiences, but every time I tried to write about it I would start sobbing. I couldn't write about what it was like to be alone trying to help your husband with no help. So I decided that I would write a book about what it was like in Vietnam, the normal effects of that on people, how that affects families, and how to get better. I started going to meetings of the International Society for Traumatic Stress Studies, where all the people who had done the first work on PTSD were. They became friends of mine. They were very supportive. They helped me with anything I wanted to know. I read every book, including all the scientific literature, that was written by people who understood PTSD at that time.

I also interviewed about sixty veterans. That was really hard. At the time I wasn't very good at taking care of myself. I would go out and do three interviews, and I would come home and sit down. If I needed something on the other side of the room, I would have to crawl for it. I would be just totally exhausted. Their stories were incredibly painful. I can remember one guy. We were sitting in McDonald's in Gainesville, Florida, talking about what it was like to be in the Mekong Delta. I was always trying to get the details because it's easier to understand if you understand that there were sores on his shoulder, he was carrying sixty pounds, and stuff like that. He was telling me what it was like to go out at night for a night position and squat down and cover yourself with your poncho because it was raining. You had to turn the radio up real high, and you were waiting for an ambush. All of a sudden he turned bright red, and he started shaking like a leaf. I said, "Are you okay? What's happening?" I felt terrible. Obviously something was happening to this guy. He said to me, "I'm just remembering what it was like to be afraid." He was nineteen when he was there, and most of those guys were quite often afraid for that whole year that they were there. I've never been afraid like that in my life, but his story made a really big impact on me.

We can't change the past. We can learn from the past. I'm in a twelve-step program. The way I've learned to deal with the things that I did that were wrong in the past is, number one, to understand that they were wrong. I always thought I was right. I never did anything wrong that someone else didn't make me do. Today I know that that's not true. I've never done anything like My Lai either, but I do know that it works to say I was wrong and then to make amends. Just talking about My Lai is making amends. Saying I was wrong is making amends. Talking about it helps you to see what you did and if there's something you should do about it. How do you make amends to the Vietnamese people for that? You can start collecting medical supplies and sending them to Vietnam or something like that.

After telling me their stories, some of the veterans had a real hard time, but they were willing to talk to me because they wanted to help other veterans. They trusted me because I am married to Bob and most of them had read *Chickenhawk*. They really care about him so they really care about me. Bob never told any of the bad things about me, like my thinking for twenty-five years that I was always right and he was never right. He leaves that out of his books, but I was like that. That gave me a great "in" with them. They knew that I was married to a veteran and that I had stayed with him. I hadn't given up, even when things were really shitty. That was part of it, but the other part of it was that I listened to them. A lot of them would say, "Well, I'm not going to talk about that." I would say, "Okay," and we would talk about little things, like what was in their packs and stuff like that. Eventually they would tell me other things.

Listening is an important part of the process. When you see somebody who tells something, and you know that it's at cost to themselves but that they're doing it to help other veterans, you know that they're doing something. They're paying back; they're making amends.

Early on, they may have told part of these stories, and people weren't listening. People told them to shut up. People told them not to swear in front of their mothers. People told them that they didn't want to hear about it. People told them they were murderers. People wanted to know how many people you killed and whether you killed any babies, and that kind of stuff stops people from talking forever. It happened after World War II. There is a lot of mythology about World War II, but the people who were in parades after World War II were the guys who were still in America. The combat veterans got back later, and what they got was people telling them in some line at the grocery store, "You know, while you guys were over having fun in Europe we couldn't get good cigarettes." There is no answer to that. You either kill the person or you walk off. Most World War II guys walked off.

I think most people want to talk about this. Some people had a harder time than others. Some people went through worse stuff. One of the things that I really believe about post-traumatic stress disorder is that it's only luck if you don't get it when you've been through something very traumatic. If you have a supportive environment, you may not get it, but your luck may change. Your wife may be killed in a car wreck, and then you'll get it. There was a long period when people would say, "Well, I don't have a problem like all those veterans." You don't have a problem yet, is my answer. You may have a problem, and you may never have a problem. It wasn't until the 1980s that Congress passed a bill saying that, if you were a POW from any war, we are going to presume that you have PTSD and that all of your physical problems were caused by your POW experience. Before that, they just threw them away. They couldn't get help.

Jonathan Shay

[*To add to the discussion of the issues of war atrocity and personal trauma, Shay shares the following Vietnam veteran combat narrative from his book*, Achilles in Vietnam, *pp. 3–4:*]

There was a LURP team from the First Brigade off of Highway One, that looked over the South China Sea. There was a bay there. . . . Now they saw boats come in. And they suspected—now, the word came down [that] they were unloading weapons off them. Three boats. At that time we moved. It was about ten o'clock at night. We moved down, across High-way One, and along the beach line, and they put us on line while these people are unloading their boats. And we opened up on them—aaah.

And the fucking fire power was unreal, the fire power that we put into them boats. It was just a constant, constant fire power. It seemed like no one ever ran out of ammo.

Daylight came [long pause], and we found out we killed a lot of fisher-men and kids.

What got us thoroughly fucking confused is at that time you turn to the team and you say to the team, "Don't worry about it. Everything's fucking fine." Because that's what you're getting from upstairs.

The fucking colonel says: "Don't worry about it. We'll take care of it." Y'know, uh, "We got body count!" "We have body count!" So it starts working on your head.

So, you know in your heart it's wrong, but at the time, here's your su-periors telling you that it was okay. So, I mean, that's okay then, right? This is part of war. Y'know? Gung-HO! Y'know? "AirBORNE! AirBORNE! Let's go!"

So we packed up and we moved out.

They wanted to give us a fucking unit citation—them fucking maggots. A lot of medals came down from it. The lieutenants got medals, and I know the colonel got his fucking medal. And they would have award ceremonies, y'know, I'd be standing like a fucking jerk, and they'd be handing out fucking medals for killing civilians.

[*To provide some perspective on atrocity, Shay offers the following observation from Herbert C. Kelman's* "The Social Context of Torture"]:*

To understand participation in massacre, it is less important to explore the forces that push people into performing such violent acts than to explore those forces that contribute to the weakening of moral restraints against performing these acts—acts that people would normally find unacceptable. Within this framework, I proposed that *authorization* [pro-

---

*In *The Politics of Pain: Torturers and their Masters,* ed. Ronald D. Crelinsten and Alex P. Schmid (Boulder, Colo.: Westview Press, 1995).

tecting the state against threats to its security] helps to define the situation in such a way that standard moral principles do not apply: The individual is not acting as an independent moral agent and therefore feels absolved of the responsibility to make personal moral choices. Through *routinization* [being part of the state's security apparatus], the action becomes so organized that there is no opportunity for raising moral questions and making moral decisions: The action is divided among many individuals and sub-units of the organization; each individual carries out routine tasks without having to think of the overall product created by these tasks; the use of euphemisms further enables individuals to avoid the meaning of the tasks that they are performing; altogether, the actions come to be seen as part of a normal job rather than participation in a massacre. Finally, *dehumanization* [designating the targets as enemies of the state and excluded from the state's protection] makes it unnecessary for actors to view their relationship to the victim in moral terms: The victim is excluded from their moral community.

Shay

Ultimately, in order to heal, someone must tell his story in a context of trust. This is not to say that there's an instant cure that comes from catharsis, from screaming, bleeding, vomiting, dying, and then being reborn. It doesn't work that way, that just retraumatizes. People have to get solid enough that they can face telling their story with their safety, sobriety, and self-care intact. It's sometimes a long struggle to build that foundation, but there isn't a single approach to recovery that doesn't require this process of rebuilding authority over memory by telling the story.

When the combat veteran retells his story several times, it's part of the whole process of creating a cohesive narrative. It's more like training to run the marathon than telling it once and you are done. The point is to achieve authority over memory, and a flashback is not memory. A flashback is a reliving. It's memory that is stored in a different form than "ordinary memory." The real healing seems to come when the ordinary memory is recovered and reconstructed with the feelings that went with the event, and with the knowledge of the context of the event, with the bodily sensations that went with it. When that sort of whole cohesive picture of consciousness is reconstructed, a major piece of recovery usually has taken place.

The people that I work with are in, and continue to be in, tremendous moral pain. The moral dimension of trauma is enormous, and any account of trauma that leaves that out is a fatally incomplete account. If you just focus on terror, on disgust, and on grief, you miss a major dimension that ruins people's character. People can generally recover spontaneously from the terror and grief of warfare if there hasn't been a significant element of moral betrayal. It is a painfully simple truth that, if the moral integrity of the armed forces is preserved throughout a war, people can recover from most of the war itself. That's not to say that war itself doesn't always create terrible situations of moral conflict and devastation. If the armed forces keep themselves together as a moral structure, however, the damage is far less.

Many of the men that I work with feel guilty about things that most people would say that they have no reason to feel guilty about. One man, for instance, feels guilty that his friend died rather than himself in a mine explosion. He had jumped off their tank at the same spot and the mine hadn't gone off. Now, he feels guilty about that. I've also worked with men who have had the experience of killing unarmed civilians. To feel guilt in either instance is a sign of one's surviving humanity. It is an assertion that there is still justice in the world. It is keeping the dead alive and keeping contact with one's former ethical self.

I don't regard forgetting as a legitimate goal of therapy. I don't regard the elimination of guilt as a legitimate goal of therapy, because, for most of the men that I work with, their dignity and their humanity is bound up in that guilt. What I try to help them do is to express that guilt in more constructive and less self-destructive ways. I have one man who occasionally has a virtual lust to chop off his fingers, and it's very definitely connected with things that he did that he feels so guilty about. I'm not trying to remove that guilt in any sense but to help him live a life of a human being now.

Karin Thompson

Discussing the impact of trauma, particularly combat trauma, may help us to understand one facet of the impact of events such as those which occurred at My Lai from the perspective of veteran survivors. Being in a war and experiencing atrocities continue to exert a powerful influence over the lives of the men and women who were there. To learn more about the impact of severe trauma, read Judith L. Herman's *Trauma and Recovery*.

As I began talking at the VA to veterans who had served in combat in Vietnam, I was moved and affected by many aspects of their stories and their lives. One of the things I was most struck by was the enormous and lasting impact the Vietnam War had made on its soldiers. The Vietnam veterans that I have seen experienced a trauma twenty or more years ago, and yet they feel as if it happened yesterday. The war, for them, is very much in the present and immediate. It is with them all the time.

Although it has only been called post-traumatic stress disorder since 1980, the phenomenon has been recognized and written about as long as there have been wars. Dr. Shay has pointed out that Homer's *Iliad,* written in the eighth century B.C., has a lot to teach us about the impact of war on soldiers. During the late nineteenth century, Dr. Jacob Mendes DaCosta, a physician, was the first to study a group of physically sound yet psychologically symptomatic American Civil War veterans. They complained of heart pain but there was no evidence of cardiac disease, and DaCosta called it "soldier's heart." During World War I the term "shell shock" described the results of artillery shell concussions on the brain. The signs of shell shock were also seen in soldiers exposed to the emotional stress of fear and terror during combat. In 1945, R. R. Grinker and J. P. Spiegel proposed that "battle fatigue" was a stress reaction unique to war. The American Psychiatric Association's *Diagnostic and Statistical Manual* (DSM) has historically included some form of diagnosis that attempted to account for stress reactions, and in 1980, as a result of clinical recommendations and clinical trials, the DSM-III introduced the category of post-traumatic stress disorder. Since that time, research and clinical reports from around the world have confirmed the presence of PTSD in veterans of all cultures and countries.

One of the largest and most comprehensive studies of PTSD among Vietnam veterans is R. A. Kulka's *National Vietnam Veterans Readjustment Study.* This is a study that was mandated by law to establish the prevalence and incidence of PTSD and other psychological problems in readjusting to civilian life among Vietnam veterans. More than half (53.4 percent) of male veterans and nearly half (48.1 percent) of female veterans have experienced clinically significant stress reaction symptoms at some time in their lives. This represents about 1.7 million war veterans. These rates are much higher than rates for veterans who did not serve in combat or rates for civilians. Further, the rates are higher because they were exposed to trauma in combat, not because of some other predisposing characteristic. Similar prevalence rates of PTSD have been found to exist in veterans of World War II, the Korean conflict, and Operation Desert Storm.

What is PTSD? First of all, it begins as a normal reaction to an abnormal event. War is not normal. Almost anyone who goes to war will come back with some adjustment problems. When the problems last a long time and begin to impair a person's social and interpersonal functioning, then we call it PTSD. The DSM-IV identifies the following criteria for post-traumatic stress disorder:

A. Exposure to a traumatic event
B. Persistent reexperiencing of the traumatic event
C. Persistent avoidance of stimuli associated with the trauma and numbing of general responsiveness
D. Persistent symptoms of increased arousal
E. Duration of symptoms in B, C, and D is more than one month
F. The disturbance causes clinically significant distress or impairment in social or occupational functioning.

Under criterion A, "the person has been exposed to a traumatic event in which both of the following were present: (1) the person experienced, witnessed, or was confronted with an event or events that involved actual or threatened death or serious injury, or a threat to the physical integrity of self or others, and (2) the person's response involved intense fear, helplessness, or horror."*

Traumatic stress can result from very different events, including war, natural disaster, sexual abuse/assault, other types of assault, and being held captive, for example, as a prisoner of war. Certain professions are at high risk for development of PTSD due to the nature of their work, including police officers, emergency workers, and firefighters.

The type of trauma that occurred at My Lai is extraordinary because of the loss of control, loss of human connection, and loss of meaning. Unfortunately, the events that unfolded at My Lai, although extraordinary in their capacity to overwhelm, did not comprise an isolated incident. Many veterans have told me over the years that "incidents like My Lai" happened often in Vietnam and that atrocities were perpetrated by both sides.

Part of the trauma that is inherent in being a combat soldier is that he or she may be forced to become a perpetrator of abuse and annihilation. Combat soldiers not only witness the death and destruction around them, and possibly get killed, but they must themselves become killers and destroyers. Unfortunately, much of what is required to be a "good" soldier in combat

---

*American Psychiatric Association, *Diagnostic and Statistical Manual of Mental Disorders,* 4th ed. (Washington, D.C.: American Psychiatric Association, 1994), 427–29.

may come into conflict with one's preexisting values. Characteristics of a "good" soldier in combat include following orders, hypervigilance, learning to dehumanize the enemy, and becoming adept at emotional constriction. The military does an excellent job of training soldiers to do these things. Infantrymen who could not do these things were likely to be those who were killed in combat. Many veterans describe, often to their horror in retrospect, that they began to enjoy the killing or to feel driven to kill by events they had witnessed. They had seen their buddies killed or mutilated, not only by enemy soldiers but also by civilians and children. In a large study of Vietnam veterans seeking treatment at VA PTSD clinics, approximately one third had witnessed atrocities and close to one third participated in atrocities. Veterans who witnessed or participated in atrocities are often the ones who are most symptomatic. According to Judith Herman in *Trauma and Recovery,*

> The violation of the human connection, and consequently the risk of PTSD, is highest of all when the survivor has not been merely a passive witness but also an active participant in violent death or atrocity. The trauma of combat exposure takes on added force when violent death can no longer be rationalized in terms of some higher value or meaning. In the Vietnam War, soldiers became profoundly demoralized when victory in battle was an impossible objective and the standard of success became the killing itself, as exemplified by the body count. Under these circumstances, it was not merely the exposure to death but rather the participation in meaningless acts of malicious destruction that rendered men most vulnerable to lasting psychological damage. [p. 54]

In some ways, PTSD can be thought of as the manifestation of these characteristics carried over to the present day.

The connection to self and others is damaged. Veterans often have great remorse over their actions in Vietnam. Frequently they will disown that part of themselves, speaking of the person they were before Vietnam, which seems almost irretrievable, and the person they are now. Many feel that a part of themselves died in Vietnam; some wish they were dead. They are sometimes disconnected from their emotions about what happened, which is a part of the numbing. They may talk about a completely horrible event with little or no emotion, or there may be a tear running down their cheek but an inability to identify the emotion that goes with the tears. Their loss of connection with others is shown in their feeling detached or estranged from others, or sometimes an inability to have loving feelings for others. Many veterans express an inability to know love.

Constrictive symptoms also interfere with anticipation and planning for the future. Many veterans, even after being back from the war for years, do not expect to live very long. As a result they do not make a lot of plans for the future. A related phenomenon is avoidance of war-related stimuli (things that are reminders of the war). This disconnection can be viewed as an attempt to deny a part of one's experience. By trying to forget the trauma (which one cannot), he or she tries to ensure avoidance of emotions.

Another symptom cluster characteristic of PTSD is reexperiencing. The traumatic event is relived as if it were occurring in the present through nightmares, flashbacks, and intrusive thoughts. The fear and rage that were present at the time of the war are present again and just as powerful. Veterans exhibiting these symptoms are often overwhelmed by emotion, which can feel very frightening and out of control.

The third symptom cluster is hyperarousal. Normal, adaptive reactions to threat and danger become permanent states of arousal. This is often seen in the form of sleep problems, irritability, difficulty concentrating, hypervigilance, and exaggerated startle response. People with PTSD have an elevated baseline of arousal; their bodies are always on the alert for danger. Unexpected loud noises will make the traumatized person jump in a fashion that is more pronounced than in other people. They also have trouble tuning out repetitive stimuli. For example, they can't habituate a loud noise like a pile driver.

The nature of PTSD is such that the symptoms tend to be phasic, which means that at any given time a traumatized individual may exhibit some symptoms but not others, and these may be different from the symptoms that are exhibited at another time. Avoidance and numbing phases alternate with intrusion or reexperiencing phases. The instability produced by these periodic alterations may lead to an appearance of unpredictability. Sometimes memories and emotions are flooding in, and other times the detached numbing and lack of remembering predominates. Over time, intrusive symptoms diminish and numbing symptoms come to predominate.

For veterans who require treatment in working through their combat experiences, several approaches are shown to be effective in reducing the symptoms of PTSD. All of the approaches have in common restoring the human/community connection, finding meaning, and regaining control. The stages of recovery include moving from unpredictable danger to reliable safety, from dissociated trauma to acknowledged memory, and from stigmatized isolation to restored social connections. For most combat veterans with PTSD, recovery from the war is a lifelong process.

Robert Jay Lifton

The most authoritative study of PTSD among Vietnam veterans was published in 1990. It gives evidence for something close to 480,000 American men of the 3.14 million who served in the Vietnam theater still suffering in 1990 from post-traumatic stress disorder. Adding the findings for women, which now have been systematically gone into, you get nearly 830,000 people still suffering in 1990 from what is called at least partial post-traumatic stress disorder. These are tremendous human costs, even though society has tried to relegate Vietnam veterans to stereotypical powder kegs and druggies. Indeed, Vietnam veterans have had problems with violence and with drugs. Nonetheless, that stereotyping is a way of avoiding the more profound issue of the human costs of that war, that atrocity-producing situation. At least that human cost has been recognized.

Beginning in 1970 and over the next three to five years, we saw amazing changes taking place in veterans with whom we worked, sometimes over months, sometimes over weeks. The changes were not insignificant. These were changes in their worldview, in extricating themselves from their war, but also in their sense of male macho. It was seen in their condemnation of what used to be called the "John Wayne thing," which was the simple structure of silence, courage, loyalty, protection of women (who were supposed to be obedient), and quick resort to violence when any of these principles were violated. As we discussed those issues, Vietnam veterans were sensitive enough to realize that this had to be overcome but that there were some noble traits, such as courage and loyalty, which had to be extricated and put into better use, better channeling. There were many aspects of the transformation, but it had to do with learning to feel, as we used to say in those rap groups, and getting over racist dehumanization and psychic numbing. This too had enormous significance for psychological theory. Of course, some of the aspects of self stayed the same. Not everything changed in people, but still, there were significant changes.

MILITARY LESSONS LEARNED

**Walter E. Boomer, Henry L. Mason, Hays Parks,
Harry G. Summers, Jr.**

What should the U.S. military have learned and, indeed, what has it learned from the failure represented by the Vietnam War in general and the My Lai massacre in particular? Harry Summers, Walter Boomer, and Hays Parks are military professionals who have directly confronted these questions in their careers. Political scientist Henry Mason is a scholar of the Nazi genocide of the European Jews. Although each acknowledges harsh realities and mistakes in American conduct, they also find positive responses to the Vietnam experience.

The author of influential books on the wars in Vietnam and the Persian Gulf, Summers maintains that the Vietnam War was primarily, but not entirely, a conventional war but that it was not perceived or fought that way. The U.S. military was at a low point in 1974–1975 because of the failure in Vietnam. There was a tendency within the military to blame General William Westmoreland (Summers thinks unfairly). Regardless of blame, the military returned to basics after Vietnam. Renewed attention to conventional training and tactics resulted in great success in the Persian Gulf War.

Boomer, a retired general who commanded all U.S. Marines in the Gulf War, says he left Vietnam very dissatisfied with the military's performance. U.S. forces just "flailed away," losing men often to unseen enemies through mines and booby traps. He believes that the United States really tried to avoid civilian casualties in Vietnam, but there were civilian casualties all the same. Rotating officers every six months was a bad policy because it denied the young marines the benefits of experienced leadership in the field. He is not sure it was ever possible for the corrupt South Vietnamese government to win the hearts and minds of the people regardless of what the Americans did. Vietnam, Boomer asserts, "helped us relearn our profession."

According to Parks, who is now a civilian lawyer for the U.S. Army, the armed forces today are extremely professional and moral. The military has studied My Lai, and today troops are taught the law of war. The law of war is an explicit command responsibility, and "hot lines" and other measures exist now to ensure that atrocities or misconduct get reported and investigated. Senior officers today will not tolerate breaches of the law of war.

Mason identifies a number of comparisons and contrasts between My Lai and the Holocaust. Research shows that one fourth of the Jews killed died in My Lai-like fashion, that is, gunned down by ordinary men who were neither exceptionally virtuous nor sadistic. There are other similarities, but there are also key differences. Most of the German executioners had not experienced warfare and had not been brutalized by combat. The lesson is to avoid the kind of war where atrocity-producing situations occur. Also, leadership must be strong and precise. When atrocity occurs, the reality must be acknowledged and confronted. In Nazi Germany the true horror of the concentration camps was not allowed to penetrate public consciousness, but in the United States the voices of Ron Ridenhour and Seymour Hersh and the moral courage of Hugh Thompson did reach through.

Harry Summers

It's very important to keep in mind how time- and space-sensitive the Vietnam War was. There wasn't one Vietnam War; there were many wars, maybe a million Vietnam Wars. There may have been a Vietnam War for everyone who served there. To focus on My Lai perpetuates the myth that the war was primarily a guerrilla war waged against black-pajama-clad guerrillas who were very poorly armed and very poorly equipped. That mind-set began very early in 1964 when it was true, and for many people it never changed.

It really made a difference where you were in Vietnam and what you were doing. If you were in the Third Marine Division along the DMZ, you had nothing to do with guerrillas. You were fighting a regular war against North Vietnamese regulars, who were probably better armed and better equipped than you were. The North Vietnamese 122mm artillery at Khe Sanh, for example, unleashed everything they had to pound the U.S. base there in 1968. All the marines could do in response with their 105s was make a lot of noise and not do much damage. As Ron Spector says in his book *After Tet,* the Third Marine Division was fighting World War I. A little further south, the First Marine Division was engaged in pacification efforts using Combined Action Platoons, and they, indeed, were dealing a lot with the black-pajama-type guerrilla. In the Central Highlands around Dak To, the guerrilla war was almost nonexistent. Combat was against North Vietnamese regulars, as had been the case in 1965 with the First Cavalry Division at the Battle of Ia Drang, one of the first major battles of the war. As Neil Sheehan said on the front page of the *New York Times,* the entire nature of the war had changed at Ia Drang. What had been a low-level guerrilla war was now a war between the regular forces of North Vietnam and the United States. Further south in III Corps, where I was in 1966–1967, the guerrilla was a threat but not much of one. The main threat to the First Infantry Division was the main force VC battalions, regiments, and divisions. A little further south, the Twenty-fifth Division in Hau Nghia Province again went back to the guerrilla war, and the Ninth Division in the Delta was fighting a guerrilla war against the black-pajama-clad guerrilla.

The point is, there were many wars going on simultaneously, and I think that sometimes gets forgotten. Another thing that gets forgotten is that, even where guerrilla war existed, it essentially ended with the Tet Offensive in 1968. For the next seven years, a period longer than World War II, the war was primarily waged between the regular forces of North Vietnam and the regular forces of the United States and South Vietnam. Again, the incredible complexity of the Vietnam War needs to be realized.

To the point of lessons learned, my second book, *On Strategy II,* is subtitled *A Critical Analysis of the Gulf War,* which is really a misnomer. It should have been subtitled "Forging Victory from Defeat," because what I tried to do in that book was analyze how we got from the defeat and demoralization of the military in 1973–1975 to the forces we took into the Persian Gulf. It's a remarkable story. It begins at, of all places (and as an army officer I hate to admit it), the Naval War College in 1972. When Admiral Stansfield Turner took over as commandant there, he said there had been enough of this fallacy, that had existed since World War II, that the entire nature of war had changed with the atomic bomb. The view was that all conventional strategy, all conventional history, and, more important, all conventional experience had no relevance, and only the so-called wizards of Armageddon had the right answers. We bought it, although it almost assured the army and marines and their conventional forces of no role in modern war. The Korean War was a conventional war, but it was dismissed as an aberration. Atomic weapons would win wars. What that view did to the study of tactics and strategy in the army is almost impossible to believe. As I said in my first book, *On Strategy*, the purpose of the military according to the old rules is to destroy the enemy on the battlefield so you can break his will to resist. We thought we were in a new kind of war in Vietnam intended to win hearts and minds and all of the rest of this baloney. It had almost no relevance to Vietnam because, as I said, even though the guerrilla war disappeared in 1968, the war continued for another seven years. Whatever the center of gravity was in Vietnam, it was not the guerrilla.

Stansfield Turner said we were going to go back to basics. We were going to go back to the study of Alfred Thayer Mahan, Sir Julian Corbett, and Carl von Clausewitz, and we were going to relearn the fundamentals of our profession. The renaissance began at the Naval War College at Newport, Rhode Island, then went to the Air War College at Maxwell Air Force Base, and finally went to the Army War College at Carlisle Barracks.

About 4 percent of the officer corps with about twenty years of service is selected for the war colleges. Every general officer in the army is a war college graduate, although not all war college graduates are generals. At the air college and war colleges is where the real revolution took hold among people who had been company commanders and platoon leaders in the Vietnam War. When Stansfield Turner put in his reforms at Newport, the feelings were so high about Vietnam within the service that he said you couldn't teach a rational course on the Vietnam War. Instead, he forced them to learn the Peloponnesian War. If you learn the Peloponnesian War, he said, they could also be learning about Vietnam and in time the discussion would lead in that direction. Again, the revolution that took place in the services was a return to basics and to fundamentals. One of the commandants of the Marine Corps at the time said that finally we were going to get the Marine Corps out of Vietnam and back into amphibious warfare where it belonged.

As I said in my book, one of the saving graces for the nation was that most of the officer corps in the army didn't blame the American people or the Congress or the president for the failure in Vietnam. They blamed General Westmoreland. It was terribly unfair, but nevertheless, to his credit, he took the heat from the officer corps and prevented a kind of stab-in-the-back theory that never developed in the ordinary armed forces after Vietnam. Westmoreland could have made a case against President Johnson and President Nixon and the rest of them. He could have come up with a satisfactory stab-in-the-back theory, but that didn't develop because Westy took the heat. After my book came out, he called me up and said reading that was like somebody kicking him in the stomach. I said, Well sir, if you read the next sentence (which he hadn't done), it said that it was terribly unfair.

In any event, the attitude among career officers was not so much recrimination as it was to ask what the hell went wrong and to get on with correcting it. We saw within the army a return to basics and a return to fundamentals. There was a reorientation toward conventional war that had not been true really since prior to World War II. There was a return to the importance of Clausewitz, for example, who had learned from the French Revolution what the founders of this country had learned from the American Revolution. That parallel made Clausewitz uniquely qualified to be the philosopher of choice for the American armed forces. We saw in the Gulf War the result of the lessons learned from Vietnam.

Major General Jim Johnson, the commander of the Eighty-second Airborne in the Gulf War, said, "You know, the lesson of Vietnam for me as a member of the younger generation, as a captain, was seeing my senior officers compromised and fall victim to the body-count syndrome and look the other way." The most damning book on the Vietnam War by a professional officer is *The Twenty-five Year War* by General Bruce Palmer, who was the commander of II Field Force Vietnam, then headed U.S. Army Vietnam (USARV), and finally was vice–chief of staff of the army. He makes a heavy indictment of the Joint Chiefs of Staff, who knew things were not going right in Vietnam, who knew we were violating the principles of war, and who still sat on their hands and did nothing. The feeling of the younger generation of the Vietnam War officer corps was that we weren't going to do that, we weren't going to allow that sort of thing to happen. We were going to speak up if it became necessary. We saw that behavior in the Gulf War. One of the great ironies of the Vietnam War was that the two senior commanders in the Gulf, General H. Norman Schwarzkopf and General Colin Powell, had both served in the Americal Division where the My Lai massacre took place. In any event, as General Johnson's remark indicated, we had a generation of officers who wouldn't temporize with these kinds of issues.

Of course, the great challenge is what the following generation is going to do. What are they going to do when it comes to a crisis of moral character? Let me tell you, physical courage—you either do it or you do not do it—is easy. When it comes to moral courage, however, you can talk yourself out of it in a heartbeat. There are all kinds of excuses. In war, courage comes in moral decisions all the time. You may not get promoted; you may get passed over. You may get booted out, but at least you can shave every morning, put on your makeup every morning, and look yourself in the mirror every morning.

The most poignant story that I heard from the Vietnam War was when I was teaching at the Army War College. Harold K. Johnson came to give a talk. Harold K. Johnson was the chief of staff of the army during the Vietnam War and probably the most moral officer we've ever had in that job. Johnson was a lieutenant colonel in the Philippines at the outbreak of World War II and was in a Philippine scout battalion. He was captured, took part in the Bataan Death March, ended up in a Manchurian prison camp, and came out of it weighing about eighty-five pounds. In the Korean War, he commanded a battalion, then took over an adjacent regiment, and watched his battalion cut down almost to the man when the Chinese intervened. He had seen battle several times over. He was a man who, as chief of staff, kept a Bible and a Boy Scout manual on his desk and lived by them. General Palmer said that the worst chewing-out he ever got in his life was in the middle of a briefing when he said "goddam" and Johnson stopped him and said, "General, I would take it as a personal favor if you not take the Lord's name in vain in my presence again." Johnson started off by writing a letter personally to every family of a soldier who was killed in Vietnam. Of course, it soon became impossible to do that. He told me that at one point he was so disgusted that he started over to see President Johnson, to turn in his four stars, to resign as chief of staff of the army, and to tell the president that he would have no more part in participating in American soldiers being killed needlessly. "And then on the way to the White House," he said, "I thought better of it and thought I could do more working within the system than I could by getting out." The tag line of the story came when he said, "And now I will go to my death with that lapse in moral courage." About two months later he died. That was the most poignant display I ever heard.

Failure at the very top, failure of leadership was something that most of us who served in Vietnam said to ourselves, if we got the chance, we weren't going to do. That revulsion against the way things happened in Vietnam set off this renaissance that ended up with the army and the military that you have today, which in my mind is probably the finest military we've had in the nation's history. There were some positive lessons learned in Vietnam and put into execution.

Walter Boomer

There were a lot of wars there. I came away from Vietnam the first time and the second time—and why I volunteered to go back I'm not really sure— very unhappy with the way the war was being fought. My first experience was with the guerrillas outside of Danang. We didn't know how to fight that kind of warfare, in my opinion. We flailed around day after day, lashing out here, lashing out there. I never recall during my entire experience as a company commander getting one piece of intelligence that was worth a plug nickel. We just seemed to flail, and of course, once you do that you give the advantage to the guerrilla. He then is able to choose the time of battle, and that is exactly what he did.

For those companies in that kind of situation, he would wait until you made a mistake, and it was inevitable that you would make a mistake. You were operating day after day after day with troops who began to get tired. Despite everything that you could do to keep them pumped up and happy, it was just impossible. If you made a mistake, the guy on the other side would seize upon that mistake, and he would kill an entire squad just like that. Ten, eleven, twelve guys—it was not unusual to have them wiped out. That was very painful for us. Mines were everywhere in that part of the country— everywhere. Everywhere you turned there was another mine. Some were rather crude, but it didn't make any difference. It would take your leg off. Some more sophisticated mines could take out five to ten people at a time. The constant emotional and psychological drain from having to put up with that day after day, in addition to losing your comrades, was an insidious thing.

Therein came the argument, I think, that we would fight this war a different way. Maybe we could win the hearts and minds of the people; maybe we could learn how to fight the guerrillas on their own terms. To a degree, we made a valiant stab at that on the Marine Corps side. For those of us who were involved in guerrilla warfare, that seemed to make sense because what we were doing sure as hell did not make any sense.

The declaring of free-fire zones and the firing of tens of thousands of artillery rounds, from my point of view, meant nothing. It just became so crazy after awhile. Occasionally we had some successes. The most successful operation I ever had as a company commander came when we developed our own intelligence as a company. We conducted this thing on our own by ourselves. In essence we had a very successful fight with a VC platoon and won, and I thought, boy, maybe we had finally done something right. Lieutenant General Lewis Walt, commander of III Marine Amphibious Force, came back and in essence called me a liar. He said I really didn't have anything to do with it; I just happened to stumble upon it. I said, "Yes, sir." That piece of the war we had a very difficult time dealing with.

We subsequently moved farther north, where the enemy was as described by Colonel Summers, but here again it was a very difficult situation for us. They seemed to pick and choose the time in which we would have to fight. It would be a conventional fight: marine against North Vietnamese soldier, U.S. soldier against North Vietnamese soldier. Occasionally there would be some good intelligence, but I never had the good fortune to participate in one of those operations. When we had good intelligence that could bring all of our power together, we inevitably won. They took extreme losses. Man for man, the young American could fight just as hard as the young North Vietnamese and did—just as bravely and with just as much courage.

The problem was that there didn't seem to be any coherence to what we were doing. When the units that we fought got tired of fighting, they melted back across the DMZ, and, of course, we weren't allowed to pursue. They melted back into Laos, and, of course, we weren't allowed to pursue. While indeed it was a conventional war, it was fought on their terms. From the perspective of a twenty-eight-year-old company commander who had his kids—though they weren't kids—die in his arms, it was a very, very discouraging situation.

It was a frustrating war. We didn't understand it very well. We didn't know how to fight it very well. Certainly the political leadership in Washington was absolutely clueless. David Halberstam has said very succinctly and very clearly that it was a political failure. On the military side at the senior level, it was also a military failure. I would concede to them, though, that it was a very, very complex situation.

We have discussed civilian casualties, but if we move away from My Lai, what kind of warfare did we practice? I will go to my grave believing that most of us tried to the best of our ability not to create civilian casualties.

Despite that fact, we had them, and that too was part of this flailing around that we seemed to be doing.

In addition, we had some policies that were very distasteful to most of us. To this day, I have never had a reasonable answer to some questions from any of those who were running that war. Most of them have now passed away. I never understood our personnel policy. This was a very complex war. It required intense concentration and learning, if you were going to be able to beat the enemy on his grounds. Yet every six months we pulled out our commanders, our officers, and replaced them with somebody else. We didn't do that for our enlisted ranks; oh, no. Quite frankly, I will never forgive my service in this regard. The reasons given were that the officers were tired and six months was about as much as they could take. It was garbage. What I think we really wanted to do was rotate as many people through those command positions as we could so everybody could get their ticket punched. It was wrong. It was wrong because we deprived our youngsters of the best leadership that could have been available. You no sooner had learned how to fight this guy these six months, if you were smart enough to make it six months, and you were gone. In came the new guy. I think it was a morally reprehensible situation. I was bound and determined that we weren't going to do it in Desert Storm. Fortunately, Desert Storm didn't last that long.

What did we learn? Colonel Summers has summarized that very well. I would add one point on winning the hearts and minds of the people. Even though philosophically I think that approach had some merits in parts of the country during certain times, I'm not sure that it would have been successful overall. Regardless of whether he liked or disliked the Vietcong, the Vietnamese farmer hated the South Vietnamese government. The South Vietnamese government in my view was absolutely corrupt. We could see it everyday. District commanders getting their rake-off. District commanders setting up roadblocks and causing the peasants to have to pay. I don't know how in the heck you could win the hearts and minds of the people unless somehow we could have improved that situation. I always felt that, if we were going to commit young Americans to that fight, we should have say-so at the local level as to whether or not an official should be removed because of corruption. We could play no part in that. There was nothing that we could do, nothing we were allowed to do.

I went back again in 1971–1972 and found that the South Vietnamese were doing no better than we had done and probably worse. They were not up to par by any stretch of the imagination with the North Vietnamese forces.

The South Vietnamese airborne and ranger units and their marines were up to par with the North Vietnamese forces, but the rest of their troops were not. They were doomed, and, of course, we had cut and run so the handwriting was on the wall.

The unhappy military professional whom Colonel Summers so well described existed throughout the ranks. We continued on. We tried to improve, and gradually there was a breakthrough. During the Gulf War all of the commanders were Vietnam veterans, and we were determined not to make the same mistakes again. I can tell you, and I believe this very sincerely, if something had come down from Washington like a body count for Desert Shield/Desert Storm, General Schwarzkopf, Lieutenant General Chuck Horner (U.S. Air Force commander), Lieutenant General John Yeosock (U.S. Army commander), and Walt Boomer would have offered their resignations, pure and simple. We would have walked away from that battle. Fortunately, at the senior levels the lessons had been so well learned that we were not asked to do that kind of thing. We went back to the basics of our profession, and indeed we improved upon them. We have a military today that knows how to fight. They rely on speed; they rely on decentralization. Perhaps if nothing else came out of Vietnam, it helped us relearn our profession.

Hays Parks

The quality of the individual service person today is the best. I lecture at schools and units in all the military services. I go out and meet with people in all of the four services, and I am in awe. Whether you're talking about the privates, lance corporals, airmen first class, officers, or what have you, they are extremely professional and extremely moral. I am very impressed with what is happening.

In 1972 as a direct result of the My Lai incident, education in the military services was reviewed. It was found to be rather erratic. In 1972 there was a Department of Defense directive written to establish an overall law of war program. It did two things that were a direct result of My Lai. First, it established training standards for all people. Every single individual would receive law of war education commensurate with his or her duties and responsibilities. Second, the law of war was made a command responsibility. There are now IG "hot lines" that don't go through the chain of command. A My Lai–type incident would be reported today.

There were several failures at My Lai. One of them was that nothing was reported, and second was that the investigation was carried out by Colonel Oran Henderson in his own unit. We now take it away from the commander. Let him get back to fighting the war, and let the professional criminal investigators come in and determine what happened. To a large degree, this is what we did in the Marine Corps in Vietnam. The call would generally come from the battalion commander saying he just had an incident in his area. A professional criminal investigator and a lawyer would go down, look into it, determine what had happened, and report to the commanding general. If some action was necessary, that action would be taken, but the idea was that the commander has to fight the battle. He should not be running his own investigation. He is not a professional investigator to begin with, and he has to let the chips fall where they may. We haven't actually had problems with that.

The training of individuals with regard to the law of war has increased tremendously. It is done at all levels. It is done in the accession training for all personnel. It is done in all schools. It is done in all units. The requirement is laid on the commanders that their personnel will understand the duties, responsibilities, and obligations under the law of war. The training is better structured if it's in the units.

Colonel William Eckhardt said that, when he was in Vietnam, there were six judge advocates in his division to cover 150,000 soldiers. In the First Marine Division, a force of approximately thirty thousand marines, we had eighteen lawyers, three times as many. We also had division commanders who were very aggressive in saying get these things investigated, and if we have a case to prosecute, prosecute it. In all the services we have young judge advocates now who enjoy being in the military. They jump out of airplanes, for example, and they enjoy being out there and getting as dirty as anybody else. The deputy operations officer of the most forward deployed armored unit during Desert Storm was a female army captain judge advocate. She was there as the legal adviser to that unit, but she was also acting as an operations officer. That is the kind of quality that we're getting. The relationship between the commander and the judge advocate today has been very effective. The feeling of the commanders is that we are not going to make the mistakes that may have occurred in Vietnam. We are not going to let that kind of thing happen, and we are going to get that word out to our people.

We have also tried to institute the KISS principle, that means "Keep It Simple, Stupid." We have nine basic rules. We state them positively rather than negatively, such as, "Marines treat prisoners of war with dignity and respect." They are very simple like that. The rules are discussed over one-hour periods in the units. We get a dialogue going, whether it's E-1s, E-2s, or senior enlisted men, asking them to tell us what the rules mean to them from a military standpoint, not from a legal standpoint. It has been quite satisfactory, and the response has been good at all unit levels. We have had people from the International Committee of the Red Cross (ICRC) come and observe what we are doing, and they have said we have the best law-of-war training program in the world.

The other thing that has happened has been a real leadership role taken by our senior officers in saying we will not tolerate misbehavior in combat. It has been a very clear moral leadership on their part. In Desert Shield, I observed any number of U.S. Army commanders, who had been lieutenants and captains during the Vietnam War, taking time while preparing to fight Desert Storm to go down to individual companies. They would say, "Sit down. I want to talk to you. Now let me tell you, first, this is what you can expect of combat, and, second, this is what I expect of you and your behavior." General Boomer tells me that what he experienced in the marines was very much the same. The people of my generation were going to the new generation and saying, "Look, we've been there. There were certain mistakes made in Vietnam, and we don't want this to happen again." That moral leadership came through.

The behavior in Desert Storm was superb. Granted, it was a four-day war. The American casualties were very light. It was not as complex in that you didn't have civilians in the battlefield as we had in Vietnam. That did make a big difference. On the other hand, we did in fact capture 69,968 Iraqi prisoners of war. Once again, the Red Cross told us that no one has treated prisoners of war better in any war in all the time the ICRC has been in existence. The conduct was exemplary.

There was a Serious Incident Report (SIR) that came down after we had crossed into Kuwait. This involved a Marine Corps unit. It was around midnight, and they were very close to the Kuwait City airport. This unit was basically a very light roadblock on a main service road. There should have been no civilian traffic in the area. Around midnight a car came toward them with its high beams on and traveling at a very rapid rate of speed. As it approached the military vehicles there, it came to a screeching halt about two hundred meters short of the Marine Corps position. It blinked its lights down, up, down, up and then drove closer. There were three men in the car. A man jumped out from the backseat and started yelling something in Arabic, apparently thinking he was facing an Iraqi military unit. He got no response. The car's lights blinked up and down a few more times. He got no response. At that point, he or the man in the right front passenger seat pulled out a pistol and fired. That was a serious mistake on his part. Thirty-seven seconds later, the marines stopped firing. All three of the men had been either killed or seriously wounded. The marines approached the vehicle, found that one of the men was still alive, and began to give medical treatment, when all of a sudden someone through night-vision goggles detected an Iraqi armored unit approaching the position. The marines abandoned the position and reported back to brigade that they had an incident in which they thought some people, who might have been civilians, were injured or killed.

The next morning at first light a military police unit was sent out to investigate. The three men who had been in the vehicle were gone. The vehicle was still there. The military police took photographs of it and searched it. Underneath the right front seat was a Soviet-made pistol, but, more important, under the floor mat in the right front side were two Iraqi identification cards for members of the Iraqi secret service. The marines recognized the pictures as being of the two men in the front seat. This was a situation in which members of the Iraqi military had carried out a hostile act in firing a weapon at the marines, who responded as they were authorized to do. Because they had been trained not to mistreat noncombatants, however, the marines immediately had made a report and the matter was promptly investigated. It was one of those fortunate situations in which we did everything right.

That example shows the results of the increased law of war training. If there is a bright side to My Lai, it is that the military, as it looked at the Vietnam War itself, got the message and said you cannot ever let this happen again in the United States military. My Lai is not what America is like.

Henry Mason

I want to go back to My Lai in a rather narrow sense. I want to use the literature on mass killings and genocide, and see how the My Lai incident fits into that. There are some similarities and there are considerable contrasts. In the genocide of the Jews, more than one fourth of the Jewish victims, more than 1.5 million, were killed in My Lai–like fashion. More than half of the Jews were killed in gas chambers at Treblinka, Sobibor, and Auschwitz, but the first method of killing Jews resembled what happened at My Lai, except in proportion. Quite a bit of literature is available on that part of the genocide of the Jews.

Christopher Browning, in *Ordinary Men: Reserve Police Battalion 101 and the Final Solution in Poland,* goes into great detail about the people in this German unit that committed mass murder. He uses German judicial records, oral history, and psychological and psychiatric studies. The first similarity with My Lai is obvious in Browning's title. These were ordinary men. In fact, the people in Battalion 101 were mostly middle-aged. People who were more ambitious were in the armed forces, the army or Waffen SS, not in the German police pool. These ordinary men came from Hamburg and from average or somewhat below average settings in society.

The main lesson from the realization that these were ordinary men is that this can happen at all times, to all kinds of men, under certain circumstances. We have talked about the new army, the new navy, and the new marines, but even these people under certain circumstances can become the ordinary men who failed at My Lai and in so many much bigger situations in World War II. We must realize that ordinary men can do these kinds of things. The "Calleyization" of My Lai is a great mistake. It wasn't his peculiar character that led to this thing.

The second similarity between My Lai and Battalion 101 is dehumanizing as an ideological precondition to massacre. The notion of "just Jews" had been preached for quite a few years by the time Battalion 101 went into operation, and obviously paralleled the "just gooks" attitude in Vietnam. Most of those killed in the Battalion 101 executions were older men, women, and children. The majority of those killed at My Lai were of the same categories because of dehumanizing, which societies permit and to which American society is not a stranger. In organizing for war, we have to watch ourselves very carefully to prevent the dehumanizing element from becoming the easy way to get good morale. That very important lesson is being carried out, as Hays Parks has noted.

The third similarity is the following. In Lieutenant Calley's outfit quite a few men did not participate in the killing and got away with that without any problem. The same was true for Battalion 101. Browning estimates that close to 20 percent of the battalion's manpower (they were not soldiers in a real sense) did not participate and got away with it. After the war, when judicial proceedings took place, no duress was ever found for those who participated, not even "putative duress," which means that they thought they were under duress. These killings can take place because a majority exerts peer pressure, and that is precisely what I think happened. There is a tolerant majority, tolerant enough to permit some people not to participate, but also tolerant of the acts that take place. The lesson certainly is that we must find ways to get a moral sense into the peer pressure and have it predominate in such situations, if that is possible. One way to do that is through leadership. Even the commandant of Battalion 101, a Major Trapp, publicly declared that he didn't like these tasks, yet he said he had to follow orders. There is potential in these extreme situations for effective dissent.

The fourth similarity is in the judicial process. The postwar Germans brought some of these people to court, and Calley and others were brought to court. It didn't work in either case. In the German case, political pressure—the cold war—was responsible for early releases of the few who were sentenced. There were eight-year sentences given to some of the officers, and five-to-six-year sentences given to some of the lower ranks. None of them served more than three years. One can argue that political pressure was responsible also for Lieutenant Calley's serving hardly any time of his sentence of life in prison at hard labor. Judicial action must be more effective and must remind others of what happened with Battalion 101 and, in our case, My Lai. Statistically, at least, the increased number of military prosecutors today may take care of future situations. What may be more difficult to take care of in a future situation, however, is precisely the political pressures which seem to crop up in these situations.

Finally, another point of similarity is the problem of facing the past. The Germans have a word, *bewältigen,* which means coping with or coming to terms with. It turned out to be extremely difficult in Germany to come to terms with precisely these killings. One could argue that the Germans have coped with Auschwitz and the gas chambers, but some observers think that the Germans have not really been able to cope with the first wave of killings, such as those by Battalion 101. I'm not so sure that our own acceptance of My Lai as a historical fact is complete or that the historical lesson has been fully learned. My Lai may not be considered a lesson worth learning in a real sense. If My Lai is viewed as an aberration, then other problems seem to become more important. While in the German case there is no doubt about the tremendous mass of guilt, we certainly have not as a people agreed upon the guilt in such events as My Lai in the Vietnamese

War. In Germany, as far as Auschwitz is concerned certainly, impressive public opinion efforts were undertaken in the media, in high schools, and in elementary schools. We have not really done that, and perhaps the parallel is not sufficient to warrant it.

The contrasts between My Lai and Battalion 101 are equally obvious. The German killing commandos were not related to the war. They had nothing to do with the military effort. The particular towns where the Jews were killed were first conquered by the army, and then after a while—two or three days—the killing commandos came in. The army was far gone by that time. The people who committed the crimes hadn't experienced the brutality of war. Hamburg hadn't yet been bombed when these killings took place in 1941 and January and February 1942. As Browning says, the men hadn't been brutalized by war. It was the killings that brutalized them. We have the extreme genocidal act in a sense, the one least related to war. Before the killings took place, the Jews themselves had no idea of what was going to occur. Some Jews, not having been informed by the Soviets about anti-Semitism in Germany, even greeted the German army as liberators.

The very opposite is Lieutenant Calley's case. Nothing could have been more war-related than the My Lai scene. It was, of course, a Vietcong tactic to place civilians in the total immersion of the war effort. So, the contrast could not be starker between My Lai and Battalion 101. There was a total noninvolvement in war and a total separation between the military and the ones doing the killing in the German case, and there was a total combination of that in the My Lai incident.

The lesson here, of course, is to avoid the kind of war where this kind of immersion among civilians is possible for the enemy to exploit. That is obviously one of the reasons why we might not want to go into Bosnia or Somalia. In his important book, *Just and Unjust Wars,* Michael Walzer says that in that kind of situation you simply cannot conduct war.

A second contrast relates to what we call authorization in genocide studies. Authorization is crucial, but authorization of the killing is almost always cloaked and in stages. The killing commandos originally were simply called *Einsatzgruppen* or special-task squads, and they were used for all kinds of purposes, including cleaning of streets and jobs like that. How did they suddenly get the task of killing? They didn't get it suddenly. There was a very gradual process in which the authorities looked ahead to see whether all of this could be carried out. The authorization was never clear and was always cloaked and in stages. At first only "bandits" were to be executed. Then there were the political commissars of the Soviet army. Then there were military-age male Jews, and then, finally, all Jewish males, females, and children. It came in stages, yet, within two or three weeks every member of the battalion knew that he was authorized to kill and that he was supposed to do these kinds of killings.

The authorization in the Calley case is at the opposite end of that. Lieutenant Calley perhaps believed that he had the authority to do what he did, but that is by no means certain. In any case the lesson is obvious: Army leadership at all levels must be strong and precise, particularly in these kinds of situations. There is a potential Calley everywhere, and a potential Calley must not be permitted to "Calley-it." There must be very precise command instructions on these most delicate problems. It is on these kinds of problems very often that authority is not very clearly expressed.

A third contrast is routinization. At first Battalion 101 was depressed, angered, embittered, and shaken by this kind of order. Major Trapp at one time thought of resigning. After a while, however, they accepted the duty and carried it out very faithfully. It was the routinization of mass murder that they exhibited in their further proceedings in the next six to seven months of war. There is a threshold where the first fright of the act gradually is accepted by these ordinary men. That did not occur, as far as I can tell, in the case of Calley's platoon and company. They did not do a repeat of My Lai in other villages. Routinization has a very crucial threshold, however, and holocaust genocide studies pay a lot of attention to these thresholds. For example, if a pogrom situation becomes a genocide situation, certain thresholds have been crossed. In the Battalion 101 case, one could clearly see when that threshold was being crossed.

One more difference between My Lai and the German army was in what we call messengers and reversers. At My Lai but also in Battalion 101, there were people who protested. There were people who sent information through channels. Attached to the German army in the east were some five battalions like Battalion 101. Noting what these battalions were doing, a special army team, a major and two lieutenants, wrote up what was actually taking place and sent it up through channels. Nothing happened. There were a few attempts at lower German army level to try to get some kind of accounting of what actually was taking place because no written order had ever established the necessity of the killing. In any case, it didn't get anywhere. In our case obviously it did get somewhere. My Lai was of such a character that the messenger's message did penetrate. Ron Ridenhour's letter, quite a while after the fact, of course, did get to the proper places. Seymour Hersh did penetrate to the places where there were facts that could be publicized. No reverser has ever been as effective as Lieutenant (Warrant Officer at that time) Hugh Thompson. There were German reversers in other situations, but nowhere ever was it possible to use a helicopter to place yourself between troops and an act of obvious war crime. Nowhere else was it possible to get another helicopter to transport potential victims. It was an incredible act, but it was possible in our system. All of these kinds of situations seem to have messengers and potential reversers in them, but they were obviously much more effective after a while in the My Lai situation.

There is one final point of perspective on My Lai. The Netherlands has a dark experience with "police actions" when the Dutch were attempting to get back their colonies in 1946–1947. Only now are they trying to get at some of the incidents, the My Lais, that happened at that time. The official Dutch historian of the World War II period had originally called them "war crimes," but he was persuaded to rename them "excesses." These "excesses," fifty years later, are now being tackled. Dutch observers have praised our speedy and efficient action in the My Lai case. My Lai is our event, but there have been other My Lais that have not been developed as far as our own, however dissatisfied we might be about our own self-examination.

10

THE MYSTERY OF MY LAI

Tim O'Brien

Tim O'Brien was a grunt, an infantryman, during 1969 in Alpha Company, Fifth Battalion, Forty-sixth Infantry Regiment, Americal Division. Pinkville—that is, the area around My Lai—was often his unit's area of operations. He has powerfully recorded his own Vietnam witness in several highly acclaimed works of memoir and fiction, including *Going after Cacciato, If I Die in a Combat Zone,* and *The Things They Carried.* His 1994 novel *In the Lake of the Woods* probes directly into the darkness of the My Lai massacre. Here, he argues forcibly that the individual American officers and enlisted men who participated in the My Lai murders remain today legally accountable and unpunished for their crimes. Why they did what they did, he says, is an inexplicable mystery.

As it was twenty-five years ago, the subject of My Lai is still confusing. It's full of tensions and full of differing opinions and differing interpretations. Some of the bitterness is still there. Some of the ignorance is there. It's as overwhelming now as it was then. The only area of possible consensus is that the massacre actually happened. Twenty-five years ago, there were a lot of people saying that it just didn't happen. As far as I can tell, there hasn't been a lot of other progress.

My Lai is a symbol of genocide or of atrocity. That's fine, but as a fiction writer I thought that in writing *In the Lake of the Woods* I would try to particularize it. I made up a lot, which you have to do, and I invented a lot. Despite all the invention and all the making up, you hope that in a novel there's a gut-turning feeling, a sense of presence or immediacy that's hard to get at through nonfiction, when you have to go by what we know factually. When you're writing about any subject, fiction doesn't depend on what really happened in the world. It depends on what happens in the heart, in the gut, in the spirits of people. I hope that my passages of descriptive writing about My Lai get to the heart and get to the gut of readers through make-believe and through invention.

QUESTION: In *The Things They Carried,* you describe something your narrator, if not you, did to the man who didn't take care of a wound. It seems to be a smaller version of crossing a line that you or the narrator should not have crossed. You say, "I was Nam—the horror, the war" [235].

O'Brien

That's the truth. That's all of us, civilians and soldiers; the gender doesn't matter. In all of us, I think there are seeds of evil, seeds of sin, the potential for it. Everything I've ever written about in my life, whether it's about Vietnam or not, has to do with whether those seeds are going to grow or not. If they do grow, what's going to happen to the human being in which they're growing? In my own life, partly in Vietnam and partly outside of Vietnam, I've done bad things and done them for reasons at the time I thought were right. I wish I hadn't done them.

When you're telling stories about a war or particularly about My Lai, what you're trying to get at ultimately is to reach through the book and grab the reader by the throat and pull him into the novel and say this could happen to you. This could happen to you, Miss Jones in Sioux City, Iowa; and this could happen to you, Clem down in Arkansas; and this could happen to you. We all have a capacity for evil, to commit it, no matter whether you're a Mormon or a Muslim fundamentalist or a Methodist. If the situation is extreme enough, if the heart is under enough pressure, if you need to be loved badly enough, if you've watched enough death, you could be in these very shoes I'm in now. It's not a foreign experience.

QUESTION: Did the peculiar nature of the Vietnam War cause the line at My Lai to be hazy for these guys?

O'Brien

In part, yes. Vietnam was a war that was essentially purposeless and aimless. I mean that in a literal sense. There was nothing to aim at physically, nothing to shoot. Ninety percent of the casualties that we took in my unit, which operated in the My Lai area, were from land mines. How do you kill a land mine? How do you shoot back at it? You can't. It's inanimate. It's already dead. If you have ten or eleven guys die in the course of a month, where the ground itself seems to be killing you, you begin to feel a sense of frustration and a sense of rage that intermix until your blood starts to sizzle. That's probably what happened to Charlie Company that day. Something began to sizzle in their blood. It exploded.

QUESTION: Some people have said that the villagers were mysterious, didn't seem to pick a side, and somehow could avoid the mines, and that on occasion little kids or women would be booby-trapped and used as weapons. Does that in any way explain what happened in My Lai, where the soldiers may have made the villagers into the enemy?

O'Brien

The villagers probably were made psychologically into the enemy, but I never saw any kids carrying hand grenades and stuff like that. It was a big myth that was taught to us in boot camp. It was a bunch of bullshit—women with razor blades in their vaginas and all kinds of absolute bullshit. There were no mitigating circumstances. It was mass murder. If Paul Meadlo or Charles Hutto or Max Hutson or any of those guys were to go up and blow someone away right now—fire a round into his stomach—you would put him in jail. If he did it to twenty-five more people, and if he shot someone's head off and shot him in the balls and decapitated him, you would probably have him in jail. If you're in Georgia, you would put him in the electric chair. Well, what happened to the guys at My Lai? One guy goes to prison for four and a half months. Now, how many other people there admitted on camera to shooting twenty-five people and weren't even prosecuted? What about those of us who went through exactly what Charlie Company went through? I went through exactly what they went through in the same place, and we weren't killing babies.

I experienced the same frustrations, but I didn't cross that line. There is an axiological line, a line between rage and frustration on the one hand and murder on the other. Although I experienced exactly what those people experienced in the same place, we didn't cross the line. The question then becomes why. Why did those people cross the line? Why didn't we cross the line? That's the abiding mystery. That's what is so frustrating and why everyone is so confused. The mystery is why did these guys do it and not the others. That's the mystery of evil that Joseph Conrad writes about in *Heart of Darkness.* No one knows what makes the blood sizzle to the point of pulling that trigger and watching those guts explode. It's a mystery that's going to remain a mystery.

Ron Ridenhour's and Hugh Thompson's heroism is a mystery, too. One wonders if, on another day, Thompson might not have landed. Or if, on another day, the guys in Charlie Company wouldn't have begun pulling those triggers. Maybe it was something in the temperature. Maybe it was that first burst of gunfire, and someone else shot. If that second person hadn't been nearby, the second person wouldn't have shot. All those variables are so mysterious and so beyond us now as to be utterly inexplicable.

I just finished reading a book by Gary Gilmore's brother Michael Gilmore. He grew up in the same family as Gary Gilmore.* Michael Gilmore turned out to be a writer for *Rolling Stone,* although both brothers grew up in the same family and experienced pretty much the same stuff.

What would have happened to Ron Ridenhour if he had been sent to Charlie Company and had been there that day? Those are the things that are utterly inexplicable. There is a certain frustration and a tension because you cannot explain the inexplicable. It makes me go out and want to smoke cigarettes because I've resigned myself to the knowledge that evil is one of these things that is almost like crankcase oil. It seeps into your veins, it's there for awhile, and then it seeps away. If you try to define it, you're trying to do what the disciples did who wrote the Gospels in the Bible. There are certain things in the world that are mysterious. What happened at My Lai

---

*A convicted murderer who was killed by a Utah firing squad in 1977 after refusing all efforts to delay the execution.

that day in the souls of those people is a mystery, just as it was a mystery at Lidice [Czechoslovakia, 1942], at Little Big Horn, and in Bosnia.

Calley was only one of many people who committed murder that day, but he wasn't a scapegoat. He should be in jail for the rest of his life. How can he be a scapegoat if he confessed to shooting women and kids and babies and old men? How can he be a scapegoat, since he did it? Scapegoats don't do anything. He is literally not a scapegoat. Language has to mean something. It's like calling you a murderer. You say you didn't murder anybody, and I say I didn't mean you actually murdered anybody. Words have to mean something. Scapegoat means someone who didn't do anything but who is being falsely accused of doing it. I disagree with those who try to somehow build up a wall between Calley, Calley's acts, and Calley's murders on the one hand, and those people above and beneath him on the other. He was guilty of murder; he ought to be in jail, but so should a lot of other people.

Some people say Calley was an incompetent officer, but incompetence is no excuse, nor is IQ. Nothing is an excuse for murder. That was murder. It seems to me commonsensical. A man pulled the trigger on a gun. He admitted doing it and that he killed babies and shot them in the head. He is guilty of murder. That's not to say that other people shouldn't be prosecuted, too. They should have been. Hutson, Hutto, Meadlo, Gary Roschevitz, Floyd Wright, Varnado Simpson—those people should be in jail. They should be in jail. Why aren't they?

The question about people up the line has bugged me. There are two issues. One issue has to do with the cover-up. That's one kind of crime. Another crime is murder. Both are crimes, but there is a tendency for some strange reason to want to turn attention to Koster and to Henderson and to Barker—the guys in the helicopters in this little chain of command. I'm not here to pronounce judgment on anyone whose acts I'm not aware of, but I am here to pronounce judgment on those who I know confessed to murder. We're talking about confessed murderers.

QUESTION: Was it your experience that the war was compartmentalized and run by lieutenants?

O'Brien

I'm talking about the guys on the ground who were pulling triggers. PFCs, sergeants, and spec. fours were killing people. Calley wasn't always around these guys. They were doing it on their own in different places.

He wasn't directing a murder. There were also murders happening off in the adjacent hamlet. These were people like me, PFCs and spec. fours committing murder. Calley, the lieutenant, was a murderer, but so were the other people. They should be in jail. I don't see how one can feel anything else but that.

QUESTION: If Hugh Thompson could see what was going on there, those guys in higher authority could see it from their helicopters, too.

O'Brien

I'm not saying they aren't culpable. They are culpable of not stopping it. They are culpable of covering up. They are culpable of various felonies. They should be tracked down and prosecuted like any war criminal, but that doesn't mitigate or take away from the crimes being committed on the ground by the people pulling the triggers. They are all guilty, but the people on the ground are guilty of shooting babies in the face. Henderson is guilty of allowing it to happen. If he in fact knew about it and didn't stop it, he is guilty of dereliction of duty, I suppose, and also of moral crime. There are all kinds of crimes having to do with covering it up, which are felonies too, but to me the most important issue has finally got to be what's being covered up. A bunch of people committed murder, 504 murders, on a terrible March Saturday morning in 1968. We know who they are. They've confessed, many of them. The evidence is overwhelming, and not a damn thing happened to most of them.

QUESTION: You say it's a mystery, but isn't part of the answer politics?

O'Brien

I don't give a shit what the justification is. I'm sure that part of it is politics, but who cares? They committed murder. If I were a prosecutor, I'd try to find some way to bring these people to account for murder. Adolph Eichmann was tracked down years and years later and sentenced to death.

QUESTION: Is there any way for America to begin to heal these wounds?

O'Brien

I don't think that the wounds should be healed. We live in this weird culture where we think everything can be helped and healed, even if somebody goes out and shoots someone. I think that we've healed the wounds too well, if anything. The country has obliterated the horror that was Vietnam. To the Vietnamese people who lost whole families or lost legs and arms, we've healed it too damn well. We've obliterated it from the national consciousness, just as we obliterated what happened to the American Indians. My Lai now is just a footnote in a history of a war that is also a kind of footnote. A thousand years from now, Vietnam will be like the Battle of Hastings or Thermopylae, and My Lai will be a word that will cause people to scratch their heads. Maybe it will be forgotten entirely. My job as a writer is to create stories that can last, if they are well told. Homer gave us what we have of the Trojan Wars, and Stephen Crane gave us a lot of what we have of the Civil War. Stories are a way to somehow keep memory alive, to keep picking at the scab.

QUESTION: Was the body count a contributing factor in all of this, as a problem of the war and at My Lai?

O'Brien

Bodies are counted when they are shot, and so you call in three dead VC. That does nothing to explain what happened at My Lai that day. It's absolute nonsense. Seven-thirty in the morning a company of soldiers arrived in this village and for four hours systematically killed 504 people. Three weapons, I believe, were found off in the outlying areas. There was no enemy incoming fire; they just killed civilians. They put them in a pile and shot them to death. What has body count got to do with that? Nothing. It doesn't motivate a soldier on the ground. It had nothing to do with it.

QUESTION: But the argument goes that a villager body equals a VC body.

O'Brien

I know that's how the argument goes. I'm saying the argument is untrue. They shot innocent people. It's a mystery. That's why you're asking me the questions. Read Michael Bilton and Kevin Sim, *Four Hours in My Lai*, and read the testimony of some of the guys who actually did it. I'm thinking of Fred Widmer. He's like me, and he was there. "I don't know what happened. I can't explain it. I look back twenty-some years. How could I have done this? That wasn't me." These are his words, more or less. It's a mystery to him. In the same way it's a mystery to a lot of people when they leave a

cocktail party after having somehow said something very stupid and embarrassing. They jerk awake in the middle of the night, saying, "How could I
have done such a stupid, silly thing?" Our behaviors are not always planned,
and they are not always explicable, even to us. Evil is a mysterious thing.
It's a mystery even to this day. If I could get into Calley's skin or the skin of
Paul Meadlo or the skin of Varnado Simpson, I think I would be saying:
"How could I have done it? What happened to me that day?" I think the
answer would be, "I don't know. I don't know. I don't know."

11

. . . .

HEALING THE WOUNDS

**Stephen E. Ambrose, Walter E. Boomer,
William G. Eckhardt, Kiem Do, John McAuliff,
Tim O'Brien, Hays Parks, Ron Ridenhour,
Jonathan Shay, Harry G. Summers, Jr.,
Tiana (Thi Thanh Nga), Kathleen Turner,
Marilyn B. Young**

Drawing upon the witness of others and on their own varying experiences, several participants reflect on the nature of the wound represented by My Lai and Vietnam, on how and to what extent these wounds can be healed, and to what extent healing is even desirable. Many of the voices in this chapter have been heard elsewhere in this volume, but added here are Marilyn Young, John McAuliff, Kiem Do, and Tiana (Thi Thanh Nga). A historian, Young is the author of *The Vietnam Wars,* a critical examination of the objectives and methods of the American war in Vietnam. McAuliff was an antiwar activist during the war who has long championed reconciliation between the people of the United States and Indochina. Kiem Do is a veteran of the South Vietnamese armed forces. The daughter of a South Vietnamese official, Tiana is an actress and film maker who has offered her own approach to healing through her film *From Hollywood to Hanoi.*

Although the predominant view here is that My Lai was an exceptional event, certainly in the magnitude of the lethal violence against civilians if not in terms of the wanton individual assaults, there is a strongly dissenting opinion that My Lai was all too characteristic of the American conduct of the war. No one denies that some American atrocities did occur in Vietnam, and all condemn the notion of body count. The counting of Vietnamese bodies made killing—not territory or prisoners or defectors or political following—the measure of military success. If there had been no war, there would have been no killing of civilians by Americans. This truism leads some to conclude that the war itself is the wound. It is impossible to erase the damage done to the Vietnamese who suffered and died. How do Americans individually and collectively atone for that destruction? Not all Vietnamese are innocent. Today some who fought for Hanoi during the war question the judgment of their leaders who stubbornly demanded that the Vietnamese people endure the enormous costs that they did. On both sides, young men and women died because of old men's decisions.

Regardless of whether My Lai was aberration or operation, it happened. Regardless of what choices Vietnamese leaders made, Americans must struggle with their own psychological and moral demons. There are treatments for PTSD, but are there treatments for guilt? The old adage says that justice delayed is justice denied, and in practical terms any further legal accountability for the murders at My Lai is probably gone. Not gone, however, is the possibility that something similar could happen again or that it could be covered up. The U.S. military made explicit changes in its training procedures and leadership expectations as a result of My Lai. In America's democratic tradition, the military remains only a reflection of the larger society. The public must know that with war comes atrocity-producing situations. If war cannot be avoided, then vigilance and commitment must remain steadfast throughout the entire society to ensure responsible leadership—leadership that will maintain discipline in the face of violence and preserve justice under the stress of war.

Kathleen Turner

We have learned from the experiences of members of the military, the media, and the literary community. We have benefited from experts in history, psychology, communication, sociology, and political science. We have accounts of atrocities and bravery, of courage and skullduggery, and contained therein are eloquent statements and electric exchanges. The depth

and breadth and remarkable freshness of the wounds is striking, even decades later. What have we learned? Are we healing the wounds or picking
the scabs?

Jonathan Shay

There are a whole lot of folks on all sides of each issue saying pretty clearly,
either out loud or inside themselves, that he is too blockheaded, too liberal,
too conservative, too radical, too reactionary, or too whatever for me to even
bother to talk to. I hope we can recover the sense that we're all in this together. I hope people will simply remember that the essence of democracy
is safe struggle, with an equal emphasis on safe and struggle. Democracy is
struggle. Where we really get into danger is when we cease to struggle with
each other.

Marilyn Young

It's also important to recognize that the divisions are real. The divisions
need to be faced and thought about, and any other kind of healing is just a
sealing over and a making things go away. The divisions were real, and they
remain real. To stay divided at the end is okay, rather than to accept the
kind of false healing that occurs and that has occurred in the United States.
In order to heal the wounds of the Civil War, "Blue and Gray" (that was
the phrase) marched together against the Spanish in 1898. That was a rotten way of healing. The Gulf War was a rotten way of healing.

What was the wound? The wound was the Vietnam War itself, the reasons it was fought, the way it was fought, and the way no senior political
leader has ever confronted that even for a nanosecond. To the leaders, it
was either Ronald Reagan's noble crusade or Jimmy Carter's quite incredible arithmetic that the damage was mutual—I don't know what scale he
uses. It's the kind of thing that is not confronted and not faced.

Harry Summers

After twenty-five years we at least can hold a civil dialogue. It's not that
we're going to change our views and suddenly become converts to one side
or the other, but we can talk about it. I was very struck by Henry Mason's
comments about the German example, and especially the comment that
these were ordinary people in Battalion 101. The American soldiers at My
Lai were ordinary people. In its first reaction, the army thought Charlie
Company was a bunch of thugs and that for some strange reason all of these

misfits had come together in one unit. We found to our horror that that wasn't true. If anything, they were above average, and that really shook the institution. The only variable that could be found was leadership, and, as Dr. Mason notes, that requirement remains constant. As General Boomer emphasized, somebody has got to say: "No. This just is not done and will not be tolerated in this unit." There was a failure to do that on the part of Medina, on the part of Calley, and on the part of the sergeants as well. I spent ten years as an enlisted man, and the noncommissioned officer has a grave responsibility here. He failed just as well. Fortunately, we had people like Hugh Thompson and Ron Ridenhour who knew the right thing to do and who, to their credit, wouldn't shut up.

Walter Boomer

We can never be satisfied with what we've done in terms of preventing other My Lais. I hope those of us on the military side didn't leave the impression that we think that everything now is fine. It's not a situation where we have a few classes in place, and we talk about this a little bit, and therefore My Lais in the future are going to be prevented. It's something that we need to keep in front of ourselves. It's something that we need to continue to talk about.

Ron Ridenhour

I had no idea and was gratified to learn that there has been so much emphasis in military teaching on My Lai. I hope that training somehow reverberates through into people's conduct on the battlefield. I'm sure that it will in some instances, hopefully in most, and, even more hopefully, in all. I'm also reminded, however, that some people have witnessed the same sort of phenomena in police work. The guys go through the police academy, but as soon as they hit the street, the officer in the car who is breaking them in says: "Okay, you've been through the academy. Now you're on the street. Forget the book. I'm going to teach you how it really works." I hope that isn't happening, and I'm sure that efforts are being made to see that it doesn't.

I was struck by Bill Eckhardt's eloquent explication of his experience and his clear outrage when he learned about My Lai. I was reminded that the vast majority of people who were in the Army at the time, especially in the officer corps, understood that and felt the same way. I am troubled, however, about the fact that we really had two policies in Vietnam much of the time. There was the front-channel policy, or regular army policy, and the back-channel policy. The back-channel policy was what the spooks [covert agents] were pursuing, all the intelligence community stuff, the Phoenix Program [to identify and eliminate enemy political cadres], and all of the special-operations-group operations. In many instances, these went far across the line. The Phoenix Program, especially, was a classic example of what went beyond the pale. Those, too, were policies of the American government, and the U.S. Army and the military participated in them to some extent.

The main lesson that the American government learned in Vietnam was that Vietnamization in a certain way worked, and it became the policy that our military and government pursued for the next decade at least, certainly well into the Reagan administration. They learned that, as long as we had Americans pulling the triggers on people of color in foreign lands, the public might very well be outraged about that. If we changed that policy and had Asian and Latin American boys pulling the triggers on Asian and Latin American people, however, the public and the press would be less concerned. Thus the policy of counterinsurgency could continue to be and did continue to be the policy pursued, especially in our client states in South America and Central America. To what extent is law-of-war training provided to the officers and the enlisted men from South America and Central America, who come up to the School of the Americas and then go back to their countries and employ the same old tired policies in their own countries against their own people?

Hays Parks

We bring in foreign military officers to the School of the Americas to expose them to democracy. In the amount of time that they're here, we present to them American values. Some will take more from that than others. We can't make a bad person into a good person in the amount of time we have them. We also use the United States military as military ambassadors in a number of countries. In fact, the Marine Corps was referred to during the Vietnam War as "ambassadors in green." At this time, we're involved in human rights training in any number of nations, not only in Latin America but in the former Soviet Union. We've had teams go to the Ukraine, Moldova, and just about every country in the former Soviet Union. They are marine officers, naval officers, and army officers. That's the good side of this. It's a start, and the military has been asked to do this.

At the same time, anybody who thinks a one-hour or a one-week lecture will turn around cultures is fooling themselves. About three years ago the

United States military sent into Rwanda two mobile training teams right behind two ICRC teams. They had both sides sit down in the same classroom, and they taught them democratic principles and gave them human rights training. The participants all said it was great stuff, and you know what happened right after that. We're making an effort with the resources given us, but I don't think that we can ever presume that our effort alone is going to fix the problem completely. It needs a lot more than that.

William Eckhardt

It was my privilege to lead a U.S. military delegation to Romania. The basic essence of that was to listen and to give some encouragement and to try to help them with demilitarizing their incredibly militaristic regime. It was my privilege on another occasion to talk to the ministers of defense of the former Warsaw Pact countries or their representatives for an hour on the role of the military in a democracy. We're engaged in democracy, but it's slow work.

A hero of mine is Elihu Root, a lawyer who as secretary of war founded the Army War College and as secretary of state won the Nobel Peace Prize. Root had a vision that you try to prevent the unleashing of the hounds of hell—war—but that sometimes that can't be done. For thousands of years we haven't been able to do that, so what one must do as the alternative is to study war very carefully for two very valid reasons: first, to prevent war, and second, if one must fight, to expend the least amount of lives and treasure possible. We desperately need an educated populace who can vote intelligently. War is a painful topic. You cannot have any discussion on national security without dealing with your past as well as the present and the future. The more that our citizens realize their responsibilities, the better they can exercise those in a democracy, and the better off we all are.

John McAuliff

The military has learned far more and dealt far more comprehensively with the My Lai experience than has civilian society. There are memories that all of us repress from that whole period. Hearing the dramatic eloquence of Ron and Hugh and learning how the army courts and Bill Eckhardt sought to deal with My Lai have inspired me and made me feel that something has to happen in American society that hasn't happened yet. Maybe we need to get Steven Spielberg to do Ron and Hugh's story. Somehow the kind of perceptions that are in this kind of a discussion have to enter into the larger popular culture. It was the larger popular culture that refused to deal with what had happened at My Lai in terms of holding anyone responsible for it. It's easy to say that it was just Richard Nixon, but it wasn't just Nixon. I remember how relieved everyone was at the time that they didn't have to come to terms with the problems that had been revealed.

Shay

We've seen some evidence that there has been culture change in the military that hasn't penetrated to the vast numbers of people who consider themselves supporters of the military. The average person will say, "Well, of course you have to dehumanize the enemy." That's their common sense of it, but the serious military people are questioning whether it's safe for the soldier to do that, and whether respect for the enemy's military capacities isn't the better key to the soldier's surviving and effectively fighting. You find the average person saying, "Well, of course there are no rules of war. You can't fight a war by Hoyle." Yet within the military, we see evidence in many quarters of a culture change that says if we shed our commitment to the fundamental ethic of the soldier, then we're doing ourselves terrible damage as an institution and as a nation and sowing the seeds of military defeat. There has been significant culture change, and I think the military has to get the civilian population to hear that.

Young

The question is, who is the enemy and what is the war? It's not an abstract question. Vietnam was in part fought the way it was fought because of the kind of war it was. It became a war against a very large part of the population north and south. Free-fire zones were daily My Lais. The questions concern the nature of the war, who the enemy is, why you are fighting, and the culture of the military. I'm impressed by what I've heard from the military people. There is bravery and courage even in a dishonorable war. The question is, how do you get this country not to fight dishonorable wars? That's not the military's responsibility, since the military is under civilian control. It's a question of what the country's goals are and, given that the workings of this democracy are imperfect, where and when and how the civilian population as a whole gets to choose who it thinks its enemy is.

Summers

The slide toward My Lai can be seen in the terror-bombing of World War II. In 1936 the Army Command Staff College published a book on strategy that said that any civilized nation that bombs civilian populations would be totally beyond the pale. As Stephen Ambrose has pointed out, it wasn't too many years later that we were running fire-bomb raids on Dresden and Tokyo. The slide toward involving the civilian population in war certainly had some terrible precedents.

One of the reasons the military has been so successful in dealing not only with My Lai but with other things is that, in the late 1960s and early 1970s, we stared into the abyss. The military was in such bad shape in such areas as racial relations, discipline, and drug problems that the security of the United States was in great peril. I don't think that anybody outside the military realizes how bad it was. The feeling in the services was that we had to do something and do something drastic. We had to get back to fundamentals, to the basics of the military profession. We did it because we were scared. Thank God we did it successfully. We owe a debt to the leaders in a time of disintegration, to General William DePuy and the rest of them, who stood up for principle and said we've got to put the military back in touch with fundamental considerations and did. That's an untold story that outside of the ranks of the military is not known.

Parks

We do have a job to do within the military. Law-of-war training is something that is constant. We consider it part of leadership, and we consider it part of being a professional military. If I speak anywhere, I use a picture from My Lai, so that we never forget that this is the kind of conduct we will not tolerate and that it is not consistent with being in a professional military organization.

There is a considerable ignorance of warfare and the law of war among our elected leaders, members of Congress, and the general public. If you go back twenty-five years to the time that Lieutenant Calley was charged, the American Legion was collecting money for him and peddling a forty-five-RPM record played to the tune of "The Battle Hymn of the Republic." Part of it went: "My name is Rusty Calley; I'm a hero of the land." There is a general ignorance within the American public. They look at war as a bunch of stuff where we just go out and kill everybody and let God sort them out. That's not the view of the military. It's not the role of the United States military, however, to educate the people of the United States. In fact, there are some rather specific federal restrictions on our doing that, probably for very good reasons, some would say. There's a sort of self-policing that goes on within the military, but at the same time, we also have to appreciate that when you send men and women to battle it's not a pleasant experience. You can't make war a nice event. So you have to balance the two of those, but there is a major educational process that needs to go on within this nation.

Tim O'Brien

Perhaps something can be said, too, about the 504 Vietnamese who died that day in March 1968, and about the suffering of the Vietnamese. I served as a foot soldier in the My Lai area about a year after the massacre occurred, and my unit helped pull security for the village when the investigation began. We lost man after man in that area through land mines or sniper fire, but the dead civilians, through napalming and through H&I [harrasment and interdiction] fire and through artillery rounds coming down, far outnumbered our casualties. It ought to be said, too, that out among us now in this nation there are some fifty human beings who took part in the massacre that day who are still driving trucks and selling insurance and peddling jewelry and who didn't go to jail. They suffered in no way whatsoever, except personal, psychological suffering. My unit in Vietnam experienced precisely what Charlie Company experienced—the frustration of land mines, snipers, and not finding the enemy—but we never crossed the axiological line between rage and homicide. They crossed it. It was murder. There was no punishment. Something ought to be done about it.

Summers

At that time, my feeling as an infantryman was that Calley and Medina ought to have been hung and then drawn and quartered and the remains put at the gates at Fort Benning to remind all who enter of the consequences. The reaction against that view from both left and right was overwhelming. The right, as was mentioned about the American Legion raising funds, said, "Well, poor old Rusty Calley is just a victim of the antiwar movement." The antiwar movement's position was, "Well, everybody's doing it, so why blame Calley?" The bastard fell through the cracks, and that should never have happened. I'm sure that most military people would agree that they ought to have suffered a most draconian punishment as a reminder, and a constant reminder, that this is absolutely beyond the pale.

I talked with Admiral Thomas Moorer, who was chairman of the Joint Chiefs of Staff and who released Calley as he was directed to do by President Nixon. He is a very distinguished naval officer and I have great respect for him, but he said, "Well, of course, Calley was faced with these babies, children throwing hand grenades and this, that, and the other." I'm reminded of the stories that go around about people who go to Mexico, buy a chihuahua, come back, and find out that they bought a rat. It may have never happened, but it's part of the mythology of what happened. Part of the mythology of Vietnam is the little children with hand grenades. It may have happened, but I never heard of it, and nobody I knew ever heard of it. Still, it's one of the persistent myths of the war, and it was even repeated as a defense for My Lai by one of the participants.

Kiem Do

I'm not condoning that type of barbaric massacre, but we need more fairness in our discussion. You have to understand the special aspect of the war. We need to develop that more and present it to the public. I've seen people accusing the American GI, and I'll tell you one thing. In spite of those massacres, the American GI is still the best that I have ever encountered. I'm talking about the Chinese, the French, and the Japanese. I have no respect for them.

In the Vietnam War context, you were dealing with an enemy who didn't care about body count. Ho Chi Minh said, "You can kill one hundred of my men; I don't care. I only need to kill one guy of yours, and we will still win the war." Body count didn't mean a thing for them. Colonel Summers said he hadn't seen any nine-year-olds or thirteen-year-olds participating in the war. I can give you proof—myself. I was recruited by the Vietminh when I was twelve years old. I spent my time pulling the string of the mine to blow up the railroad station. I've seen kids used many times in the Vietnam War. During the Tet Offensive, many of the enemy that we killed in front of our headquarters were so young that they weren't much taller than their rifles were long.

Some people claim that you have to dehumanize yourself in order to survive in war, but I think the war dehumanizes you whether you know it or not. At that time when I saw the kids lying grotesquely across the street from our headquarters, I didn't feel anything. I didn't feel any emotion, and I was born and raised in a conservative family heavily influenced by Confucianism. That night I told my wife there was something wrong with me. The war had desensitized me, and I had dehumanized my enemy. That was the type of war we were in, and we have to find a way to deal with that different type of war. War is atrocity. War is killing. If you have to resort to war as a last resort, you have to win the war. You can't just go halfway. In order to win the war, you have to know what your enemy will do to win the war, and you have to counter it.

Eckhardt

You behave professionally on the battlefield, and if you don't, you lose wars—lesson learned from My Lai. What do we do in the future and how do we avoid those sorts of things? You avoid it in a democracy with accountability. If you look at the Gulf War, you'll notice a very unique thing. You'll notice that when there were allegations of misconduct, there was placement of the facts very quickly in the public arena, so that people could make decisions. About three or four days after an allegation, you had facts or a response so that people could be held accountable. That's the only way I know how to respond to those sorts of things.

Boomer

I don't buy the theory that there were a lot of My Lais. My Lai was indeed an aberration. Four hundred people killed, five hundred—we're not really sure of the number. I'm relatively certain that it didn't happen in any other place during the decade that we fought there. There were atrocities. Colonel Parks, who was a Marine Corps lawyer, has described the cases that we tried. Over a decade, with three million Americans there fighting a very difficult war, we did have atrocities, but My Lai was an aberration. My Lai was an absolute failure of leadership from the brigade commander to the platoon commander. When you have that kind of failure of leadership in that sort of situation, the My Lais spring up.

Stephen Ambrose

Anybody who has studied war for a long time isn't going to be surprised by what happened at My Lai. In regard to the nature of this particular war and to the enemy being willing to go to any length, war is always awful, unspeakable. It has gotten a lot worse in the twentieth century because technology has made the killing so much worse. The range at which a man can do harm has become so much greater in the twentieth century. The rise of totalitarian ideologies has played a very significant role in this, whether that ideology is Japanese militarism, Nazism, or communism.

What happened at My Lai primarily was a failure of leadership. It was a failure of leadership starting at the very top with the president of the United States. We haven't had enough talk about the presidents of the United States during the Vietnam War. It was a failure of leadership on the part of the Joint Chiefs. It was a failure of leadership on Westy's part, and on down—corps, division, battalion, down to platoon level. There were several failures of leadership.

What we are most in need of in the United States today is good leadership. It distresses me greatly that my own profession, the historical profession, as a part of what is happening with the society as a whole, has turned against leadership. It has become scornful of leadership, not just critical but scornful of leadership. Bob Dillon's song "Don't Follow Leaders" came out about the time of My Lai. If you don't follow leaders, you're going to be in big trouble. You have to have good leaders, however, and you aren't going to get good leaders if you have a society that discourages the study of leadership. We need to recognize the importance of leadership and how important it is to train people to be leaders. We can't do it if we're constantly denigrating leaders in the way we teach our history and in our general societal approach to the past.

Young

I thought one of the problems with totalitarian places is that they *have* leaders, who are in fact their problem. Surely it depends on where leaders are going. Leadership is an abstract quality. It doesn't mean anything. We've had lots of leadership. It's just rotten a very good deal of the time. Somebody said that if Harvard boys had been leading the troops, My Lais would not have happened. This notion was contradicted by the presence of Hugh Thompson. Hugh Thompson didn't go to Harvard; Jack Kennedy did. So I don't think that a Harvard education really protects us very much.

Military people tell me that My Lai is explicitly rejected, and that's a good thing that I do want to recognize. I would like more, but I surely want to recognize that. I don't think the nation *should* heal, not before it has dealt with what has happened in Central America, where, in fact, one sees the damage done from a failure to change more deeply than even an explicit rejection of My Lai entails.

As for Ho Chi Minh's statement that you will kill ten of our men for every one of yours that we kill, we must remember Winston Churchill's statement that "we'll fight them on the beaches; we'll fight them everywhere." What was that about, other than you keep killing us and we're going to keep killing you back? This is the standard statement of patriotism. It's not a statement of a wicked, provocative leader who says, "Ah, those Americans, they're really good people; I'm going to provoke them into being very bad to me." That has been stated as the strategy of the other side. I don't believe it for a minute, not for a minute.

Shay

I have for my whole life loathed the social institution of war. Since working with combat veterans for the last several years, I've come to be able to embrace within myself the paradox of continuing to hate the institution of war as I always did but to respect the soldier. My worry is that there is a missed opportunity, or a potentially missed opportunity, to come together over these issues. The responsibility has to be squarely in the hands of the civilian leadership, and this is what the military wants. I just want to point out that the humanity of the soldier is something to be treasured. It's my experience from working with combat veterans that it is indeed the very humanity of the soldier that has been so terribly wounded by participation in operational doctrines such as search and destroy, which they had no possibility of opposing except by making martyrs of themselves. I'm talking about grunts now; I have never had an officer as a patient.

Tiana

Americans are loved in Vietnam. Anyone who has been back to Vietnam in the last ten to fifteen years knows that the Vietnamese respect and love the Americans—in the north, the central, and the south. Not all, I'm not here to speak for every single Vietnamese. Americans are loved for the example of the humanitarian efforts of the American Vietnam vets who have been going back to Vietnam. I know a vet who recently went back, Tim O'Brien. The Vietnamese at Son My, at the My Lai site, told me that this American came back, that he really cared, and that he said, "My God, we should have bombed these people with love." We should bomb these people with love. What can we give them? We can give them books because they're learning English. We can give them chalk for their chalkboards and antibiotics for their children who are dying from simple lack of antibiotics.

McAuliff

One of the elements that we have to deal with is that there were people in My Lai and there still are people in My Lai. We're not just talking about a moral drama or a question of who we are as a people, but we're talking about a population and a country that, after April 30, 1975, continued to exist. It screwed up on its own, but it also faced tremendous problems caused by the kind of war that we fought. I would submit that our inability to deal fully as a civilian population with My Lai has not been so different from our inability as a country to deal with real normalization with Vietnam, whether that is diplomatic, political, economic, or cultural. American actions have had consequences, and we need to feel responsibility for the consequences.

AFTERWORD

· · · · · · · · · · · · · · · ·

Twenty-five Years After

Randy J. Fertel

As the fellow who, in a not entirely sane moment, conceived of organizing a conference, entitled "My Lai Twenty-five Years After: Facing the
Darkness and Healing the Wounds," to commemorate the twenty-fifth anniversary of the disclosure of the My Lai massacre, I have been asked to write
a few words about why we gathered, three hundred strong from all over
America, on the Tulane University campus on a balmy weekend in December 1994. First, however, I must explain—as I did then—that the purpose
of the conference was not to train a searchlight on the men who crossed a
line in a village at My Lai, Quang Ngai Province, Vietnam. We came together, not to point fingers, nor to accuse men of doing something we cannot imagine ourselves doing, but rather to try to understand what happened
to ordinary Americans and ordinary Vietnamese on March 16, 1968, and
to seek to grasp something of the significance of those events.

Hence we gathered not on the twenty-fifth anniversary of the massacre
itself but on the anniversary of its disclosure. This gave us occasion not merely

to consider the wrongs done that day but to recognize the heroism and brav-ery of those who brought those wrongs to light: Hugh Thompson, who landed his helicopter and tried to stop the killing, and then lodged the first official complaint; Ron Ridenhour, who wrote the letter to Congress that forced the government to reopen the case; Seymour Hersh, who broke the story and went on to write two books, one on the My Lai massacre and another on the smaller but no less dastardly massacre in My Khe, perpe-trated on that same day not four miles away; William Eckhardt, whose Sisyphean task as chief counsel for the government was to bring the perpe-trators to trial. We gathered to hear their witness twenty-five years after the fact, and the witness of Vietnam veterans (American and Vietnamese) and high-ranking military personnel, experts in the law of land warfare, poets and fiction writers, photographers, film-makers, and scholars in history, lit-erature, sociology, political science, and psychiatry.

Our announced goal, suggested by the conference title, was *healing:* fac-ing the darkness of the My Lai massacre to heal the wounds inflicted on the American conscience by that event and by the war of which it was a part. This goal was almost immediately challenged. Tim O'Brien and Wayne Karlin, two brilliant fiction writers, were adamant in their view, shared by many, that to heal meant to forget, and that the atrocity in My Lai must never be forgotten. Indeed, as Harvard psychologist Judith Lewis Herman points out, "the ordinary response to atrocities is to banish them from con-sciousness." She continues, however:

> Atrocities . . . refuse to be buried. Equally as powerful as the desire to deny atrocities is the conviction that denial does not work. Folk wisdom is filled with ghosts who refuse to rest in their graves until their stories are told. Murder will out. Remembering and telling the truth about ter-rible events are prerequisites both for the restoration of the social order and for the healing of individual victims.[1]

Thus healing demands in fact not forgetting but remembering. Robert Jay Lifton, who gave the conference's first plenary address, was instrumental in developing the rap sessions in the early 1970s that were among the first set-tings where Vietnam Veterans were able to tell their stories and out of which the post-traumatic stress disorder diagnosis was developed.[2] They told their stories that weekend and we did our best to hear what they said.

In truth, we in America have never truly listened to what Vietnam veterans experienced in Vietnam. We did not listen when they returned to the World, as they called it. We had no idea of what it meant to return from the jungle to San Francisco in the space of twenty-four hours, or what it meant to be spat on and called baby-killers. We did not listen to them when Hollywood portrayed them as crazed and drugged and ready to kill at a moment's notice or no notice at all. And we do not listen to them today, when we argue ideologically about whether we should have fought the war or how we should have fought the war.

One of the lessons of the conference was that, if we are to hear the veterans clearly, we must understand that the war itself—irrespective of its causes and regardless of its justice or injustice—was, as Lifton argues, an atrocity-producing situation. Given the ambiguity of the enemy, our official commitment to measuring success by body count, and a variety of other conditions, the very nature of the war invited men to cross lines that nothing in their upbringing, and no one in their churches and families and schools, had prepared them to understand. Many carry the wounds of their crossing still.

What kept us then and keeps us now from listening? Perhaps the most formidable obstacle to true listening is ideology. The degree of ideological polarization in America has scarcely decreased since the 1960s, and indeed may be greater now, in the age of Rush Limbaugh, than it was then. Limbaugh, who argues that we are in the midst of a cultural revolution, is wrong only in asserting that it began with Reagan; it began with Vietnam.

Anyone who lived through the 1960s remembers the absolute qualities of that decade's polarities. For those born later, a personal story might help convey them. In August 1969, my father and I—nineteen years old—drove through the jungles of the Yucatan peninsula while my brother, Jerry, just a year older, prepared himself in boot camp for the jungles of Vietnam. All my father wanted to know was, "If called, will you serve?" I temporized as long as I could, but finally I told him I would not. That was when my father stopped the car and tried to put me out into the Yucatecan jungle.

The point of the story is not my relationship with my dad, but rather that in the midst of our fight we were no longer talking about my brother and the dire experience he was about to face. All we were talking about, all we were expressing, were our ideologies. We did not bother—nor could we then have found the skill or the sangfroid—to examine the premises of those ideologies. And yet only by such examination can we hope ever to hear one another, can we hope ever to empathize with another's point of view. It is only by such examination that we can hope ever to find some middle ground.

Real listening, I believe, took place that December weekend at Tulane, and I know that for many it was a powerful emotional experience. The strength of the conference lay in its diversity and the many disciplines represented, and in its balance. Never before, conferees told me again and again, had they attended a conference where both sides of the ongoing debate about the Vietnam War were present. Such balance speaks to the humanities' central commitment to the proposition that every argument must have more than one side, and that truth can best be found not through the adoption of an ideology but through the consideration of opposing points of view. Truth, we believe, lies in the middle. At the heart of the liberal arts enterprise is the development of empathy, the experience of imagining another's position. Wherever we stand, the Vietnam War invites such an enterprise, challenging us to consider both poles of the hawk–dove debate, as well as the point of view of our former enemy.

If empathy was not invariably the rule during the conference, and if discussion often grew heated, still there was listening. If the conference's polarities were no less sharp than those of the time we came to discuss, still there was consensus on one point, one key question that dogged the consciousness, and conscience, of every participant: Was the My Lai massacre an aberration or was it somehow representative of how the United States fought the Vietnam War?

For the military professionals at the conference, certainly, the My Lai massacre was an aberration, the result of a leadership problem that was due, among other things, to President Johnson's decision not to call up the reserves. This point of view was articulated by General Walt Boomer (USMC ret.), Colonel Hays Parks (USMC ret.), Colonel Harry Summers (USA ret.), and Colonel William Eckhardt (USA ret.), chief prosecutor of the My Lai cases in 1970–1971. Colonel Summers, veteran of Korea and Vietnam, had this to say:

> When word of My Lai first broke, I thought it was an antiwar propaganda scheme. . . . [At first] the Army investigators thought that this was, by happenstance, a bunch of losers, that there were a bunch of thugs in this company who had come together by accident of assignment. They started looking into that, however, and found out that the company was above average. It had more high school graduates, more people who had at-

tended college, and more college graduates than an average rifle company. So that did not wash. The only variable they could find was leadership, and it comes down to that.

Colonel Parks concurred:

> Lieutenant Calley did not deserve to be in the United States military, much less to be an officer in the United States military. . . . When you had a leadership breakdown at the brigade, task force, company, and platoon level, My Lai occurred. Had there been any strength in leadership at any one of those levels in expressing the intolerance [of breaches of the law of land warfare] that certainly was my experience in Vietnam, My Lai would not have occurred.[3]

The opposite view, that Vietnam was an "atrocity-producing situation" and that the My Lai massacre was representative, was articulated by Robert Jay Lifton, the eminent psychiatrist, by Seymour Hersh and David Halberstam, both Pulitzer Prize winners, and by Ron Ridenhour. Ridenhour forcefully argued that the My Lai massacre was not an aberration but an operation, one of many strategic tools in the military's kit, a tool that commanders could choose to employ as needed:

> Within a few years, if you stopped most Americans on the street who were politically conscious and . . . asked them what My Lai was, they would say: "Well, wasn't that where that lieutenant . . . went crazy and killed all those people?" My response to that is, not exactly, not at all. It was where an operation occurred and where there were two massacres, and Lieutenant Calley was one of many officers who, albeit too enthusiastically, followed orders. That was my impression, and I just consider that whole period the education of Ron, where I learned something significant and deeply troubling about our society.

For Ridenhour the My Lai massacre was the result of policy, not accident, and a policy that has continued through surrogates in Guatemala and El Salvador where hundreds of atrocities—of which El Mozote is only the best known—were perpetrated.[4] For Ridenhour, then, to mistake the representative nature of My Lai is to betray the past; to misunderstand the massacre is to allow its deliberate repetition. For the military professionals at the con-

ference, on the other hand, construing My Lai in this way betrays the past
in another way. To do so, they argued, eradicates the distinction between
murderers and soldiers—between the few who lost their moral bearings in
the midst of a moral wilderness and the many who served honorably and in
good conscience.

So, inevitably, for much of the conference we debated the nature of the
Vietnam War and its aftermath in terms not dissimilar to those of 1969. As
Tim O'Brien said, the conference felt like a time warp: "hawks at the throats
of doves . . . all the division, confusion and ambiguity" of twenty-five years
before. Armed with such contradictory premises and conclusions, the doves
and hawks cannot be said to have overcrowded the middle ground that
weekend.

But what if both sides are right? In many significant ways the My Lai
massacre was an aberration. There is compelling logic to a kind of numerical assessment: since most soldiers did not perpetrate atrocities, since most
never crossed a line that they learned to regret, the My Lai massacre cannot
be representative. But it is also possible that the minority report can nevertheless be symbolically apt, that it can penetrate to a certain truth about the
war. Take, for example, the testimony of Jeff Needles, a supply sergeant
stationed in Quang Ngai province:

And when they came out of My Lai, I heard the stories they came back
with. I didn't know whether they were true because I wasn't there. If they
were true, it meant my company had murdered people, it meant I had
helped by making sure the weapons worked, it meant my friends were in
serious trouble because they had been taught their job too well. It meant
speaking out against something I was told was right but deep within me,
I knew wasn't right, it meant because of lies I had been told I was sitting
in the middle of a useless war, it meant if I died in Viet Nam my life would
have been used and wasted, it meant that each day as I did my assigned
job, I was contributing my small share to keep the war going, it meant
the men who already died and the men who were going to die were throwing their lives away, it meant I was helping to continue something I felt
was wrong. It meant if I decided not to do my job anymore I would be
sent to jail and court-martialed. It meant a lot of people would think I
was a traitor to my country because I didn't believe in the war anymore,
it meant some of the people in the company and outside the Army would
hate me because they wouldn't understand why I had changed my mind,

it meant I would get a dishonorable discharge, it meant I would find it hard to get a job, it meant losing the privileges of the G.I. Bill for schools and hospital care, it meant hardships on my parents. It meant a lot of bad things I didn't want to think about, based on stories I wasn't sure were true. So I decided to forget about it.[5]

Needles neither raped nor pillaged; all he did was supply. Yet he felt, with compelling logic, that he too crossed a line. Again and again, authors of combat narratives put atrocities at their thematic centers, so much so that it has been said atrocity is the primal scene of Vietnam fiction.[6] To name just a few, James Webb, who served in Vietnam and later as secretary of the navy, does this in *Fields of Fire,* as does Philip Caputo in *Rumor of War* and Tim O'Brien in *The Things They Carried* and *In the Lake of the Woods.* Something is going on here.

All of which is meant to urge that to wrap our minds around the My Lai massacre and to begin to heal that wound we need to learn to hear "both/ and," not just "either/or." Yes, in significant ways the My Lai massacre was utterly an aberration. But that truth is neither gainsaid nor belied by admitting that in some important and significant ways the massacre was also representative. If we can agree for the moment that it both was and was not representative, then perhaps we can begin to listen to those like Needles, Caputo, and O'Brien who feel compelled to say that they participated in something that feels even today like a wound. Only then can we both honor veterans' service to their country and listen to them when they express their doubts and anguish about that service.

Only if we listen can we help Vietnam veterans heal their wounds. Only if we listen can we begin finally to heal what has been called the Vietnam syndrome. I hope that by keeping the My Lai story before the American public, the Tulane conference and this book contribute in some way to that important task.

NOTES

1. Judith Lewis Herman, *Trauma and Recovery* (New York: Basic Books, 1992), 1.

2. See Robert Jay Lifton's book on that experience, *Home from the War: Learning from Vietnam Veterans* (1973; reprint ed., Boston: Beacon Press, 1992). See also Jonathan Shay, *Achilles in Vietnam: Combat Trauma and the Undoing of Character* (New York: Atheneum, 1994).

3. Colonel Parks assiduously reminded the conference audiences that he spoke as a citizen and not as a representative of the Army Judge Advocate General's Corps.

4. Compare Wayne Karlin's recent analysis. My Lai, he writes, "was the face the war had always been rushing to become, the subtext Calley read correctly from the tactics of body count and free-fire zones and jellied fire from the sky on farmers' huts, from the answers to our many questions: *What do you want? Bodies. How many? Many. Whose? Vietnamese. Which? Vietnamese.*" Wayne Karlin, *Rumors and Stones: A Journey* (Willimantic, Conn.: Curbstone Press, 1996), 28 (emphasis is Karlin's).

5. Quoted in Lifton, *Home from the War*, 312.

6. Philip Beidler, *Re-writing America: Vietnam Authors in Their Generation* (Athens: University of Georgia Press, 1991).

APPENDIX A

• • • • • • • • • • • • • • •

Ron Ridenhour's Letter of
March 29, 1969

After returning from Vietnam, Ron Ridenhour spent several weeks drafting the following letter. He mailed it to his congressman, Morris Udall of Arizona, and to thirty other prominent officials, including President Richard Nixon, Secretary of Defense Melvin Laird, and several members of the congressional leadership. It is quoted from William R. Peers, *Report of the Department of the Army Review of the Preliminary Investigation into the My Lai Incident,* vol. 1, *The Report of the Investigation,* pp. 1-7–1-11.

> Mr. Ron Ridenhour
> 1416 East Thomas Road #104
> Phoenix, Arizona
> March 29, 1969

Gentlemen:

It was late in April, 1968 that I first heard of "Pinkville" and what allegedly happened there. I received that first report with some skepticism, but in the following months I was to hear similar stories from such a wide variety of people that it became impossible for me to disbelieve that something rather dark and bloody did indeed occur sometime in March, 1968 in a village called "Pinkville" in the Republic of Viet Nam.

The circumstances that led to my having access to the reports I'm about to relate need explanation. I was inducted in March, 1967 into the U.S. Army. After receiving various training I was assigned to the 70th Infantry Detachment (LRP), 11th Light Infantry Brigade at Schofield Barracks, Hawaii, in early October, 1967. That unit, the 70th Infantry Detachment (LRP), was disbanded a week before the 11th Brigade shipped out for Viet Nam on the 5th of December, 1967. All of the men from whom I later heard reports of the "Pinkville" incident were reassigned to "C" Company, 1st Battalion, 20th Infantry, 11th Light Infantry Brigade. I was reassigned to the aviation section of Headquarters Company 11th LIB. After we had been in Viet Nam for 3 to 4 months many of the men from the 70th Inf. Det. (LRP) began to transfer into the same unit, "E" Company, 51st Infantry (LRP).

In late April, 1968 I was awaiting orders for a transfer from HHC, 11th Brigade to Company "E," 51st Inf. (LRP), when I happened to run into Pfc "Butch" Gruver, whom I had known in Hawaii. Gruver told me he had been assigned to "C" Company 1st of the 20th until April 1st when he transferred to the unit that I was headed for. During the course of our conversation he told me the first of many reports I was to hear of "Pinkville."

"Charlie" Company 1/20 had been assigned to Task Force Barker in late February, 1968 to help conduct "search and destroy" operations on the Batangan Peninsula, Barker's area of operation. The task force was operating out of L. F. Dottie, located five or six miles north of Quang Nhai city on Viet Namese National Highway 1. Gruver said that Charlie Company had sustained casualties; primarily from mines and booby traps, almost everyday from the first day they arrived on the peninsula. One village area was particularly troublesome and seemed to be infested with booby traps and enemy soldiers. It was located about six miles northeast of Quang Nhai city at approximate coordinates B.S. 728795. It was a notorious area and the men of Task Force Barker had a special name for it: they called it "Pinkville." One morning in the latter part of March, Task Force Barker moved out from its firebase headed for "Pinkville." Its mission: destroy the trouble spot and all of its inhabitants.

When "Butch" told me this I didn't quite believe that what he was telling me was true, but he assured me that it was and went on to describe what
had happened. The other two companies that made up the task force cor-
doned off the village so that "Charlie" Company could move through to
destroy the structures and kill the inhabitants. Any villagers who ran from
Charlie Company were stopped by the encircling companies. I asked "Butch"
several times if all the people were killed. He said that he thought they were,
men, women and children. He recalled seeing a small boy, about three or
four years old, standing by the trail with a gunshot wound in one arm. The
boy was clutching his wounded arm with his other hand, while blood trick-
led between his fingers. He was staring around himself in shock and disbe-
lief at what he saw. "He just stood there with big eyes staring around like he
didn't understand; he didn't believe what was happening. Then the captain's
RTO (radio operator) put a burst of 16 (M-16 rifle) fire into him." It was so
bad, Gruver said, that one of the men in his squad shot himself in the foot
in order to be medivac-ed out of the area so that he would not have to participate in the slaughter. Although he had not seen it, Gruver had been told
by people he considered trustworthy that one of the company's officers, 2nd
Lieutenant Kally (this spelling may be incorrect) had rounded up several
groups of villagers (each group consisting of a minimum of 20 persons of
both sexes and all ages). According to the story, Kally then machine-gunned
each group. Gruver estimated that the population of the village had been
300 to 400 people and that very few, if any, escaped.

After hearing this account I couldn't quite accept it. Somehow I just
couldn't believe that not only had so many young American men participated in such an act of barbarism, but that their officers had ordered it. There
were other men in the unit I was soon to be assigned to, "E" Company, 51st
Infantry (LRP), who had been in Charlie Company at the time that Gruver
alleged the incident at "Pinkville" had occurred. I became determined to
ask them about "Pinkville" so that I might compare their accounts with Pfc
Gruver's.

When I arrived at "Echo" Company, 51st Infantry (LRP) the first men I
looked for were Pfc's Michael Terry and William Doherty. Both were veterans of "Charlie" Company, 1/20 and "Pinkville." Instead of contradict-
ing "Butch" Gruver's story they corroborated it, adding some tasty tidbits
of information of their own. Terry and Doherty had been in the same squad
and their platoon was the third platoon of "C" Company to pass through

the village. Most of the people they came to were already dead. Those that weren't were sought out and shot. The platoon left nothing alive, neither livestock nor people. Around noon the two soldiers' squad stopped to eat. "Billy and I started to get out our chow," Terry said, "but close to us was a bunch of Vietnamese in a heap, and some of them were moaning. Kally (2nd Lt. Kally) had been through before us and all of them had been shot, but many weren't dead. It was obvious that they weren't going to get any medical attention so Billy and I got up and went over to where they were. I guess we sort of finished them off." Terry went on to say that he and Doherty then returned to where their packs were and ate lunch. He estimated the size of the village to be 200 to 300 people. Doherty thought that the population of "Pinkville" had been 400 people.

If Terry, Doherty and Gruver could be believed, then not only had "Charlie" Company received orders to slaughter all the inhabitants of the village, but those orders had come from the commanding officer of Task Force Barker, or possibly even higher in the chain of command. Pfc Terry stated that when Captain Medina (Charlie Company's commanding officer Captain Ernest Medina) issued the order for the destruction of "Pinkville" he had been hesitant, as if it were something he didn't want to do but had to. Others I spoke to concurred with Terry on this.

It was June before I spoke to anyone who had something of significance to add to what I had already been told of the "Pinkville" incident. It was the end of June, 1968 when I ran into Sargent Larry La Croix at the USO in Chu Lai. La Croix had been in 2nd Lt. Kally's platoon on the day Task Force Barker swept through "Pinkville." What he told me verified the stories of the others, but he also had something new to add. He had been a witness to Kally's gunning down of at least three separate groups of villagers. "It was terrible. They were slaughtering the villagers like so many sheep." Kally's men were dragging people out of bunkers and hootches and putting them together in a group. The people in the group were men, women and children of all ages. As soon as he felt that the group was big enough, Kally ordered an M-60 (machine-gun) set up and the people killed. La Croix said that he bore witness to this procedure at least three times. The three groups were of different sizes, one of about twenty people, one of about thirty people, and one of about forty people. When the first group was put together Kally ordered Pfc Torres to man the machine-gun and open fire on the villagers that had been grouped together. This Torres did, but before everyone in the group was down he ceased fire and refused to fire again. After ordering

Torres to recommence firing several times, Lieutenant Kally took over the M-60 and finished shooting the remaining villagers in that first group himself. Sargent La Croix told me that Kally didn't bother to order anyone to take the machine-gun when the other two groups of villagers were formed. He simply manned it himself and shot down all villagers in both groups.

This account of Sargent La Croix's confirmed the rumors that Gruver, Terry and Doherty had previously told me about Lieutenant Kally. It also convinced me that there was a very substantial amount of truth to the stories that all of these men had told. If I needed more convincing, I was to receive it.

It was in the middle of November, 1968 just a few weeks before I was to return to the United States for separation from the army that I talked to Pfc Michael Bernhardt. Bernhardt had served his entire year in Viet Nam in "Charlie" Company 1/20 and he too was about to go home. "Bernie" substantiated the tales told by the other men I had talked to in vivid, bloody detail and added this. "Bernie" had absolutely refused to take part in the massacre of the villagers of "Pinkville" that morning and he thought that it was rather strange that the officers of the company had not made an issue of it. But that evening Medina (Captain Ernest Medina) came up to me ("Bernie") and told me not to do anything stupid like write my congressman" about what had happened that day. Bernhardt assured Captain Medina that he had no such thing in mind. He had nine months left in Viet Nam and felt that it was dangerous enough just fighting the acknowledged enemy.

Exactly what did, in fact, occur in the village of "Pinkville" in March, 1968 I do not know for *certain*, but I am convinced that it was something very black indeed. I remain irrevocably persuaded that if you and I do truly believe in the principles, of justice and the equality of every man, however humble, before the law, that form the very backbone that this country is founded on, then we must press forward a widespread and public investigation of this matter with all our combined efforts. I think that it was Winston Churchhill who once said "A country without a conscience is a country without a soul, and a country without a soul is a country that cannot survive." I feel that I must take some positive action on this matter. I hope that you will launch an investigation immediately and keep me informed of your progress. If you cannot, then I don't know what other course of action to take.

I have considered sending this to newspapers, magazines, and broadcasting companies, but I somehow feel that investigation and action by the

Congress of the United States is the appropriate procedure, and as a conscientious citizen I have no desire to further besmirch the image of the American serviceman in the eyes of the world. I feel that this action, while probably it would promote attention, would not bring about the constructive actions that the direct actions of the Congress of the United States would.

Sincerely,

(signed) Ron Ridenhour

APPENDIX B

• • • • • • • • • • • • • • •

Excerpt from Peers Report of March 14, 1970

After receipt of Ron Ridenhour's letter of March 29, 1969, the U.S. Army began an investigation of the My Lai incident through the Inspector General's Office and the Criminal Investigation Division. These efforts began to confirm portions of Ridenhour's allegations, and in November 1969 Army Chief of Staff General William C. Westmoreland and Secretary of the Army Stanley R. Resor directed Lieutenant General William R. Peers to begin an inquiry. Westmoreland and Resor specifically instructed Peers to examine all investigations from the date of the My Lai incident, March 16, 1968, up to the date of Ridenhour's letter. Although the Pentagon was concerned primarily with learning more about the possible cover-up of criminal activity by higher officers, Peers's four-volume report (volume 2 was actually thirty-three books containing twenty-thousand pages of testimony) included extensive details of the crimes themselves in My Lai and My Khe during the period March 16–19, 1968. It also detailed the criminal actions to suppress information about those crimes. This excerpt summarizes some of Peers's findings and is taken from William R. Peers, *Report of the Department of the Army Review of the Prelimi-*

nary Investigation into the My Lai Incident, vol. 1, *The Report of the Investigation*, pp. 12-1–12-4.

On the Basis of the Foregoing, the Findings of the Inquiry Are as Follows:

A. CONCERNING EVENTS SURROUNDING THE SON MY OPERATION OF 16–19 MARCH 1968

1. During the period 16–19 March 1968, US Army troops of TF Barker, 11th Brigade, American Division, massacred a large number of noncombatants in two hamlets of Son My Village, Quang Ngai Province, Republic of Vietnam. The precise number of Vietnamese killed cannot be determined but was at least 175 and may exceed 400.

2. The massacre occurred in conjunction with a combat operation which was intended to neutralize Son My Village as a logistical support base and staging area, and to destroy elements of an enemy battalion thought to be located in the Son My area.

3. The massacre resulted primarily from the nature of the orders issued by persons in the chain of command within TF Barker.

4. The task force commander's order and the associated intelligence estimate issued prior to the operation were embellished as they were disseminated through each lower level of command, and ultimately presented to the individual soldier a false and misleading picture of the Son My area as an armed enemy camp, largely devoid of civilian inhabitants.

5. Prior to the incident, there had developed within certain elements of the 11th Brigade a permissive attitude toward the treatment and safeguarding of noncombatants which contributed to the mistreatment of such persons during the Son My operation.

6. The permissive attitude in the treatment of Vietnamese was, on 16–19 March 1968, exemplified by an almost total disregard for the lives and property of the civilian population of Son My Village on the part of commanders and key staff officers of TF Barker.

7. On 16 March, soldiers at the squad and platoon level, within some elements of TF Barker, murdered noncombatants while under the supervision and control of their immediate superiors.

8. A part of the crimes visited on the inhabitants of Son My Village included individual and group acts of murder, rape, sodomy, maiming, and

assault on noncombatants and the mistreatment and killing of detainees. They further included the killing of livestock, destruction of crops, closing of wells, and the burning of dwellings within several subhamlets.

9. Some attempts were made to stop the criminal acts in Son My Village on 16 March; but with few exceptions, such efforts were too feeble or too late.

10. Intensive interrogation has developed no evidence that any member of the units engaged in the Son My operation was under the influence of marijuana or other narcotics.

B. CONCERNING THE ADEQUACY OF REPORTS, INVESTIGATIONS AND REVIEWS

11. The commanders of TF Barker and the 11th Brigade had substantial knowledge as to the extent of the killing of noncombatants but only a portion of their information was ever reported to the Commanding General of the American Division.

12. Based on his observations, WO1 Thompson made a specific complaint through his command channels that serious war crimes had been committed but through a series of inadequate responses at each level of command, action on his complaint was delayed and the severity of his charges considerably diluted by the time it reached the Division Commander.

13. Sufficient information concerning the highly irregular nature of the operations of TF Barker on 16 March 1968 reached the Commanding General of the American Division to require that a thorough investigation be conducted.

14. An investigation by the Commander of the 11th Brigade conducted at the direction of the Commanding General of the American Division, was little more than a pretense and was subsequently misrepresented as a thorough investigation to the CG, American Division in order to conceal from him the true enormity of the atrocities.

15. Patently inadequate reports of investigation submitted by the Commander of the 11th Brigade were accepted at face value and without an effective review by the CG, American Division.

16. Reports of alleged war crimes, noncombatant casualties, and serious incidents concerning the Son My operation of 16 March were received at the headquarters of the American Division but were not reported to higher headquarters despite the existence of directives requiring such action.

17. Reports of alleged war crimes relating to the Son My operation of 16 March reached Vietnamese government officials, but those officials did not take effective action to ascertain the true facts.

18. Efforts of the ARVN/GVN officials discreetly to inform the US commanders of the magnitude of the war crimes committed on 16 March 1968 met with no affirmative response.

C. CONCERNING ATTEMPTS TO SUPPRESS INFORMATION

19. At every command level within the American Division, actions were taken, both wittingly and unwittingly, which effectively suppressed information concerning the war crimes committed at Son My Village.

20. At the company level there was a failure to report the war crimes which had been committed. This, combined with instructions to members of one unit not to discuss the events of 16 March, contributed significantly to the suppression of information.

21. The task force commander and at least one, and probably more, staff officers of TF Barker may have conspired to suppress information and to mislead higher headquarters concerning the events of 16–19 March 1968.

22. At the 11th Brigade level, the commander and at least one principal staff officer may have conspired to suppress information to deceive the division commander concerning the true facts of the Son My operation of 16–19 March.

23. A reporter and a photographer from the 11th Brigade observed many war crimes committed by C/1-20 Inf on 16 March. Both failed to report what they had seen; the reporter submitted a misleading account of the operation; and the photographer withheld and suppressed (and wrongfully misappropriated upon his discharge from the service) photographic evidence of such war crimes.

24. Efforts within the 11th Brigade to suppress information concerning the Son My operation were aided in varying degrees by members of US Advisory teams working with ARVN and GVN officials.

25. Within the American Division headquarters, actions taken to suppress information concerning what was purportedly believed to be the inadvertent killing of 20 to 28 noncombatants effectively served to conceal the true nature and scope of the events which had taken place in Son My Village on 16–19 March 1968.

26. Failure of the Americal Division headquarters to act on reports and information received from GVN/ARVN officials in mid-April served effectively to suppress the true nature and scope of the events which had taken place in Son My Village on 16–19 March 1968.

27. Despite an exhaustive search of the files of the 11th Brigade, Americal Division, GVN/ARVN advisory team files, and records holding centers, with few exceptions, none of the documents relating to the so-called investigation of the events of 16–19 March were located.

APPENDIX C

• • • • • • • • • • • • • • •

Why Study Vietnam?

Jerold M. Starr

This sketch of significant facts that attest to the continuing importance of the study of the Vietnam War is from *The Lessons of the Vietnam War,* edited by Jerold M. Starr (Pittsburgh, Pa.: Center for Social Studies Education, 1996).

Americans Killed and Wounded

Carved into the black granite wall of the Vietnam Memorial are the names of over 58,000 Americans officially acknowledged as killed in the Vietnam War. A 1969 Gallup Poll found that fifty-five percent of Americans personally knew someone who had been killed or wounded in Vietnam. Some of these family and friends can be seen still mourning at the Vietnam Memorial on any given day.

Many survivors have accepted their loss as necessary, even honorable. In contrast to World War II, however, the grief of many other survivors has been aggravated by the thought that the cause was not just and the sacrifice futile. Heather Brandon quotes one father who despairs that, though many years have passed, his wife still wears black and his house "will never see light again." Since his son was killed "there's no parties, there's no weddings, there is no nothing." Looking into space, the man recalls painfully:

> Every time I turn around, even if I go into another room, I see something. The picture, the gun. We used to hunt together. Fishing, he was with me like a little puppy dog. He wouldn't get away from me at all. Anything I needed, I had from him: "Hey Sam." "Yes, Dad." Boom. It's mine. Now, what happens? So many things I remember. If he would be sick, that would be another story. Not this way. This was a slaughterhouse way.

A retired lawyer laments to Myra MacPherson:

> Here's the horror of it. We lost our only child there, a Marine, in 1968. . . . I counseled my son to go. I'll bear the burden of that for the rest of my life. I feel I killed him. When parents lose a son in war, they're supposed to be silent and lick their wounds. It's time parents became radicalized. You clutch your teenage son to your bosom, and don't let your government send him to Central America or the Middle East. They'll lie to you in the name of national interest.

Large though they are, the numbers also do not measure all the costs to the over 300,000 men who were wounded in Vietnam, 154,000 of whom required hospital care. The jungles and rice paddies of Vietnam were seeded with booby traps and mines that ripped legs away at the knee, shattered spines, amputated arms. Ground troops on both sides carried automatic weapons designed to lay down "walls of fire."

Ironically, while the technology for killing and maiming had been perfected, so too had the ability to save lives. Helicopter evacuation teams rushed wounded men to MASH units where medical teams stemmed the bleeding and labored to patch a shattered young body back together.

Rick Eilert, a combat Marine wounded in Vietnam, describes the excruciating pain patients suffer when their wounds are cleaned and the dressing changed:

> The doctor began to pull the bandages from the area around his tail bone. I saw Smitty grasp the frame of the side of his rack. He held on so that his knuckles turned white. He didn't groan or scream. He just closed his eyes

and buried his head in the mattress. The doctor took tweezers and began to pull foot after foot of packing out of the wound, it, too, dripping pus and blood. I saw perspiration dripping from Smitty's brow, down to the mattress and the floor. Awaiting the second half of the process, Smitty rolled on his side to face me and said, "the damn enlistment posters never said nothing about pain. It sounds naive, but I never thought that getting wounded involved so much agony."

During the year he spent recovering from his wounds, Eilert was surrounded by blind, burned, crippled, but still innocent young men. Eilert looked on sympathetically as they vainly refused to accept the obvious permanence of their injuries:

Al really believed that he would see again. His naive understanding of anatomy and body functions was not his alone. Almost all of the horribly wounded and deformed patients believed that they would fully recover, at least in the early stages of their hospitalization. Al believed that his injuries would heal—like all the wounds portrayed on TV and in the movies. The wounded in the movies were never portrayed as crippled or maimed for life. It seemed that everything like this I'd ever seen was a sham. The actors knew that their portrayals were just acting. Now all this pain and terror was real, and forever. Just think of it—forever.

Almost 7,000 Americans lost limbs in Vietnam. They are compensated according to the degree of their disablement. A veteran who has lost both legs above the knees receives $1,661 a month. One with both legs off below the knees gets $1,506; one with one leg off above the knee gets $506; and one with one leg off below the knee gets only $311 a month.

There are over 13,000 veterans judged totally disabled. Most have endured prolonged hospitalization involving multiple operations and long-term intensive care. They will spend most of their lives in and out of VA hospitals.

Psychological Wounds

Many more came back physically intact, but psychologically wounded. It is estimated that during their lives more than half of all Vietnam veterans will have suffered some of the symptoms of Post-traumatic Stress Disorder (PTSD). The symptoms are many: panic and paranoia, chronic anxiety, nightmares or flashbacks to traumatic events, survivor guilt, depression, and emotional numbness. Many have trouble sleeping, some turning to drugs or alcohol for escape.

Certainly, survivors of other wars have suffered from similar symptoms. In the past it might have been labeled shell-shock or battle fatigue. Due to the peculiar nature of the Vietnam War, however, the rate of psychological impairment of its veterans is over twice that of the other wars (approximately 15 percent), almost four times that of other wars if we include partial impairment.

Vietnam was not a conventional war in which uniformed troops battled over strategic territory. Progress was not measured in terms of how much land was gained or people "liberated" from the enemy. Ferocious battles were fought over what seemed to GIs like meaningless objectives. Many were killed or wounded for territory that was abandoned soon after, like the infamous Hamburger Hill. Summing up his frustration, one combat soldier demanded: "What am I doing here? We don't take any land. We don't give it back. We just mutilate bodies. What . . . are we doing here?"

Instead, progress in the war was measured by kill ratios and body counts with no provision for certifying identities. U.S. soldiers were disillusioned to discover that many of the people they were sent to save regarded them as the enemy. And any of them at any time could bring sudden death. Many learned to shoot first and ask questions later. Robert Jay Lifton writes: "To a degree unparalleled in our earlier wars, combat in Vietnam involved the killing of women, children, and the elderly: some of whom were armed fighters, some of whom were killed inadvertently, and some of whom were killed in retaliation for deaths caused by their countrymen." In therapy sessions Vietnam veterans go over and over the terrible anguish they felt in trying to distinguish civilians from combatants and their nagging guilt for inadvertently killing innocent people.

Many veterans were burdened further by drug addictions picked up in Vietnam. For those desperate for an escape from their anxieties drugs were cheap and available. By 1970, GIs could buy 96 percent pure heroin (compared to 3–10 percent back home) in a multi-dose vial for a mere two dollars. According to a 1971 survey, a shocking 29 percent of U.S. Army personnel in Vietnam used heroin or opium. More than half of them became addicted.

A 1971 Harris Poll shows 26 percent of veterans using drugs after their return home, 325,000 of them heroin. In the first five years after their return,

Vietnam veterans suffered a 69 percent higher rate of accidental poisonings, mostly drug overdoses, than U.S. soldiers assigned to other countries.

To make matters worse, veterans came home to a troubled economy. For the first five years after the war, Vietnam veterans averaged over 6.0 percent unemployment, about a third higher than for veterans after World War II.

Some responded to the above dilemmas by committing suicide or turning to crime. Studies show the suicide rate for Vietnam veterans to be 65–75 percent higher than for non-Vietnam veterans, putting the total figure at perhaps 7,500 young men. A 1979 Presidential Review Memorandum found over 400,000 Vietnam veterans in some trouble with the law, including 29,000 in state and federal prisons.

Other casualties of the war would include the 3,200 young men imprisoned because they refused to participate in the war. Many were subjected to beatings, forcible rape, and solitary confinement. There also were about 100,000 youth who chose exile in Canada or elsewhere. By the time it was over between 750,000 and two million young Americans were in some form of legal jeopardy for their resistance to the war.

Social and Political Costs

There were social and political costs as well. For many Americans, the early 1960s were a time of hope. Throughout the South blacks were challenging segregation and demanding their right to vote. Congress passed major civil rights and voting rights bills; President Johnson declared a "war on poverty"; and the apathetic 1950s seemed to be giving way to a period of social and political progress. Young, idealistic Americans were leading the way.

Twenty-five years later it seems clear that national pride was another casualty of Vietnam. Between 1966 and 1976 public opinion polls show that every major institution in American life suffered a loss of public esteem. The biggest losses occurred during the peak years of the war, 1966–1971.

The biggest loser was the government—no longer perceived as an instrument of progress, but rather as huge, remote, and self-interested. The proportion of Americans with "a great deal of confidence" in the executive branch of the federal government plummeted from 41 percent in 1966 to 11 percent in 1976. Great confidence in Congress fell from 42 percent in 1966 to 9 percent in 1976; great confidence in the military fell from 62 percent in 1966 to 23 percent in 1976. Pollster Louis Harris found that, by the end of 1971, the vast majority of Americans agreed that politicians make false promises, are not appointed on the basis of merit, are in politics to make money for themselves, and take graft.

Similar results have been obtained by the Institute for Survey Research (ISR) of the University of Michigan. ISR researchers found a drastic decline in the number of Americans who said they could trust the government in Washington to do what is right "at least most of the time"—from 76 percent in 1964 to 37 percent in 1974. The proportion believing the government is getting "too powerful for the good of the country and the individual person" rose from 44 percent in 1966 to 69 percent in 1976. While the government certainly deserved criticism, it might be proposed that this widespread cynicism lowered the standards Americans have held for their leaders, leading to the present level of banality at the top.

Loss of U.S. Prestige

Why were we in Vietnam? One answer was provided by Assistant Secretary of Defense John McNaughton, who in 1966 stated: "The present U.S. objective in Vietnam is to avoid humiliation . . . to preserve our reputation as a guarantor, and thus to preserve our effectiveness in the rest of the world." President Johnson spoke frequently of "not losing face" in Vietnam, and President Nixon sought "peace with honor." It is very ironic, then, that staying the course in America's longest war should lead to a significant loss of U.S. standing in the world community. That, however, is what happened.

In 1973, George Gallup polled 341 leaders from seventy different nations concerning their perceptions of the United States in Vietnam. Among those polled were public officials, diplomats, bankers, corporate executives, physicians, attorneys, educators and media executives. The findings were that 86 percent thought the U.S. lost prestige by its involvement in Vietnam; 66 percent thought the U.S. military intervention in Vietnam had been a mistake; 55 percent did not think communism suffered a setback in Southeast Asia as a result of the war; only 26 percent thought it did; 59 percent thought the U.S. should help to rebuild North Vietnam; only 24 percent were opposed.

Economic Costs

In terms of dollars and cents, Vietnam was the second most expensive war in American history. The government estimates direct military expenditures at $168 billion. Other costs like payments to other countries providing military support, interest on debts incurred by the government to subsidize the war, and payments for veterans' benefits balloon this figure into the hundreds of billions.

As with all wars, these costs will continue to grow through the years. There presently are almost a half-million active compensation cases from Vietnam. The VA has paid out about $120 billion to date and provides an additional seven billion dollars or so every year for compensation, loan guarantees, educational assistance, vocational rehabilitation, and medical services. If Agent Orange–related diseases are ever acknowledged by the government, medical treatment and other costs will add billions more to this total.

A less visible but no less significant cost of the war was the damage done to U.S. economic stability. As the war escalated, many in the business world became concerned about its long-term effects. Louis Lundborg, chairman of the board of the Bank of America, gravely informed the Senate Foreign Relations Committee: "The escalation of the war in Vietnam has seriously distorted the American economy, has inflamed inflationary pressures, has drained resources that are desperately needed to overcome serious domestic problems confronting our country, and has dampened the rate of growth of profits on both a before- and after-tax base."

As many leading economists explained, price inflation is basically a function of how much money is competing for how many goods. Over a million Americans were employed directly in the war effort. This helped keep employment high, but without contributing to the production of consumer goods. As more wages competed for what goods there were, prices naturally went up. As prices rose, labor began demanding higher wages.

The result was a spiral of inflation that lasted until the recession of 1982. The inflation was compounded by President Johnson's decision to continue his domestic war on poverty without raising taxes. Inflation averaged about 1.3 percent per year over 1960–1965, and then climbed to 6 percent by 1970.

In order to control the inflation, the Federal Reserve Bank raised interest rates on loans, making it harder for people to borrow for houses and cars. This led to a 750,000 a year decline in new housing construction and a fall off in new car sales. This, in turn, led to layoffs in manufacturing and increased pressure on social services.

Few people can comprehend the magnitude of these figures. To give some idea, however, consider alternative uses to which the money spent on the war might have been put. In 1972 economist Robert Lekachman suggested that, just for the annual direct cost of the war at the time, the government could have rehabilitated all urban slum housing in this country, creating many construction jobs in the process. Of course, no one is saying that any money not spent on the Vietnam War would have or even should have been spent on social programs. Such comparisons, however, do make the trade-offs in our overall national security even more concrete for leaders and citizens.

Instead, the money was used to subsidize the heaviest barrage of concentrated firepower in the history of human warfare. The United States exploded over fifteen million tons of bombs and ground munitions in Vietnam. This is over four times the tonnage of air and ground munitions that the U.S. used in all theaters of war in World War II and is equivalent in destructive force to about six hundred Hiroshima type bombs. As a result, many acres of Vietnam's once verdant landscape are pockmarked with twenty-six million bomb craters. In addition, the U.S. sprayed over eighteen million gallons of poisonous chemical herbicides to destroy over five million acres of forest and croplands, about the size of the state of Massachusetts.

The human costs are staggering. Over two million Vietnamese were killed; over four million were wounded; and over ten million were made refugees by the war. Multiply these figures by five to get an estimate of what it would mean for the United States. Comparatively speaking, the Vietnamese death toll was about twenty-five times that of the U.S. in World War II; the totally disabled toll about fifty times that of the U.S. in Vietnam.

Conclusion

Over the years, the American public has been consistently critical of the war. A 1987 national survey by the Chicago Council on Foreign Relations found that 66 percent of those polled agreed that the "Vietnam war was more than a mistake; it was fundamentally wrong and immoral."

At the same time, we must be concerned that large segments of the U.S. public cannot specify what were the mistakes committed in our nation's Vietnam policy. If they cannot do that, the lessons of that tragic experience are lost to decision makers and citizens confronted with similar regional conflicts in Central America, the Middle East, Africa, and elsewhere. For example, a 1985 ABC News/*Washington Post* poll found that 57 percent did not have a "clear idea" what the war was about and 33 percent did not even know which side the U.S. supported.

The situation is even more extreme for American youth who have no personal experience of the war. Clearly, unless our generation undertakes responsibility for teaching Vietnam, all cultural memory of the war will disappear with us. According to Georgetown University's Alan Goodman, the very same foreign and military policy making establishment—assumptions, objectives, procedures—that took the U.S. into Vietnam is still in place.

Why teach Vietnam? Because as Santayana has warned: "Those who do not learn from history are condemned to repeat it." And this nation—great as it is—could not afford another Vietnam.

SOURCES

Brandon, Heather. *Casualties.* New York: St. Martin's Press, 1984.

Eilert, Rick. *For Self and Country.* New York: Morrow, 1983.

Lifton, Robert Jay. "Beyond Atrocity." *Saturday Review Magazine* (March 27, 1971).

MacPherson, Myra. *Long Time Passing: Vietnam and the Haunted Generation.* New York: New American Library, 1985.

McNaughton, John. Quoted in Len Ackland. *Credibility Gap: A Digest of the Pentagon Papers.* Philadelphia: The National Peace Literature Service, no date.

BIBLIOGRAPHIC ESSAY

● ● ● ● ● ● ● ● ● ● ● ● ● ●

The literature on the Vietnam War is prodigious, and there are many books and articles that address in whole or in part the issues raised in this book. What follows are some suggestions on where to begin further reading on My Lai, U.S. military conduct in Vietnam, and related topics. An excellent and highly recommended bibliography is Lester H. Brune and Richard Dean Burns, *America and the Indochina Wars, 1945–1990: A Bibliographic Guide* (Claremont, Calif.: Regina Books, 1992). It has sections on My Lai, war crimes, media, tactics and strategy, veterans' memoirs, military legacy, artistic and literary legacy, civilian casualties, post-traumatic stress disorder, and other specialized bibliographies.

Lieutenant General William R. Peers, *Report of the Department of the Army Review of the Preliminary Investigation into the My Lai Incident* (Washington, D.C.), dated March 14, 1970, remains one of the most concise and accurate accounts of the events in and around My Lai before, during, and after March 16, 1968. Although the full report contains tens of thousands of pages of testimony and evidence, the narrative summary is found in Vol. 1, *The Report of the Investigation*. The full text of this volume has been reprinted in Joseph Goldstein, Burke Marshall, and Jack Schwartz, *The My Lai Massacre and its Cover-up: Beyond the Reach of Law?* (New York: Free Press, 1976). Peers summarizes much of the report and adds personal reflections in his memoir, *The My Lai Inquiry* (New York: Norton, 1979). An excellent recent reexamination of the massacre and the judicial proceedings that eventually followed is Michael Bilton and Kevin Sim, *Four Hours in My Lai* (New York: Viking, 1992). This book draws upon extensive interviews with participants in the events at My Lai and with those involved in the investigations. It contains a very helpful Note on Sources and details the location and contents of archival collections relevant to the study of the massacre and its aftermath.

Several works that appeared during or shortly after the investigation and courts-martial recount the story from various perspectives. One of the first accounts was Seymour Hersh, *My Lai 4: A Report on the Massacre and Its Aftermath* (New York: Random House, 1970). Hersh also wrote *Cover-up: The Army's Secret Investigation on the Massacre at My Lai 4* (New York: Random House, 1972). Also useful are Martin Gershen, *Destroy or Die: The True Story of My Lai* (New Rochelle, N.Y.: Arlington House, 1971), Richard Hammer, *The Court-Martial of Lt. Calley* (New York: Coward, McCann & Geoghegan, 1971), Mary McCarthy, *Medina* (New York: Harcourt Brace Jovanovich, 1972), and John Sack, *Lieutenant Calley: His Own Story* (New York: Viking, 1971). A recent memoir by one of the army's principal investigators is William Wilson, "I Had Prayed to God That This Thing Was Fiction," *American Heritage* (February 1990): 44–53. Another personal retrospective is Ron Ridenhour, "Heroes at a Massacre," *Playboy* (March 1993). There is also a 1970 film, *Interview with My Lai Veterans,* that was released on videocassette by Films, Inc. (Chicago).

On the question of the extent of U.S. war crimes in Vietnam, two opposing views are presented in Vietnam Veterans Against the War, *The Winter Soldier Investigation: An Inquiry into American War Crimes* (Boston: Beacon Press, 1972), and Guenter Lewy, *America in Vietnam* (New York: Oxford University Press, 1978). See also Peter French, *Individual and Collective Responsibility: The Massacre at My Lai* (Cambridge, Mass.: Shenkman, 1972), and Herbert C. Kelman and V. Lee Hamilton, *Crimes of Obedience: Toward a Social Psychology of Authority and Responsibility* (New Haven, Conn.: Yale University Press, 1989). Telford Taylor, *Nuremburg and Vietnam: An American Tragedy* (Chicago: Quadrangle Books, 1970) examines U.S. conduct in Vietnam in light of World War II precedents. Two recent books dealing with Germany during World War II do not address Vietnam directly but raise issues pertinent to My Lai. They are Christopher R. Browning, *Ordinary Men: Reserve Police Battalion 101 and the Final Solution in Poland* (New York: HarperCollins, 1992), and Daniel Jonah Goldhagen, *Hitler's Willing Executioners: Ordinary Germans and the Holocaust* (New York: Alfred A. Knopf, 1996). See also Michael Walzer, *Just and Unjust Wars: A Moral Argument with Historical Illustrations* (New York: Basic Books, 1977).

The impact of combat and atrocity on individual soldiers is examined in Robert Jay Lifton, *Home from the War: Vietnam Veterans: Neither Victims nor Executioners* (New York: Simon & Schuster, 1973), and Jonathan Shay, *Achilles in Vietnam: Combat Trauma and the Undoing of Character* (New York: Atheneum, 1994). A provocative examination of Lifton's concept of survivor witness is in Charles B. Strozier and Michael Flynn, eds., *Genocide, War, and Human Survival* (Lanham, Md.: Rowman & Littlefield, 1996). A standard work on psychological trauma is Judith L. Herman, *Trauma and Recovery* (New York: Basic Books, 1992). On post-traumatic stress disorder, see also Patience H. C. Mason, *Recovering from the War:*

A Woman's Guide to Helping Your Vietnam Vet, Your Family, and Yourself (New York: Penguin Books, 1990), and the two memoirs by her husband Robert Mason, *Chicken-hawk* (New York: Viking, 1983), and *Chickenhawk: Back in the World: Life after Vietnam* (New York: Viking Penguin, 1993). For data on PTSD see R. A. Kulka et al., *National Vietnam Veterans Readjustment Study: Tables of Findings and Technical Appendices* (New York: Brunner/Mazel, 1990). Myra MacPherson, *Long Time Passing: Vietnam and the Haunted Generation* (Garden City, N.Y.: Doubleday, 1984), is a compelling description of the impact of the war on individual Americans.

Other works that specifically evoke the American combat experience include Christian G. Appy, *Working-Class War: American Combat Soldiers and Vietnam* (Chapel Hill: University of North Carolina Press, 1993), Eric M. Bergerud, *Red Thunder, Tropic Lightning: The World of a Combat Division in Vietnam* (New York: Penguin, 1994), and Jonathan Schell, *The Real War* (New York: Pantheon, 1987). Among the many excellent memoirs and oral histories are Mark Baker, *Nam: The Vietnam War in the Words of the Men and Women Who Fought There* (New York: Morrow, 1981), Al Santoli, *Everything We Had: An Oral History of the Vietnam War by Thirty-Three Soldiers Who Fought It* (New York: Ballantine, 1984), Otto J. Lehrack, *No Shining Armor: The Marines at War in Vietnam: An Oral History* (Lawrence: University Press of Kansas, 1992), and Harold G. Moore and Joseph L. Galloway, *We Were Soldiers Once . . . and Young: Ia Drang, the Battle That Changed the War in Vietnam* (New York: Random House, 1992). For the memoir of a conscientious objector who chose civilian service in Vietnam, see John Balaban, *Remembering Heaven's Face: A Moral Witness in Vietnam* (New York: Touchstone, 1992).

Media coverage of the war is discussed in two books by William M. Hammond, *The U.S. Army in Vietnam: Public Affairs: The Military and the Media, 1962–1968* (Washington, D.C.: U.S. Army Center of Military History, 1988), and *The U.S. Army in Vietnam: Public Affairs: The Military and the Media, 1968–1973* (Washington, D.C.: U.S. Army Center of Military History, 1996). See also David Halberstam, *The Powers That Be* (New York: Alfred A. Knopf, 1979), Daniel Hallin, *The "Uncensored War": The Media and Vietnam* (New York: Oxford University Press, 1986), and Kathleen Turner, *Lyndon Johnson's Dual War: Vietnam and the Press* (Chicago: University of Chicago Press, 1985).

Poetry and fiction offer powerful American and Vietnamese reflections on the war. For an introduction to this literature and a brief but useful bibliography see H. Bruce Franklin, ed., *The Vietnam War in American Stories, Songs, and Poems* (Boston: Bedford Books of St. Martin's Press, 1996). Literary criticism and analysis is found in John Hellmann, *American Myth and the Legacy of Vietnam* (New York: Columbia University Press, 1986), Timothy J. Lomperis, *"Reading the Wind": The Literature of the Vietnam War* (Durham, N.C.: Duke University Press for the Asia Society, 1987), and two books by Philip Beidler: *American Literature and the Experience of Vietnam* (Athens: University of Georgia Press, 1982), and *Re-Writing America: Vietnam Authors in Their Generation* (Athens: University of Georgia Press, 1991). The work of Tim O'Brien is notable, including his classic novel *Going After Cacciato* (New York: Delacorte Press/Seymour Lawrence, 1978), his short stories in *The*

Things They Carried (Boston: Houghton Mifflin, 1990), and his novel inspired by My Lai, *In the Lake of the Woods* (Boston: Houghton Mifflin, 1994). Other excellent books include Philip Caputo, A *Rumor of War* (New York: Ballantine, 1978) and his novel about PTSD, *Indian Country* (New York: Bantam, 1987), two novels by Larry Heinemann: *Close Quarters* (New York: Viking Penguin, 1977) and *Paco's Story* (New York: Penguin, 1986), David Halberstam, *One Very Hot Day: A Novel* (Boston: Houghton Mifflin, 1967), Robert Olen Butler, *A Good Scent from a Strange Mountain: Stories* (New York: Holt, 1992), W. D. Ehrhart, *Vietnam-Perkasie: A Combat Marine Memoir* (Jefferson, N.C.: McFarland, 1983), John M. Del Vecchio, *The 13th Valley: A Novel* (New York: Bantam, 1982), and two novels by Wayne Karlin: *Lost Armies* (New York: Holt, 1988) and *US* (New York: Holt, 1993). For an anthology of short fiction see Wayne Karlin, Basil T. Paquet, and Larry Rottmann, eds., *Free Fire Zone: Short Stories by Vietnam Veterans* (Coventry, Conn.: First Casualty Press, 1973).

Two excellent collections of poetry are Larry Rottmann, Jan Barry, and Basil T. Paquet, eds., *Winning Hearts and Minds: War Poems by Vietnam Veterans* (Brooklyn, N.Y.: First Casualty Press, 1972), and W. D. Ehrhart, ed., *Carrying the Darkness: The Poetry of the Vietnam War* (Lubbock: Texas Tech University Press, 1989). Some of the work of two major poets is in John Balaban, *Blue Mountain* (Greensboro, N.C.: Unicorn Press, 1982), and W. D. Ehrhart, *To Those Who Have Gone Home Tired: New and Selected Poems* (New York: Thunder's Mouth Press, 1984). See also George Evans, *Sudden Dreams: New and Selected Poems* (Minneapolis: Coffee House Press, 1991). For collections that include Vietnamese writers see Nigel Gray, ed., *Phoenix Country* (London: Journeyman Press, 1980), John Balaban, *Ca Dao Vietnam: A Bilingual Anthology of Vietnamese Poetry* (Greensboro, N.C.: Unicorn Press, 1980), and Wayne Karlin, Le Minh Khue, and Truong Vu, *The Other Side of Heaven: Post-war Fiction by Vietnamese and American Writers* (Willimantic, Conn.: Curbstone Press, 1995). A powerful literary expression by a former North Vietnamese soldier is Bao Ninh, *The Sorrow of War: A Novel of North Vietnam,* trans. Phan Thanh Hao, ed. Frank Palmos (New York: Pantheon Books, 1995).

For general works on the Vietnam War and on U.S. military performance see George C. Herring, *America's Longest War: The United States and Vietnam, 1950–1975,* 3d ed. (New York: McGraw-Hill, 1996), Gary Hess, *Vietnam and the United States: Origins and Legacy of War* (Boston: Twayne, 1990), Robert D. Schulzinger, A *Time for War: The United States and Vietnam, 1941–1975* (New York: Oxford University Press, 1997), Stanley Karnow, *Vietnam: A History* (New York: Viking, 1983), Marilyn B. Young, *The Vietnam Wars, 1945–1990* (New York: HarperCollins, 1991), David L. Anderson, ed., *Shadow on the White House: Presidents and the Vietnam War, 1945–1975* (Lawrence: University Press of Kansas, 1993), Harry G. Summers, Jr., *On Strategy: A Critical Analysis of the Vietnam War* (New York: Dell, 1984), Bruce Palmer, Jr., *The 25-Year War: America's Military Role in Vietnam* (Lexington: University of Kentucky Press, 1984), James William Gibson, *The Perfect War: The War We Couldn't Lose and How We Did* (Boston: Atlantic Monthly Press, 1986), Loren Baritz, *Backfire: A History of How American Culture Led Us into Vietnam and Made Us Fight the Way We Did* (New York: Ballantine, 1986), David Halberstam, *The Best and the Brightest* (New York: Random House, 1972), and Frances Fitzgerald, *Fire in the Lake: The Vietnamese and the Americans in Vietnam* (New York: Vintage, 1973).

On changes in the U.S. military since the Vietnam War, see Harry G. Summers, Jr., *On Strategy II: A Critical Analysis of the Gulf War* (New York: Dell, 1992), John L. Romjue, Susan Canedy, and Anne W. Chapman, *Prepare the Army for War: A Historical Overview of the Army Training and Doctrine Command, 1973–1993* (Fort Monroe, Va.: U.S. Army Training and Doctrine Command, 1993), and Robert H. Scales, Jr., *Certain Victory: The U.S. Army and the Gulf War* (Washington, D.C.: Brassey's, 1994).

PARTICIPANTS

• • • • • • • • • • • • • • •

STEPHEN E. AMBROSE is professor of history at the University of New Orleans and the author of more than twenty books on military history, political history, and U.S. foreign relations. Among his best-selling and award-winning books are biographies of Dwight D. Eisenhower, Richard M. Nixon, and Meriwether Lewis.

DAVID L. ANDERSON is professor of history and chair of the department of history and political science at the University of Indianapolis. His book *Trapped by Success: The Eisenhower Administration and Vietnam, 1953–1961* was a cowinner of the 1992 Robert H. Ferrell Book Prize of the Society for Historians of American Foreign Relations. He was in the U.S. Army, 1968–1970, and served in Vietnam in 1970 as a sergeant in the Signal Corps.

JOHN BALABAN is professor of English at the University of Miami, and a poet, translator, and fiction writer whose recognitions include a National Book Award nomination. He served civilian alternative service in Vietnam, 1967–1969, primarily on the staff of the Committee of Responsibility to Save War-Injured Children.

WARREN BELL is a journalist, university lecturer, and media consultant with three decades of experience in broadcast journalism, including a position as senior anchor and reporter at ABC affiliate WVUE in New Orleans.

WALTER E. BOOMER retired from the U.S. Marine Corps in 1994 as a general. He was commanding general of all the U.S. marine forces during Operations Desert Shield and Desert Storm and later was assistant commandant of the Marine Corps.

He served in Vietnam as an infantry company commander, 1966–1967, and as an adviser to a South Vietnamese infantry battalion, 1971–1972.

DAVID CLINTON is associate professor of political science at Tulane University and a specialist in international relations.

WILLIAM G. ECKHARDT is a retired U.S. Army colonel and is clinical professor of law at the University of Missouri–Kansas City. He was chief military prosecutor of the My Lai cases, 1970–1971. He was later on the staff of the U.S. Army War College and served as general counsel, U.S. European Command, Germany.

W. D. EHRHART is a poet, editor, and educator. His works include a large body of poetry and several memoirs, and he is the editor of the highly regarded anthology *Carrying the Darkness: The Poetry of the Vietnam War*. He was in the U.S. Marine Corps, 1966–1969, and served in Vietnam as a sergeant in combat intelligence, 1967–1968.

RANDY J. FERTEL is a visiting assistant professor of English at Tulane University and was codirector of the conference "My Lai 25 Years After: Facing the Darkness and Healing the Wounds," Tulane University, New Orleans, December 1994.

DAVID HALBERSTAM is a journalist and best-selling author who won the Pulitzer Prize for his reporting from Vietnam for the *New York Times* in the early 1960s. His numerous books include *The Best and the Brightest* and *The Powers That Be*.

GEORGE C. HERRING is professor of history and chair of the department of history at the University of Kentucky. A leading historical authority on the U.S. war in Vietnam, he is the author of a widely used textbook on the war, *America's Longest War: The United States and Vietnam, 1950–1975*.

SEYMOUR HERSH is an investigative journalist who has won many awards, including the Pulitzer Prize in 1970 for his series of articles exposing the My Lai massacre. He has written two books on the massacre and the army's eventual investigation.

WAYNE KARLIN is a novelist and editor who is chair of the department of English at Charles County Community College, St. Mary's County, Maryland. He is also on the faculty of the William Joiner Center at the University of Massachusetts. He served in the U.S. Marine Corps, 1963–1967, and in Vietnam as a combat aircrew sergeant, 1966–1967.

KIEM DO is a leading member of several Vietnamese civic and veterans' groups in the United States. He served in the navy of the Republic of Vietnam from 1954 to 1975. With the rank of captain, he held several command positions including deputy chief of staff for operations. Three of his brothers were killed in the Indochina wars.

ROBERT JAY LIFTON is professor of psychiatry and psychology and director of the Center on Violence and Human Survival, John Jay College of Criminal Justice and Mt. Sinai School of Medicine, CUNY. He is the recipient of many awards, including the National Book Award for *Death in Life: Survivors of Hiroshima*. He wrote the pioneering book on Vietnam War–related trauma, *Home from the War: Vietnam Veterans: Neither Victims nor Executioners.*

HENRY L. MASON is professor of political science at Tulane University and specializes in Holocaust studies.

PATIENCE MASON is a trained crisis-line phone counselor and author of a guide for dealing with Vietnam War–related stress. Her personal experience with and research on post-traumatic stress disorder came from her years of efforts to help her husband Robert Mason, a victim of PTSD. He has detailed his own story in two best-selling memoirs.

JOHN MCAULIFF is founder and executive director of the U.S.-Indochina Reconciliation Project, a nonprofit educational organization based in New York. He was director of the Peace Education Division of the American Friends Service Committee, 1972–1982. Since 1975 he has made countless visits to Indochina, including visits to My Lai.

TIM O'BRIEN is a novelist whose numerous honors include the National Book Award for *Going after Cacciato*. He is the author of many best-sellers, including a novel based on My Lai, *In the Lake of the Woods*. He served in the U.S. Army, 1968–1970, and was an infantryman in Vietnam in the area around My Lai, 1969–1970.

BASIL PAQUET is a poet, editor, and cofounder of 1st Casualty Press. He was in the U.S. Army, 1966–1968, and served in Vietnam as a medic, 1967–1968.

HAYS PARKS is an attorney and retired U.S. Marine Corps colonel. He is chief of the International Law Branch, International and Operational Law Division, and Special Assistant for Law of War Matters, Office of the Judge Advocate General of the Army, Washington, D.C. He served in Vietnam in the Marine Corps as an infantry officer and military lawyer.

RON RIDENHOUR is a journalist and freelance writer. During 1967–1968, he served as an infantryman in the U.S. Army in South Vietnam's Quang Ngai Province, where he learned of the events at My Lai. His 1969 letter sent to the White House, Congress, and the military prompted the investigation that led to the eventual revelation of the My Lai massacre. His journalism has been honored with the George Polk Award (1983) and the Gerald Loeb Award (1988).

JONATHAN SHAY is a clinical instructor in the department of psychiatry at Tufts Medical School, staff psychiatrist at the Day Treatment Center of the Veterans Administration Outpatient Clinic in Boston, and team psychiatrist in the Veterans Improvement Program (PTSD) of the Boston VA Outpatient Clinic. He is the author of *Achilles in Vietnam: Combat Trauma and the Undoing of Character.*

KEVIN SIM is an author, documentary film maker, and director with Yorkshire Television in England. He cowrote and directed a documentary film, *Four Hours in*

My Lai, that won an International Emmy and a British Academy Award. He also coauthored a book with that title.

JEROLD M. STARR is professor of sociology at West Virginia University and director of the Center for Social Studies Education in Pittsburgh. He is the author of a widely acclaimed curriculum for teaching the Vietnam War, and he has conducted workshops for teachers throughout the nation.

HARRY G. SUMMERS, JR., is a retired U.S. Army colonel who is an author, columnist, radio and television commentator, and editor of *Vietnam* magazine. He has written two best-selling studies of military strategy in the Vietnam War and the Gulf War—*On Strategy* and *On Strategy II.* A veteran of the Korean and Vietnam Wars, he is an Army War College Distinguished Fellow and formerly held the War College's General Douglas MacArthur Chair.

HUGH C. THOMPSON, JR., was a U.S. Army warrant officer (WO1) who was a helicopter pilot of an aeroscout team from Company B, 123d Aviation Battalion, at My Lai on March 16, 1968. Observing what he considered to be needless killing, he landed his helicopter and attempted to aid the villagers. He also reported his concerns through his chain of command. By the time of the My Lai investigations, he had advanced to the rank of first lieutenant. He was a key witness in the hearings and court-martial proceedings related to My Lai.

KARIN THOMPSON is a clinical psychologist and program director of the Post-traumatic Stress Disorder Inpatient Unit, Department of Veterans Affairs Medical Center, New Orleans. She is also clinical assistant professor in the department of psychiatry and neurology, Tulane University School of Medicine.

TIANA (THI THANH NGA) is an actress, founding director of Indochina Film Arts Foundation, and producer-director-writer of the film *From Hollywood to Hanoi.* She is the daughter of a former South Vietnamese government official.

KATHLEEN TURNER is professor of communication at Tulane University and has written on press coverage in Vietnam.

MARILYN B. YOUNG is professor of history at New York University and author of the critically acclaimed *The Vietnam Wars, 1945–1990.*

INDEX

• • • • • • • • • • • • • •